DICK⊙ MARKETING

SMART MARKETING *to* WOMEN ONLINE

Yvonne DiVita

WME BOOKS

a division of
Windsor Media Enterprises, LLC
Rochester, New York
USA

DICKLESS MARKETING: Smart Marketing to Women Online

ISBN 0-9777297-0-2

Printed in the United States of America.

Published by:
WME Books
Windsor Media Enterprises, LLC
Rochester, New York
USA

Available online at: www.WMEBooks.com
as well as other booksellers and distributors worldwide.

Special Sales:

This and other WME Books titles are available at special discounts for bulk purchases, for use in sales promotions, or as premiums. Special editions, including personalized covers, excerpts of existing books, and corporate imprints, can be created in large quantities for special needs or projects.

For more information, please contact:

Special Book Orders
Windsor Media Enterprises, LLC
150 Lucius Gordon Drive
West Henrietta, NY 14586

1-877-947-BOOK (2665)

info@wmebooks.com

Preface i

Introduction... xiii

1. What Do Women Want? 1

   Women Want to be Taken Seriously *1*

2. Lip-Sticking 17

   Be Clear and Honest in Your Sales Message *17*

3. Making friends with the F Word............................. 49

   Female-friendly Web sites *49*

4. You Don't Know Dick 73

   Getting Jane (and Dick) to your Web site to Shop, Shop, Shop *73*

5. S-E-X Sarah-Ellen Xceptions................................. 115

   Baby Boomers vs Gen Xers & Gen Ys....................... *115*

6. Ties that Bind 147

   Marketing Tools that Work Online............................ *147*

7. Meeting at the Well.. 187

   Working with Communities, Non-profits and Partnerships *187*

8. Risky Business... 217

   Ignore Jane's Buying Power at Your Own Risk!.......... *217*

9. Can You Handle It? 239

   Bad, Baad Web sites! Are YOU Guilty of these Mistakes?........ *239*

10. Was Will Eine Frau Eigentlich? 269

   Don't ask Freud What Women Want, Read On... .... *269*

Acknowledgements 283

Preface

Yes, *Dickless Marketing* means exactly what you think it means. Marketing to women. (Were you thinking it meant something else?)

In the old days, that *Dick and Jane* world of the 20th century, marketing focused primarily on men because men were the ones perceived as holding the world in the palm of their hands. In this new world, in the mobile media marketplace of the Internet, marketing perceptions are changing dramatically. More women than men shop online. *Dickless Marketing* is all about marketing to women who shop online. In the pages of this book you will learn how to successfully draw in those eager women shoppers. Then you will learn how to get them to buy, using today's mouse-to-house expediency.

THE INTERNET MEETS MR. ROGERS

The "small, small world" we were singing about in the early '70s has evolved into a world of ones and zeros; ones and zeros that have changed this globe we call Earth into a virtual Mr. Rogers neighborhood. Women are so comfortable with this new digital neighborhood that we visit it on a daily basis, and we always take our pocketbook with us. Each chapter of this book will show you that women, not men, rule online shopping—and that it's not a man holding the digital world in the palm of his hand, it's a woman.

Years of being Moms, buying all those Christmas presents, packing Easter baskets, and rewarding each other for special occasions, along with years of being office managers shopping for office supplies and conference room equipment, have prepared women for shopping mouse-to-house. We're tired of fighting traffic to get to the mall. Our lives are so crowded and busy we have little or no time to stop at strip malls or boutiques. And we're fed up with having to stand in line at the checkout counter! Shopping online is more convenient—it's easier—and it saves us money. And, it's fun. *Dickless Marketing* will reveal how the convenience, the ease, and the savings online are leading more and more women to spend their time and money at favorite Web sites. If you'd like one of those Web sites to be yours, read on.

In my career as an Internet consultant, I've worked with dozens of small and medium-sized businesses still trying to "get it" when it comes to the Internet. How do they get sales? How do they get leads? How do they find their target market online? For more than a year I have been telling them, "Get in front of the women's market." I've endured a good many quizzical frowns in response to that phrase.

To all the small and medium-sized businesses still trying to make a success of your online presence, *Dickless Marketing* is going to lure you out of the old millennium. Leave the *Dick and Jane* world of the previous century back in the schoolroom where it belongs. Forget those outmoded concepts that dictate men have the money, men control the finances, and men make the decisions on what to buy, at work and at home. Women are doing all of those things, and they're doing them online. I'll show you how to get them to do the buying part at your Web site.

Dickless Marketing is more than the title of this book, or the location of a Web site (www.dicklessmarketing.com). It's a concept. It's a focus. It's a glimpse into the female psyche to learn how the mobile media marketplace has changed how women shop. Young and old, teens to seniors, women are leaving the old millennium behind to claim the shopping territory of the Internet in the new millennium. If you have a business online and want that business to grow exponentially, get your marketing message in front of more women. How? Read *Dickless Marketing* and stop dicking around!

UNCLE DICKIE

When I was a little girl, my favorite uncle lived in the country, over a hundred miles from my city home. Though I did not get to see Uncle Dick (we called him Dickie) very often, I remember the roughhousing and fun of visiting him on Saturday afternoons, in a place where there were more trees than buildings. I remember it fondly, as clearly as I remember sunny afternoons playing hopscotch on the sidewalk in front of my house in the city, or curling up on the bed at my grandmother's house reading fairy tales.

Those memories of the mid 20th century, especially the fun days of the '50s and '60s, were a time of innocence, a time identified with "Father Knows Best" or "Leave it to Beaver." Children learned to read using the *Dick and Jane New Basic Readers.* Originally published by Scott-Foresman and Company in 1941, the *Dick and Jane* readers "conveyed the stereotypic American dream pervasive in the United States during and following WWII and the Korean Conflict. The family depicted in the Dick and Jane basals owned a spacious, white, two-story home in a well cared for suburban neighborhood. Mother stayed home while Father worked at a successful career, providing for the family's needs. A car or two, a pet dog and cat, also adorned the dream of the American family portrayed in this series." (Comment provided by D. Ray Reutzel and Robert B. Cooter, Jr, in their book *Teaching Children to Read*, New York: Macmillan, 1992).

Of particular interest to me, as I instruct you on how to market to women in a new millennium, using a new technology—the Internet— is the fact that the 20th century was mired in the dream of those basal readers. The Dick and Jane series of books approached the subject of learning to read by offering books with a limited vocabulary. The first grade reader used only 323 words. This was only half the number of words previously used in books of the 1920s and '30s, which taught children to read. Whether the approach was good or bad, whether it succeeded or not, is not my issue. My issue is to show small and medium-sized businesses that the new millennium will NOT tolerate a Dick and Jane basal-reader focus on marketing. It requires expanding your thought processes (and vocabulary) into a brave new world that extends beyond a limited, male-centered marketing perspective.

"LOOK, DICK. SEE JANE EVOLVE"

The house I grew up in was vastly different than the world depicted in those Dick and Jane readers. Women ruled my life. When I visited Uncle Dickie, it was at my grandmother's house. I went there with my mother and my brother and sister. We had fun, we read books, we played outdoors, and no one cared what gender she or he was. It wasn't until I reached puberty that I learned being a tomboy didn't mean I'd stopped being a girl. Suddenly, everyone, Uncle Dickie included, treated me differently. The imaginary worlds of those old black-and-white TV shows invaded my world and I didn't like it one bit. I could rebel in only one way—by writing.

All through my childhood, I was a writer. A year ago, the writer in me led me to the idea of writing a book about my childhood. A book of nostalgia, stories told in first person by other folks who had grown up during the happy-go-lucky '50s, '60s and '70s. While researching information for this book, those Dick and Jane readers popped up once again.

"Look, Jane, see Dick. See Dick run." "See Spot. See Spot run." I am sure these short sentences are etched into the memories of thousands of American women, and men. For me, and many others, Dick and Jane immortalize a world uncomplicated by the millions of bits and bytes thrown at us today through digital media. Boys played baseball, girls played house. As a country, peace was abundant, the suburbs sprang up like carefully tended gardens, and children reveled in playing outdoors.

I say keep the memories, but leave Dick and Jane out of your business and marketing focus. Those cute kids have faded into the wallpaper of old kitchens—brought back occasionally at large family gatherings (my family counts over 50 of us when we all get together), but they are not a part of today's reality. The truth is that Dick and Jane have no part in today's world of real-time communication over a broadband Internet connection.

My research for that book of nostalgia, much of it done online, led me to a remarkable truth. **Women are taking over the Internet.** This news sent me on a totally different path, away from the stroll down memory lane, away from thoughts of my Uncle Dickie. Yet no matter how I tried to lose my old friends Dick and Jane, they wouldn't go away. As I conducted research, the concepts they represented kept popping up again and again. My daily online research proved over and over that the Internet, this dynamic, new, eye-popping technology, was clinging to the old standard of putting Dick ahead of Jane when it came to online marketing. And yet, Jane was the one adopting it for her use in greater and greater numbers.

"Dick is not holding the digital world in his hand," I thought. "Jane is the one filling online shopping carts. Dick is only buying a toy or a CD or a gift, here and there. Why aren't more people marketing to Jane?"

This is what *Dickless Marketing* is really about—smart marketing to women online. My experience as an Internet consultant was showing me that many online businesses approach the Internet thinking they have the right answers, when they don't even know the right questions. These are the questions you should be asking: "Who is spending the most money online?" And, "What will get this market to my site to buy from me?" The answer to the first question is: women. The answer to the second question is: *Dickless Marketing.*

WOMEN ARE PROACTIVE

The National Foundation for Women Business Owners states that women are "more proactive than male business owners in adoption of this new technology," meaning, the Internet. Twenty-one percent more women than men have an 800 number on their Web site and are actively searching for qualified IT support for their online businesses.

> **Statistics show that women overtook men online in 2001. As of May 2003, 45% of Internet surfers are men— 55% are women.**

Women also have money; a Harris Interactive study shows that women control 75% of household finances and 80% of purchasing decisions. And let's not leave out shopping for family and friends. Last year during the Christmas shopping season (2002), 63% of Americans shopped online. Trust me when I say that more than half of them were women.

All of this, and more, influenced the writing of this book.

Just as schools of the 21st century have moved far beyond the Dick and Jane readers of 50 years ago, so must marketing in this new age adjust to a digital medium. Those Dick and Jane primers are stuck on the bottom shelves of bookshelves now. Computer books have taken their place on the top shelves. The computer brought with it a dramatic change not only in the way we communicate, but in the way we relate to each other—person-to-person, man-to-man, woman-to-woman, woman-to-man and man-to-woman. We need those computer books close at hand; they are our new educational primers.

During the last 10 years, since business and the new economy went hog-wild online (we will speak of the dot-bombs later; you have heard those myths and stories enough for now) a funny thing began to happen—Jane decided she liked this new technology. She pulled her chair up to the computer and told Dick he could have his turn when she was done!

This was a boon for the computer industry. With a computer in almost every home, and with Jane wanting online time as much as Dick, many homes went the way of the TV, deciding they needed multiple computers. In addition to the one Jane is using to shop, there is one for Dad, and one for each of the kids, or at least an extra one for the kids to fight over—I mean, to share.

Jane's affection for this new technology goes beyond the shopping aspect. It allows her to communicate with family and friends at the click of—dare we say it—a mouse. The Internet opened the door to a new world for Jane. A world of fun and frolic, convenience and delight, excitement and education. The Janes of today's world do not shy away from mice, mechanical or otherwise. We also kill our own spiders and many of us take care of our own cars. Shopping online is becoming as natural as scrambling eggs or taping our soap operas.

In the United States and across the world, Jane is influencing the majority of sales and marketing online. In her nightgown at midnight, in high heels during her lunch hour, in sweats after a morning run through the park, or in jeans and T-shirt while the kids nap, she is online looking for deals. She shops on Mondays, on Tuesdays, on Wednesdays; why, she even shops on Thursdays and Fridays, and on weekends, both Saturday and Sunday. When she finds bargains, she tells all of her friends—in one of the hundreds of women's communities online. The gender wars, (let's say gender differences) continue offline, in the workplace and in the home with no clear winner, but the war online is over. Dick is just not the online shopper that Jane is!

COMPLETELY DICK-LESS

I have been fortunate to experience employment in both large and small companies during my climb to self-sufficiency. During my employment years, I noticed something peculiar—most of the people I worked with, both male and female, were locked into a Dick and Jane world that belonged in history books, not in our offices.

Memories of the senior-level managers in the Internet companies I worked at during the last five years or so were still fresh in my mind as I began writing this book. These were men who often relied upon the decisions of other men, or groups of men with one or two women [such as myself] thrown in, caught in that old dirt world of the previous millennium. If there was any mention of Jane, or what Jane, as a reference to females, might want, I don't remember hearing it.

> The bricks and mortar world—think shopping malls and physical stores—is sometimes called the dirt world. I will refer to it as such throughout *Dickless Marketing.*

In their world, Dick was the primary focus. Jane was ignored or included as an afterthought. While researching for *Dickless Marketing,* I uncovered a whole cadre of marketing still directed at

Dick, as if Jane hadn't made it out of the "Leave it to Beaver" world of the last century—the one where women stayed home while men worked, and no one talked about money. If you're online and you're making the same mistake ignoring the women's market, you're cutting out **more than half** of your possible sales prospects!

It's time to focus your marketing campaign on the gender that does the most buying. While it's true that Dick shops online, he does not spend the time and money Jane does. You will find, as you read on, that in the end, Dick often lets Jane do his shopping for him, anyway!

I feel a special connection to the "Dicks" in my life, through the numerous engagements and parrying of wits we have shared. It is partly because of them that *Dickless Marketing* exists. While they were busy studying marketing trends and perfecting their golf swings, I was busy interviewing Jill and Jane, and learning that, by golly, Jill and Jane have been out of the kitchen for decades!

In several chapters of this book, you will see that the dirt world is slowly recognizing the value of marketing to Jane. But, I submit that the greater portion of it is still mired in the previous century where Dick ruled. What surprised me is that even online Jane is still being ignored by both the Fortune 500 and also the small to medium—sized business market (SMBs). *Dickless Marketing* is going to teach you about the shopping habits of females who shop online, both consumers and businesswomen, because Jane is the one holding the world in her hand in this century.

I will be sharing statistics, stories, and suggestions substantiated either by personal experience, or intense research. This book is intended for all businesses—whether the CEO is male, female, or a shared partnership. The Internet has room for us all—its Welcome sign is non-gender, non-denominational, and without prejudice.

A DICK AND HIS TOOLS

My readers, both male and female, contributed conflicting opinions on the content of this book. Some readers felt I stereotyped men as "Dicks"; not the cute little boy from the Dick and Jane readers, but the "Dick" played by actor Tim Allen in the popular '90's sitcom, *Home Improvement.* For anyone not familiar with the top-10 rated TV series, Tim played the host of a home improvement cable TV show called "Tool Time." His character repeatedly grunted like a pig, talked cars, tools, and sports, and had a "man's perspective on life"— an identity which Tim, himself, described as the DICK identity. If that identity is reflected in some parts of *Dickless Marketing* it's because it suited that paragraph or point. 'Nuff said.

Other readers felt I was too kind or not kind enough to women, especially when writing about careers, business, appearance, and being a Mom. Some readers commented that I was focusing too much attention on the U.S. and not being diverse enough. I was as gentle and kind, or as critical and pointed, about women as I needed to be, when I needed to be. The focus on the U.S., with the diversity covering only the Hispanic market and the African-American market, was deliberate. In my next book, I will expand our horizons and go global. That book will include the groups I did not talk about this time around.

During the writing of *Dickless Marketing* I carried out extensive research; I read countless books on marketing, some of which focused totally on marketing to women, although they did not cover the Internet in any detail; I read and highlighted hundreds of articles from marketing experts, sales experts, and Internet experts. I scoured dozens of marketing, sales, and Internet-related newsletters for relevant content.

In addition to my research, I relied on personal business experiences stretching over a 10-year period. The stories told in this book are not unique. I am not alone (nor is my gender alone) in having endured rude and/or embarrassing incidents at the hands of senior level managers mired in that good old boys world of Dick and Jane— managers of both genders, by the way.

Happily, I can report that many women I know, and many women I don't know but with whom I have shared e-mails, told me inspiring stories about partnerships with the men in their lives. Each woman had a story to tell—a story about how a male manager or friend went out of his way to help her achieve what she was so eager to accomplish. The acknowledgements in the back of this book are my tribute to the men and women who took their time to support me both emotionally and professionally as I struggled to get this book out the door.

Those friends and colleagues who lent their time and energy to help me get this book to print did so because they believed in me, all of them understood my vision—to show small business owners that online success is attainable if they focus their marketing on women because we are the big spenders online.

The work required to realize results from this guide is yours alone. It is offered in good faith, but in and of itself, it cannot bring you riches. It is in the practice of the advice that the riches will follow.

Remember, running a business, whether online or off, requires study and careful consideration. Not only should you have a well-thought out business plan, you should have a vision; where do you want to be next year, the year after, and the year after that? Why are you in business for yourself? What makes you better than your competitors? Who is your core market, that hungry group of eager shoppers ready and willing to buy from you? This attention to business strategy will influence all aspects of your business success, both online and off.

Dickless Marketing exists to help you understand the strategy of marketing to the one group of shoppers comprised of your mother, your wife, your sister, your daughter, your mother-in-law, your girlfriend and all of her friends—a group of interesting individuals who go online looking for you, every day.

Join me to learn how to:

- o Gain a better understanding of what it means to market online.
- o Get the largest group of potential buyers in the world to buy from you.
- o Get current information about the surfing and spending habits of women.

- ○ Refine and increase your knowledge of Internet marketing in general.
- ○ Gain practical advice on reaching women, from an insider's point of view.

This valuable information is only available in this handbook—the only how-to in print today that specifically addresses the issue of using the Internet to gain the trust and support of the largest and most generous group of consumers in the world—a group that operates under the mantra: Have Cash, Will Spend.

WOMEN!

Dickless Marketing

Introduction

What is the secret to online success?

The secret to online success is selling to the right market. A market composed of eager shoppers. A market composed of people who have money to spend and who are spending it online. A market composed of women.

WINNING OVER WOMEN

Dickless Marketing is going to teach you how to WOW this market. I am going to introduce you to a world in which we leave the 20th century focus of Dick and Jane behind because it is no longer relevant to shopping in a marketplace increasingly connected by the mobile medium of the Internet. In our world, you should be courting Jane as intensely as you used to court Dick because Jane is the consumer who is sold on the convenience of shopping online.

Jane has also become a respected business partner to Dick—influencing his purchasing power on a very large scale. Never doubt that Jane is more than ready to spend her money online; she is eager to do so. This is a new Jane, one who is quite capable of balancing the world in the palm of her hand.

AN OCEAN OF RICHES

The Internet is a veritable ocean of riches, so say new age marketing professionals and pundits alike. According to Frank Feather, global business futurist and the author of *futureconsumer.com* (New York: Warwick Publishing, 2000), "The home becomes the shop—a virtual mall showroom for comparison shopping and a convenience store for buying."  If you're a small business owner, identified by the U.S. census as having fewer than 500 employees or achieving $10 million or less in annual revenue, the Internet is the place for you.

All you need to do to tap into this market and make it your own is to build a Web site. Right? **Wrong!** I have studied the Internet for more than nine years. I have watched it evolve from a playground for teenagers and techies, lusting after new and exciting ways to get into trouble, into business-to-business (B2B) and business-to-consumer (B2C) arenas offering small businesses a fighting chance to make good alongside the established, logo-touting giants. Whether you're an entrepreneur just entering the business world, or whether you own a small business poised to tackle the Internet's promise of riches to be made online, there is a right way and a wrong way to go about it.

The wrong way is to jump in without due diligence. The right way is to employ considerable research. *Dickless Marketing* will teach you how the Internet influences the B2C and the B2B marketplace, and which gender is spending the most money in that marketplace—much more valuable lessons than learning how it gets those bits and bytes from your computer to mine.

WATCHING THE HOURGLASS SPIN

Doing business online is a sensible choice. This continues to be proven by the amount of money being spent online. Emarketer http://www.emarketer.com/welcome.php predicts that $58.2 billion will be spent online in 2003, and Feather notes in his book that "consumers are voting, not with their feet but with their mouse clicks and digital wallets, for the Web economy."

Yet, I continue to see small businesses and Web-preneurs jump on the Internet bandwagon like toddlers on a merry-go-round—completely oblivious to the pain they are going to feel when they fall off of that swiftly moving whirligig.

To understand how the World Wide Web (WWW) works, it helps to think of it as a library. Authors Tara Calishain and Rael Dornfest of *Google Hacks* (New York: O'Reilly, 2003) dislike this comparison, but I think it's applicable. Presently, this library contains millions of Web sites on its virtual shelves—though not all of them are listed in the e-catalog. In the old millennium that pre-teen Dick and Jane lived in, libraries used card catalogs to index every book on every shelf. Today, libraries use computer databases or e-catalogs—to index all of their holdings in a variety of media.

On the Web, search engines and indexes such as Google and Yahoo! are the equivalent of the e-catalog of a library. Search engines exist to help searchers retrieve information. They operate on computer-coded algorithms (mathematical formulas) that read the text on your site. Web sites built for looks, not content, will be left out of the search engines, or at best, will be ranked well below the top 15-20 link results the average surfer views.

Your business needs to build a Web site that contains optimal text and hyperlinks in order for the search engines to include it in their database. Think of it: the searcher wants relevant results to his or her search; the search engine wants to make the searcher happy. Web sites that look pretty, or have a lot of flashy animation and images but little text, are invisible to the search engines.

In my business as an Internet consultant I continue to meet Web-preneurs who build an online presence thinking their logo or a few images of product on their homepage is all they need to become rich. They launch a Web presence before taking time to identify how their business is going to function in this new environment. When their business gets lost in the vastness of cyberspace, very much like a good book lost on a library shelf because it didn't get logged into the e-catalog, they grumble out loud and blame the Internet, instead of recognizing their own shortcomings.

It's plain and simple: text is what searchers search for and it is also what search engine spiders need to see in order to return relevant results. In order to do this, search engines and indexes use uniquely developed code instructing their spiders what to look for or human beings who view each site individually for content and relevance. You've heard it before, I'm sure. I will confirm it emphatically: the words on your Web site can make you or break you.

Charlie Page, a successful online marketer, and owner of
www.directoryofezines.com, said as much in his August 20, 2003
newsletter.

> **"Of all the things that marketers talk about to make sales
> happen, there is one tool that stands head and shoulders
> above all the others. What is this tool? WORDS."**
> **Charlie Page**

Why should you listen to Charlie Page? Because he knows what
works and what doesn't. In 2002, he recognized the key
characteristics of a successful online business when many newcomers
to the net were still scratching their heads over how to get this Internet
business thing to work. That's when he purchased *The Directory of
Ezines*, an online business already producing a profit. Page's
continued success with this business is a very good reason to follow
his advice.

Listen to Charlie because in our everyday world words compel,
inspire, coach, bring a tear to your eye, or a laugh to your throat. On
the Web, words are the living parts of your online presence, and they
compliment the images you use, including that thumbnail shot of
yourself with "Founder/Owner" printed beneath. In my first attempt at
an online presence, I used the Yahoo! site builder to build a short
sales page. Underneath my picture I wrote, "The author in her most
recent incarnation." My WORDS generated attention. Mission
accomplished.

Too many Web-preneurs get caught up in the pretty pictures, blinking
animation, and loud audio elements that technology offers today.
They forget that inclusion into a search engine database requires good
copy (text). A high ranking requires better than good copy; it requires
descriptive copy that describes your business or product exactly, copy
that gets reader attention and attention from the search engine spiders.

Then, just when you think you're home free, when you've developed
a site with rich content that both the spiders like and your visitors like,

disaster strikes! The search engines revise their software algorithms. Your great Web site can fall from a ranking of 7th last week, to a ranking of 27th this week! In Chapter 4, "You Don't Know Dick," you will learn why that happens.

THE HAND THAT CLICKS THE MOUSE, RULES THE WEB

This is why you MUST build a solid homepage. Web usability experts Jakob Nielsen and Marie Tahir, who dissect 50 business Web sites in their book, *Homepage Usability* (New York: New Riders Publishing, 2002), say that the homepage of a Web site is "the most valuable real estate in the world." It's your front door—more people see your front door than see many of the inside pages of your site.

Dickless Marketing is going to help you construct a homepage that search engines and women will love, a homepage that directs both of them to your products page, a homepage that will get the women, at least, spending money. The vital elements of a female-friendly homepage will get women to share your site with every other woman they know.

New online business owners who haven't taken the time to understand their core market—that small group of hungry shoppers who are actively buying online—build Web sites that have little chance of getting listed in the search engines. They focus their design and content on preconceived notions of what makes a success offline, woefully uninformed about what works on the net.

Let me share a secret I learned from my many years of online research: **it's hard to read the label when you're inside the bottle.** Building a successful online business requires a visit outside the bottle, it requires learning how Web visitors react to your Web site by observing the choices they make and by asking them what they want, because they know the answer—you don't!

Territory is what it's all about. In the dirt world of physical offices, if you've chosen a good location you can move into your look, your feel, and your core market over time, using the existing traffic in your immediate area. The Internet, however, does not allow a gradual move into your location. It's imperative you understand how to get your core market to your site before you even build it. Your core market should influence your site colors, font, design, copy, graphics, and more.

Just as importantly, you need to change the way you think about marketing, because marketing online is not the same as marketing offline. Women need to be a central focus of your online marketing strategy, regardless of what you sell.

Think of it this way: millions of small businesses enter the gigantic Internet database every day, just as thousands of books are added to the library every day. We've already discussed how the search engines function as the library card catalog, now an e-catalog. Visitors to the library check the e-catalog by typing in significant search terms on a computer. Visitors to the Internet do the same. Your site will only come into their field of vision if it is optimized to show up in the top 20 results of that search. That means page one or page two.

The question is, how do you make that happen? I've already told you that search engines are particular about choosing where to place your site. They read your text and look at a few other elements, and you get placed wherever they choose to place you. It doesn't seem fair. How do you compete with the millions of other Web sites out there? After all, you're not on a busy city street or in a crowded shopping mall; you can't put up a fancy billboard to get attention. I suppose you could erect one on your local expressway, but that fleeting glimpse of your dub-dub-dub or www (also known as your URL: Uniform Resource Locator) won't be remembered by very many of the occupants in those fast moving cars, cars that are speeding by faster every year.

In a small survey of approximately 100 women from all over the U.S., I asked participants if they read billboards, and then I asked them what was being advertised on the last billboard they read. More than half responded that yes, they do read billboards. But only three could identify what the last billboard they saw was advertising, and two of those responses were incomplete, the reader could only remember part of what she saw written there.

Back in the dirt world, opening a bricks and mortar store in a strip mall allows you to put up a flashy neon sign to attract customers. Bricks and mortar stores located on the corners of busy city streets display all manner of colorful posters in their windows. Some of them even play music to attract passersby.

Yes, traditional media can help you establish an online presence. You can and should place an ad in your local paper or Pennysaver. But unless readers have your print ad in front of them when they log on to the Internet, you're out of luck. People most easily remember text they can associate with known objects or information—cows and milk; dolls and little girls; trucks and little boys; baseball and mighty Babe Ruth.

The act of "recalling" something requires more work than the average shopper cares to do. Expecting customers to recall the series of letters and/or words that make up your dub-dub-dub (www.site.com) is wishful thinking. Catchy dub-dub-dubs notwithstanding—don't rely on print ads to get you all of the Internet attention you need to make your business a success.

Online you are at the mercy of your Web design and your Web site functionality. Your online core market will not find you by following billboards, neon signs, colorful posters, or piped music. On the Internet you need to use Internet tactics and tools. Whether you're in technology, publishing, work-at-home endeavors, or a rare, unique e-commerce endeavor, your success depends on an entirely different mindset. It's a learning curve you cannot afford to ignore.

I think I hear some of you muttering that I am exaggerating the difficulties of online marketing. It can't be that hard to create a Web site, install a shopping cart, and open for business online. It only takes a few bucks and a trip to the computer store for a box of software, right? Think again. It's a lot harder than those out-of-the-box product design companies want you to know.

Dickless Marketing will show you how to build and promote your Web presence successfully. And I will also show you how to market it to the largest consumer group online today—women with cash to spend but little time to run to the mall and spend it there.

WORD-OF-MOUSE PROMOTION

The Internet seemed to offer a simple solution for commercial success in the early days of the World Wide Web. "Build it and they will come," it said. Today, smart Web-preneurs know that only happens in the movies. And yet, even movies have to market themselves properly—in all media—including the Internet, otherwise they play to empty theaters. The film industry certainly knows the value of Internet marketing.

A shining example of successful online pre-marketing for movie sales is the 1999 release of *The Blair Witch Project.* The online site SOLD the film to moviegoers before it ever hit the theaters. And, in the end, it made everyone associated with it a lot of money. *The Blair Witch Project* made millions because it was marketed by what we could call a successful "word-of-mouse" campaign.

However, there were more failures in those first years of the Web than there were successes. If we visit that far ago dot-bomb era, we can see that it was crammed with minds that bought into the *build it and they will come* promise. It was a time rife with venture capitalists and Wall Street pushing those out-of-control Initial Public Offerings (IPO's) of their new darlings, technology and Internet start-ups. Those VCs and Wall Street financiers took full advantage of this interactive, fresh avenue of gaining public attention, concerned only with their own bottom line. Ultimately, the failures spiraled down into a black hole.

I give credit to those small business owners who tried to understand the Internet and think through appropriate marketing strategies before putting their businesses online. Unfortunately, the advice they received was often from professionals who were used to making their money in the dirt world. Let's be clear here, the Web is not Woolworths Five and Dime, it's not Ben and Jerry's Ice Cream Parlor, it's not Saks Fifth Avenue, it's not Park Avenue or Boardwalk. It is innovation in technology, with more potential to support sales of almost anything—think eBay—than any other commercial venture to date. But it exists in a virtual world we are all still exploring and evaluating in order to learn how to make it work.

Marketing in the dirt world has extensive experience and testing behind it. There are thousands of print books written on how to build a business offline, from how to organize your business plan, how to word your sales copy, and how to find a good location. The content of these books comes from great minds with years of experience. You can find books that will instruct you on ad copy and print advertising, complete with lists on how to determine what time slot to put your TV ad in, how to write, produce and place radio advertising, how to network, and more. Indeed, books on how to write a business plan and how to manage your business are available by the truckload!

The words in those books are full of sound advice. The dirt world has been at this marketing thing long enough to understand how the human mind reacts to certain advertising gimmicks or direct mail pieces. It understands the constant need to evolve and recreate oneself. With each new generation of shoppers, the marketing experts in the dirt world hustle to reinvent their marketing focus to address the needs and wants of the latest trend or fad.

As the marketplace and the dominant media changes and evolves, so must the individual hoping to build a successful business. Consider this ancient Chinese proverb: "If you do not change direction, you are likely to end up where you are headed." If you are still reading books on how to do business in the dirt world, you are headed for failure online.

The World Wide Web is still a baby. Though the grown-ups in the dirt world have some affection for it, there is also wariness. How much money is this child going to steal from them? Is the child going to outperform them? Is it going to step on their toes and crush them, or merely bruise them?

At present, the dirt world treats the Web like a new electronic toy with too many strange parts making it too complicated to use effectively, even though it keeps beckoning us with all those bells and whistles. The dirt world prefers to keep the Web in the closet because they say it's rampant with problems: privacy issues, sales issues, connection issues, tax issues and more. This is a clear case of the pot calling the kettle black.

Don't buy into the dirt world's false predictions and negative news copy on Internet marketing. The dirt world doesn't understand the Internet, and you shouldn't be relying on its outmoded teachings to make your Web presence succeed. You should spend more time finishing this book.

KEYWORDS, COPY WRITING, POP UNDERS, OH MY!

A visit to Amazon.com shows the number of books written about how to be a business success online reaching triple digits, but for the most part those books delve into areas the average business owner often finds confusing and suspicious. Many of my clients express doubt when listening to a presentation on such things as Search Engine Optimization, Web copy editing, banner ads, click through rates, e-zines, newsletters, and the bane of all Internet advertising, pop-ups (or pop-unders—sneaky ads that hide under the current screen you're viewing, waiting for you to close it down so they can burst into view).

Any discussion about keywords and meta-tags, which shopping cart to use, or whether to include Macromedia flash and animation, is all mumbo-jumbo to them. They generally heave big sighs and implore me to just advise them on how build a simple site people will visit.

I have to tell clients that they need search engine optimization and meta-tags and much of the rest. What's at issue is whether or not they need all of it and whether or not they need to know every detail of how it all works. The issue is: how does marketing work in a technical venue, a virtual world, a disembodied space that can't be felt or touched? It's not like selling on TV or radio; that's old hat. There are set ways to do that. Online, you're in no man's land.

In my experience, search engine optimization, banner ads, click through rates, and all of the attendant technology that goes along with marketing a Web site are too confusing because they delve too much into the *technology* itself.

We don't open our televisions to see how they work, do we? Aren't we all pretty much happy when we click the remote and it connects us to ABC, or NBC, or the WB or whatever channel we want to watch at that moment in time? So, why do we obsess about how the Internet does what it does? Shouldn't we be just as happy to hit the boot button on our PC or MAC, click our mouse to log on and be happy that our favorite Web site opens up? Of course we should. And most of us are.

But not enough of us have taken the time to recognize that marketing online requires a new mindset, a rethinking of the natural order of things, a review of how the human mind works and how people read on a computer monitor. Once again, to make your Web presence return a solid payback, the Web-preneur has a learning curve that is unavoidable.

WHO AM I TO SAY?

The Internet is my passion. I spend twelve to fourteen hours on it, every day. I read, read, read about marketing online and then contemplate what I've read. After that I discuss what's working and what isn't with other Internet professionals. It's because I've followed the steps above that I truly feel competent to call myself an Internet expert. I know what marketing advice to offer Web-preneurs opening up shop online. I know it because I've studied it and used it myself.

Dickless Marketing is going to take the focus away from the technology of how the Internet works. You will get a short tutorial on what the Internet really is (hint: it's neither audio, video, nor print) in order to understand how to use it to your advantage. But, my true purpose is to show you how to sell to a specific market. Isn't that the reason your business is online? To sell something? And to make a profit at it?

I ask you, now, where are the experts to show you how to do that successfully online?

LOOK FOR THEM IN THIS BOOK

Don't look for them offline. It's precisely because the Internet is still so new that the hype being thrown around cyberspace is replete with unfounded information, much of it in the form of spam. A few minutes at Google or Yahoo! searching for "Internet marketing experts" turns up hundreds of thousands of possibilities.

Trust the ones who can show you they've done their homework—as I have—the ones who have followed and tested the research. Trust the ones who, instead of making wild promises of instant riches, actually give you advice that makes sense because it's being used now, and it's working. Trust the ones who can help you find your core market—that hungry group of shoppers ready to buy.

Trust *Dickless Marketing*, because I will teach you how to attract the largest, most affluent group of shoppers online today. I will show you how to build your site to attract this market, sell to this market, and keep them coming back for more!

Dickless Marketing has one purpose—to reveal the secrets of selling online to the largest consumer market in the world—a market made up of shoppers known the world over for their lavish spending habits. This consumer group is collectively referred to as **women**. Individually they are often referred to by titles such as: Mom, Sis, Aunt, Wife, Grandma, and Girlfriend. I invite you to learn more about them. In the process, you will learn how they think and how they feel about shopping online.

You will also learn which elements of your Web design and/or content are most important when selling to them. And you will learn a little bit about the female psyche.

Best of all, you will learn that when you market to women, you are also marketing to their significant others, who, generally but not exclusively, make up the second largest group of online surfers commonly referred to as men.

It's a brave new world on the Internet. If you are willing to open your mind to the new millennium where Jane is building strong partnerships with friends and relatives, and where Dick is standing right there by her side cheering her on, then you're ready to make your Web presence profitable. Read on.

FINDING THE RIGHT SPOT

As a writer, I am inherently curious. I first logged on to the Internet in 1994 just to see what it was all about. There was no purpose to my surfing other than to explore this new dimension in communication. The truth is, I resisted even using a computer for such a long time it often amazes me that I am so wedded to it today.

By the time I first logged on to the Internet, I was a confirmed keyboard expert and I expected this new game—using my computer and my phone line to talk to people in other worlds, (anyplace outside of my home state was another world, as far as I was concerned), would be a boring waste of time. But I felt I had to try it.

If you think of a small child riding her first amusement park roller coaster, you will begin to understand the pure delight I felt when I discovered how much of a playground the Internet was, a playground accessible day or night; a playground that did not discriminate against anyone—male, female, young, old; a playground that welcomed us all with open arms.

This new playground was also a new marketplace for my writing. It took me from being a non-entity slaving away over my keyboard, struggling to get published, to the joy of becoming a published author and eventually, a respected professional in sales and marketing. This crazy playground called the World Wide Web validated me in ways the dirt world never had.

It was shortly after I began logging on to the Internet that my words began getting noticed, and people began responding with encouragement. Through my own research and surfing, I lucked into some e-zines that were looking for writers and lo and behold! my writing was now bringing in an income!

I went from being a caterpillar clutching a bare tree limb in the dirt world, offering my guts to editors and publishers, papering my study with rejection slips, gritting my teeth with determination not to give up, to bursting from my cocoon, spreading my wings in glory on the Internet. I broke free of the caterpillar and flew like a butterfly lifted in an updraft. The landings were successful most of the time, but I was often blown about by winds that cared little for my self-esteem or my eagerness. I found myself flitting from one Web-group to another. There was room for participation everywhere, but I was searching for a niche.

"Look at me! Look at me!" I cried. But my voice was lost in the din. Thousands of others were singing the same tune, some better and some worse. My smile faded, I heaved a sigh. Had I come so far only to be beaten down once again by the crowd?

No! I was in the right place. It was the right time. I didn't give up. And neither should you.

The overwhelming number of Internet users—close to 700 million worldwide, as this is being written—the unbelievable number of active Web sites clamoring for attention—at the close of 2002 the count was estimated to be over 36 million—was mind-boggling, indeed, but I knew the secret, and I was determined to use it to my advantage. *Dickless Marketing* is going to reveal that secret to you.

Here it is: the secret is finding your spot online—that unique place where your core market is not only eagerly looking for you, but will buy from you when they finally find you. My spot, my niche, was in the knowledge I possessed; knowledge few other writers had expertise in. Back in those early Internet days, before we were close to 700 million strong, before millions of Web sites were clogging our browsers, I was the exception to the rule; I knew things about the Internet that others didn't.

My insight came from a stint at a telemarketing firm selling DSL—long before the world understood DSL—to graduating into jobs writing software manuals and Web content, combined with learning a bit of HTML code. I devoured everything I could about Search Engine Optimization, the only successful way, at that time, to attract visitors to your Web site. I also began writing articles about DSL, about Search Engines and how they worked, and about how different the Internet was compared to the dirt world, especially in the way people use it.

My e-mail inbox began filling up with notes from people who read my writing and—liked it! I wasn't winning awards, but, like Sally Fields at the 1985 Oscars (*Places in the Heart*), I was feeling pretty good; "They like me. They really like me!"

The untold hours of study, endless weekends of reading, days and days of confusion paid off—I was incapable of programming my VCR, but here I was, showing other people how to understand the Internet! I was earning a few hundred dollars here, only fifty dollars there, writing for recognition elsewhere, all the while continuing to study and learn everything I could about this fascinating new technology. This was worse than my need for chocolate; worse than my penchant for leafing through catalogs and not buying anything; worse than my obsession for watching *Law and Order!* I was hooked.

TWO DAUGHTERS, FOUR SISTERS, TEN NIECES...

Because of my Internet knowledge and my writing skills I was hired by high-tech start-up companies, each with a substantial online presence. The lessons I learned at the hands of the senior-level managers in these start-ups, and my background in writing, are directly responsible for this book.

> That and the fact that I have two daughters, one granddaughter, four sisters, ten nieces, two grandnieces, one sister-in-law, an outspoken mother, and dozens of women friends who all—well, almost all—shop online.

The Internet and the Web are directly responsible for my being hired at those start-ups. I owe those senior-level managers, Harvard graduates and holders of master's degrees from the prestigious Simon School at the University of Rochester, New York, special thanks.

Weighed against my Honors degree in English from a SUNY school, their credentials trumped mine, every time. There was no disputing that fact. I was reminded of it often enough, especially if I became too outspoken. In the end, the more they ignored me, the more determined I became to prove my point. (Isn't that just like a woman?) I admit that it was their sometimes-patronizing attitude that planted the seed to write this book.

The writer in me was tapping me on the noggin whispering, "If you know so much, write a book about it." Or "If you think you know more than they do, write a book about it." And sometimes, "Those guys are pretty smart about dirt world business, but you know the Internet and women—write a book about it."

No problem. Being a writer, I listened, I studied, and I took notes. In the end, my education at the conference tables of all those senior level managers taught me more than I could ever have learned at Yale or Harvard. The most important thing they taught me is that a successful online business needs more than Web statistics, more than an idea, and more than a new, improved, better than anything in the known universe product or service.

Success for Web-preneurs involves using Internet tools and tactics, along with dirt world charts and graphs.

As time passed, I came to realize that inherent in that relearning curve I've been talking about is also discovering whom your core market is. If I had a dollar for every company that came to me and confessed, "I'm so unique, I have no competition," I would be—well, not a rich woman, but I would have money to invest—and I certainly wouldn't invest it in them.

SINGING AN ONLINE ARIA

Like many writers, I am a self-made success. The Internet is all about self-made successes. It gave me the tools, the training, and the experience I needed to build my success into a tribute to the written word. I wanted to show people that words communicate everything to everyone—especially online. A picture may be worth a thousand words, but when was the last time you took a trip, brought back rolls of pictures, and then passed them around without *talking about them*?

Words are the conjunctions of communication. Words connect us to our graphics and pictures. Yes, there are photographs that leave us speechless, but I submit that even those enthralling pictures often elicit awed whispers of praise.

My writing success came because the Internet enabled me to speak to millions—not because it's easy to get published online, or because I'm a great writer (although I am, ask any one of my siblings). No, the Internet helped me cultivate success by helping me perfect my voice and get it in front of the masses.

The idea of voice is integral when studying writing. I believe that your voice is so important that you cannot be a success online until you develop that unique presence of voice that is yours alone. Voice, which includes not only your words, but also your Web design, works to persuade and promote.

Surf over to my content site www.windsormediaenterprises.com and learn more about how words work online and how to build the right tone on your Web site. For now, you need to understand that **your Web site is your voice** both on and off the Internet. It **speaks** to your Web site visitors and clients and it promotes your business universally.

Voice is the color you choose for your logo; it's the layout of your homepage design and navigation; it's an invitation on your homepage to learn more about you; it's the text on all the other pages of your Web site, put there to serve a purpose—sales, information, case studies, whatever. Online, your voice is the interaction you must have with your customers—existing and potential—to build enough credibility to convince them to buy from you.

The voice you use online will follow sales to your offline presence.

> **Jupiter Research reported that in 2002, the Internet affected $232 billion in *offline* spending.**

NOT TV, NOT RADIO, NOT PAPER

Words work with the design of your Web site to speak a language that is uniquely digital—recognizable because many clever scientists and technical folks, led by scientist Tim Berners-Lee who invented the World Wide Web, wanted the Internet to look and feel familiar—like using a computer GUI (graphical user interface) more commonly known as point and click technology.

Do not make the mistake so many new Web site business owners make and think you can throw your company brochure up on the Internet to achieve success. People read differently on a computer monitor. Your printed company brochure is not designed for computer viewing. You will learn in Chapter 4, "You Don't Know Dick," how reading on a computer is different than reading in print. You will learn where your Web visitor's eyes lock first and what information you should be putting there for her to review.

You will learn that being online is not like listening to the radio, although you can pop in a CD and enjoy your favorite songs while you surf. Music may soothe the savage beast, but it will distract your surfer if you use it incorrectly on your Web site.

And, while being online seems a lot like TV, after all, you do view it on a monitor that is very TV-ish, your computer monitor is not a TV—at least, not yet. There is an aspect that is similar—the TV remote acts like a mouse; click, click, click and you can change channels in an instant. However, with your mouse, you can click, click, click and visit places your TV will never take you. Your TV remote gets you only to the stations your cable company (or Direct TV) offers you, in whatever package you pay a nice monthly fee for.

Web surfing gives you unlimited access to worlds far beyond your living room. You do pay a monthly fee to an Internet Service Provider (ISP), but admit it; your bill from your ISP is usually a lot less than your cable bill. Yet your cable company controls your viewing. Your ISP only filters your e-mail, and you have some control over that.

Online, a surfer is in a world all her own, one that extends as near or as far as she wishes. The one with the mouse is all-powerful. She can click out of your shopping cart as easily as she clicked in.

NO SHOUTING, PLEASE!

If our voice is too loud, too soft, too convoluted, too busy, or too involved with you and not your customers, you are doomed.

> **Design does affect purchasing decisions...poor design sends people clicking to a competitor. The goal is a positive consumer experience, not flashy colors and loud music that distract the visitor from her purpose: to buy something!**

Many of my clients, in their ignorance, let the designer of their Web site determine their voice. Or they buy into the advice of marketing professionals still buried in the dirt world, insisting that louder is better, or flashier is more fun.

Why? Why loud colors and crazy animation? This isn't television, and it isn't radio. Loud and flashy does more harm than good. Studies show that the majority of Web surfers still have a dial-up connection, and your flashy, loud Web site will not download quickly enough for them. We also know that a majority of Web surfers click out of those flashy Web openings when offered a link to "skip intro," even if they have broadband and don't have to wait forever for that fun movie you spent thousands of dollars developing to download.

If your visitors have stopped by to shop—don't you hope they've stopped by to shop?—let them shop. Leave the entertainment to Spielberg and Lucas.

E-MAIL, BLOGS, INSTANT MESSAGING

As business migrates from passive actions offline such as direct mail and print advertising which traditionally have a very small return on investment (ROI), to interactive marketing online using e-mail, surveys, blogs (online diaries where visitors post comments), and portals (large Web sites that operate as directories for specific topics or industries), all of which allow your customers to meet and greet not only you but EACH OTHER, it may seem as if the scam marketer is taking over. Who can really determine truth from an e-mail or a Web site? How can shoppers really judge how sincere the person selling the product is, just from the content on the Web site? The Web is so impersonal, isn't it?

Absolutely not! The Web is more personal than any newspaper ad, than any magazine ad, than any radio ad; and it gets results better than any Yellow Pages ad. In fact, people are more comfortable sharing information on the Web, or through e-mail. With 93% of Americans hooked on e-mail, and 80% of business professionals preferring it to the phone, it's easy to get very personal online using this real-time communication tool. It's also easy to be wary of it, to be skeptical, to avoid it because the spam issue and/or the reality issue (is this person really who s/he says s/he is?) can get in the way.

Quell those negative thoughts. From the dawn of the 1990s to the sunlit afternoons of the first decade of the new millennium, the information age has been and continues to be about real-time contact. No stamps. No mail truck. No letter carrier. No waiting in line at the post office.

E-mail is the preferred method of communication of teens, moms, sisters, brothers, and business professionals. Let's also factor in that popular teen tool: Instant Messaging. The Instant Messaging market is expected to grow at an annual rate of 150% for the next three years, according to The Yankee Group. You can bet that this dynamic form of communication is going to directly impact your online success in the near future. **Ignore it at your own peril!**

THE SPAM CAN OF WORMS

And so it goes—progress makes our lives easier, but it also brings trouble. Yes, my friend, trouble, in River City, Iowa and everywhere else in the world. Trouble—in the guise of real-time contact; trouble—filling everyone's inboxes with more spam than would ever fit into our home or post office mailbox.

It's the summer of 2003, and the Internet is bulging at the seams with ads and long copy promising riches beyond measure if we would merely click on the link offered. Or invitations promising to spice up our love life with bigger body parts. Every time we open our e-mail box, eagerly anticipating that reply from cousin Jake or Mom or sis, it's guaranteed that along with our regular messages we will be bombarded by unsavory news in the form of ads formerly relegated to the back-end of print magazines—usually typed in tiny print designed to attract only the most intent.

Unsolicited commercial e-mail (UCE) arrives in the same format as all the other e-mails in the box. Savvy consumers know spam from legitimate e-mail—hint: if it resembles a two-year old's typing style, i.e., nonsense words in the subject line: "Read this for great xyensf def" it's probably spam; those extra letters are there to confuse filters. Yet, even for the best of us, one or two offers occasionally get by our radar, leaving us feeling violated. Spam reports abound, with AOL, one of the top ISPs, reportedly filtering over 4.1 million pieces of spam every day!

It reminds me of the 1957 musical, *The Music Man*, where Professor Harold Hill scammed the citizens of River City, Iowa, into buying band instruments he never intended to deliver. Oh, the price of his sweet tongue!

While Professor Hill ultimately saw the error of his ways, convinced by Marian, the librarian (a lover of words, if I remember correctly), we do not have it so easy today. Some of those multi-level marketing schemes are profitable. Most are not. Added to the mix are the hundreds of spam e-mails offering to show us nude pictures of our favorite actress or worse, nude pictures of our relatives! Regardless of their purpose or legitimacy, the fact that these e-mails exist does impact your ability to build a successful online business.

That's the bad news. The really bad news is that like junk mail, spam will probably never go away. Using filters helps, and carefully developed e-mail marketing campaigns do work. But, better minds than ours are struggling with this issue. Let's let them do their work. Our work is to make sales online. And e-mail is still a viable marketing tool if you spend some time learning how to use it properly.

READING, WRITING AND SEO

There is no way around it: you don't need to learn the technology, but you do need to learn how people use the Internet before you begin your journey down the road to online riches. The Internet is cost-effective, interactive, personal, fast, easy, and dynamic. If you have a business, and you do not have a Web presence, it's been nice knowing you.

If you are smart enough to know you need to be online, *Dickless Marketing* is here to help you. Read on to learn how to build a winning Web presence and gain inside information on the largest group of loyal customers in the world. Learn how to approach them, how to court them, and how to close your online sales with them. In the process, you will also learn how to attract their friends and relatives.

How do I know this? When asked if their online spending was likely to increase, participants (non-gender specific) in a survey by the UCLA Internet Report responded with a resounding YES! to the tune of seventy-one percent! Do the math; currently the U.S. has over 166 million homes online. Ninety-seven million shoppers bought online in 2002; that's 59% of all Internet users. If more than half of them are admitting they will be spending even more online in the future; don't you want to join the Web merchants attracting those dollars?

Of course you do. And what group of consumers would you bet is a large part of that 97 million shoppers? If you said the group known the world over for their delight in spending—in other words, women—you would be right. But, read on to learn how this large group of shoppers shops online, and what they expect from you. I think you may be surprised.

Dickless Marketing

1. What Do Women Want?

Women Want to be Taken Seriously

A Pew Internet & American Life Project study shows that more than 9 million women went online for the first time in the latter half of 2002—"revealing that women are now reshaping America's social landscape."

When 61% of women and 55% of men currently access the Internet for business and/or pleasure, you have to stop and consider who is reading your online sales message.

More than half of the time, it's a woman.

> **63% of online shoppers are women.**
> **Women influence over 95% of total goods**
> **and services purchases in this country.**

I have a favorite poem that says: "Make new friends, but keep the old. Those are silver, these are gold." Poet Joseph Parry knew what he was talking about when he composed that friendship poem more than a century ago. As long as precious metals have been worth investing in, gold has always been a better investment than silver. *Dickless Marketing* is here to show you that women who shop online are the gold standard of marketing.

One thing you need to learn about selling to women is that mouthing platitudes by offering them a two-for-one sale, or trying to appeal to their sense of family dedication is a good beginning, but women are not robotic shoppers caught by the lure of a sale or by the obvious tugging of our heart strings over and over again. Yes, we love sales, and we have a deep commitment to family and friends, but getting us to buy from you online requires some finesse, some new world thinking, and some consideration.

OF COUCHES AND REMOTE CONTROLS

Media mogul, Barry Diller, best known for The Home Shopping Network and Match.com, says, "Who cares if some customers are Web surfers and others are old-fashioned couch potatoes?"

Well, Barry, you should. There are few women in that picture. Why? Because the epitome of the couch potato is a man reclining on a sofa on a Saturday or Sunday afternoon watching sports on TV, jealously guarding his remote control.

The woman of the house is more often surfing through her day from one chore to another. In the old millennium, those long ago Dick and Jane days, she would be running errands in the family station wagon; grocery shopping; birthday present shopping; toting kids to soccer or little league; getting her hair done; any number of time-intensive tasks. Today, much of her surfing is being done online. She holds the mouse, not the remote. Her shopping is quick and convenient right from her computer.

If you're online selling products and services, I ask you, do you care if some customers are couch potatoes? You should. Barry Diller can have the couch potatoes. *Dickless Marketing* is going to help you win over the Web surfers.

> **The idea of surfing online was coined by a woman. Jean Armour Polly, a librarian, writer, and mom, wrote the first "Surfing the Internet" book in 1992.**

Lesson number one: women are different from men. Author Andrew Hacker penned an entire book on the differences between men and women (New York: *Mismatch*, Scribner, 2003) in which he identifies "a growing cultural divide as women demand equality." Hacker notes in his book that today more women than men are graduating from college. He points out that women now dominate college sports, thanks to Title IX securing gender equity in sports, signed into law by President Nixon in 1972. But he doesn't really explain what women want. How can he? His research doesn't include interviews or discussions with real women. Mine does.

If we agree that women are different from men, in ways even women might have trouble articulating sometimes, why do marketers think ads focused on selling to men will also sell to women? In a study conducted by marketing research firm Greenfield Online, when asked how they are portrayed in advertising, 91% of the women surveyed answered that they didn't think advertisers understood them. Ninety-one percent. Almost all of them.

Freud was onto something with his notorious question: "What do women want?" Yet, even now, there are still more misunderstandings than clear answers to this question.

THROUGH THE LOOKING GLASS

Women are the most important consumer base for Internet marketing, but focusing on their wants and needs online is barely noticeable. The new millennium is moving into a new decade, yet the old millennium is still clinging tightly to its coattails.

How do I know the 20th century is alive and well online? I log on to the Internet daily. In my search for information I often discover new, interesting Web sites. When I do, I click on over to the "About Us" page to get a better idea of who I'm dealing with and what do I find? An absence of women represented in senior management!

If I do happen to get lucky, the woman shown on the site is either in Human Resources, or Marketing. These are fine professions in and of themselves, but where are the women CEOs or VPs of Operations? The women I see on many, many "About Us" pages represent the female gender in fields that have always represented the female gender.

> **More women than men check out a Web site's "About Us" page.**

This is more than sad. It's a disgrace. According to Jane Eisner, writing in the Philadelphia Inquirer (*Glass Ceiling isn't Getting Any Higher*, June 2002)," only 57 women made it on the list of the 1000 highest paid executives at the Philadelphia region's publicly traded companies." Philadelphia is not unique. Women are not well represented in senior level management much of anywhere, including on the most current list of the Fortune 500. And to those of you determined to point out Carly Fiorina of Hewlett Packard and Anne Mulcahy of Xerox, I say, two women out of hundreds is laudable for them, not the gender.

Surely, you may be thinking, women have made strides in politics. Look at Hilary Clinton and Condoleza Rice. Yet, the situation in government and politics is similar to that in business. In July of 2003, there are 14 women serving in the U.S. Senate. There are 59 women in the House of Representatives. This means that 76 of the 535 members of Congress (both houses) are women (13.6% overall).

Yet women account for more than half of all U.S. jobs, a number that is expected to rise to 62% by 2010. Women also comprise half of the college graduating seniors and almost half of all MBA graduates.

The glass ceiling women have been trying to shatter for more than 40 years may be cracking, but it hasn't broken yet. Society, supported by many of those good old boys, continues to view women in a traditional sense, almost exclusively as homemakers, clerical workers, or moms who are more concerned with making dinner than with technology.

The Internet is showing a significant impact on the position of women in our society, as well as dramatically changing the way consumers act. In the next ten years, women are going to shatter that glass ceiling, and we're not cleaning up any of the broken glass lying around. We are going to be busy building businesses online or buying from other online businesses. If you want to be one of them, read on.

> **It's a Mall World After All, declares Wired magazine, July 2003. Their blurb on Amazon.com's newest slogan, "Amazon.com and you're done!" shows the rising power of personalization.**

As the new millennium confidently chips away at the glass ceiling and the good old boys network, it leaves a number of questions about doing business online unanswered.

- How do you make your Web business friendly to your visitors?
- How do you give your Web site the warm fuzzies?
- How do you gain the trust of online customers—as if the customer could actually stand before you and look into your eyes to determine the quality of your sales' ethic?
- How do you market differently to women than to men?

The answers to these questions are not contained in the simple feminist positions of the 1970s. They are also not answered by developing androgynous sales pitches. No matter how hard we try to pretend that people are people and the body parts beneath their clothes don't matter, it isn't true. Oh how we mothers tried that attack back in the '70s! In our determination to raise our children to be androgynous we gave our daughters Tonka® trucks, our boys Ken dolls, then stood back in amazement when most of them traded toys and went on their merry way.

Men are men and women are women; girls play with Barbie—or emulate PowerPuff Girls today. Boys play with hackysacks—or Nintendo. Occasionally they overlap; girls will induce boys to play house and boys will welcome a particularly sports-minded girl into their hackysack gang because she's as good at it as they are. But, fundamentally, girls and boys **think** differently. And they take those differences into adulthood with them.

Male/female differences are often the subtleties that attract us to each other, though, more often than not, they are also the reasons we can't agree on what color to paint the bedroom. When a woman's place is considered to be in the home, what color to paint the bedroom may seem a trivial decision, but ignoring a significant other's dislike for say—the color green—might cause more trouble than it's worth. If it's the woman who dislikes green, she may give in to her significant other in the bedroom, but not the kitchen. Women choose their battles carefully, with an inbred finesse that tells us when we will win, and when we won't.

These differences have significant implications for marketing. In *Marketing to Women* (Dearborn Trade Publishing, 2003), Martha Barletta notes that, "while men occupy a pyramid, women occupy a peer group." This is an echo of earlier texts that note the community aspect of women's interaction, a concept I will cover in Chapter 7, "Meeting at the Well."

And while many books today opine that women's peer groups involve only other women, don't believe it. Women like men. Male-bashing jokes are no more serious in their delivery than blonde jokes. This century, this brave new millennium, is bringing women and men closer together.

> **"Males and females, it turns out, are different from the moment of conception, and the difference shows itself in every system of body and brain."**
> **Psychology Today/ August 2003**

What it isn't doing is changing the fundamental truths inherent in our genes. Faith Popcorn and Lys Marigold, in their best seller, *EVEolution* (New York: Hyperion Books, 1998) also note that, "women process information differently because our brains are wired differently." *Psychology Today's* August 2003 article, "The New Sex

Scorecard," goes on to qualify this by noting that women have "more gray matter in their brains." Gray matter, according to author Hara Estroff Marano, "is where the brain's heavy lifting is done. The female brain is more densely packed with neurons and dendrites, providing concentrated processing power—and more thought-linking capability."

This shows that our identities as women are predetermined, to a point, by our genetic make-up. Marano's article goes on to show that women excel in language tasks and that our genetic make-up allows us to use our intuition to guide us on many fronts. The article states that women process information by tuning in to the verbal act of communication. This, I maintain, is why we approach shopping and technology differently than men.

Marano says men, "operate most easily with a certain detachment." Imagine this picture—a woman standing in the men's department at Sears, discussing size and washing instructions with the clerk, while a man is shuffling through the rack of khakis, eager to get what he came for and be on his way.

Take that scenario online, and you have a man clicking into a Web site to buy a tool, a CD, or a present for his wife, and the shopping experience is over almost before it's begun because he will not linger to look around. A woman, on the other hand, may want to talk to someone— is there an 800 number to call?— and she will certainly devote a good deal of thought to both the gift and the receiver of the gift, so much so that she may shop around at several other sites before settling on her purchase!

This fondness women have for discussing their purchases, their careful consideration of the gift or product they are buying, often leads salesmen in electronic stores or auto dealerships to become impatient with them or to talk down to them. This is why women have taken to shopping online so eagerly. There is no man to make the questions seem foolish or unimportant. Online, the woman is in control and, using either e-mail or your Web site's preferred method of contact, she can ask as many questions as she likes. A good business will be giving careful thought to how these questions are answered on their Web site.

BIRDS OF A FEATHER

Women didn't tune into the Internet as quickly as men did. Ten years ago, only 10% of online surfers were women. It was a male-dominated medium because technology was assumed to be a male domain controlled by techies and engineers. In 2002, a subtle change occurred. Women began outpacing men in Internet use.

Today, women are the commanding consumer presence online. If you plan on making sales on your Web site, marketing to us is not merely good business; it's a fundamental task you should be studying (men and women alike) as closely as you study your company's quarterly financial statement or your monthly sales figures.

Ignoring the woman's market by making the mistake of believing your products and services can be presented to us using the same ads, the same Web site copy, the same processes you use to attract men, will not endear you to us.

Forget the old millennium and that good old boys network. Join us in the new millennium and discover real answers to that persistent Freudian question: What do women want? These answers will get hundreds of women to your Web site, and we will spend more time and money than the men you are trying to attract now.

WE WANT TO BE WHO WE ARE

Despite the fact that women often congregate in groups, we want you to address us as individuals. We may be the wife of your neighbor; we may be your sister, or your mother; we may be your neighbor's mother, or a cousin or an acquaintance; but each of us is as unique and separate in our identities as birds. Like birds of a feather, we often flock together, but also like birds, we fly home to separate nests, only to re-group the next morning. Because women operate on both a collective level and on an individual level, you need to reach us as a group, but sell to us as individuals.

The *Advancing Women* network, a sub-site of Entrepreneur.com http://www.advancingwomen.com/entrepreneur.html reported in 2000 that "Women today are using the Net to route around the power structure, transcend traditional and historic barriers and, finally, liberate themselves by talking and networking with each other."

That was written three years ago. Our liberation is well into its second stage. The foundation was set when iVillage, the biggest online women's community, bought Women.com, priming hundreds of other women to build and promote communities of their own. It also showed women that a collective voice gets the most cookies (pun intended—if you don't know what an Internet cookie is, you will learn in Chapter 6, "Ties that Bind").

It's this inherent desire in women to communicate, to share thoughts and experiences with others that makes the Internet so attractive to us. We do our best to enable others. Studies even show it makes us better managers.

For example, the Center for Women's Research cites the following list of ways women use their leadership skills: http://www.nfwbo.org/

- o To create and articulate a vision (behind every successful man there is a woman, after all).
- o To set clear direction (we practice what we preach).
- o To take charge (women do what needs to be done, at home and at work).
- o To bring inspiration to the table.
- o To set high standards for performance (we want our sons AND daughters to be doctors, or at least the BEST of whatever they choose to be).
- o To assume responsibility (all right, the world crisis is all our fault—so get out of the way and let us fix it, okay?).

Between 1997 and 2002, the Center estimates that the number of women-owned firms increased by 14% nationwide, twice the rate of all firms; also, employment in women-owned firms increased by 30%—1-1/2 times the U.S. rate, and sales grew by 40%—the same rate as all firms in the U.S. http://www.nfwbo.org/key.html

That's why *Dickless Marketing* is important to the small and medium-sized businesses online. The online business model is not yet set in stone.

Dickless Marketing wants to drive out those old 20th century Dick and Jane misconceptions that still pervade the marketplace and may be preventing you from achieving the profits you deserve.

I know it's stereotypical, but it's also true: women like to shop. Shopping is fun. Case in point: my 20-year-old son has a new girlfriend, a delightful young woman who is both attractive and intelligent. She will be attending a local university in the fall of 2003 to begin her college studies. When I suggested we go to lunch to get to know each other better, she said, "Sounds good, but let's go shopping!"

The good news for small businesses online is—we also have the cash to spend, and we are spending it online. You will find out how much we spend online, and what we buy, in later chapters. Suffice it to say that women may have adopted this new technology a bit more slowly than our male friends, but we're on board now and we're taking over. The Internet is even supplanting the phone as our preferred method of communication.

Last year, mothers spent more time online either e-mailing or engaging in Instant Messaging, than their teenagers. E-mailing and IMing are better than any phone connection—they're not only instantaneous, they're free!

Look to Instant Messaging to be offering sales options for your products and services in the not so distant future.

Regardless of what you're selling—you might be a clothing outlet; you might be in the business of selling copy machines, business supplies or computers; you might be selling novelties or intimate apparel; whatever it is, if you haven't taken the time to carefully consider how your message is coming across to women, you're trotting down a muddy road full of potholes, and your profit and loss statement is going to show it.

We have the money—a February 2003 article in *The New York Times* (*Wage Gap Between Men and Women Shrinks)* cited new wage trends in favor of women. "While men's wages have failed to keep up with even the low rate of inflation, women's earnings have continued to grow, giving an important lift to many families and helping sustain consumer spending."

Drop the reluctance to get in front of the woman's market. Stop viewing us as the *weaker sex*. We are mysterious by design no less nor more than the men in our lives. Let's explore what that means.

WOMAN AS MYTH

Historically, woman has been depicted as the weaker sex, born of the rib of Adam, designed as his "helpmate." Western religions have also depicted woman as temptress. Eve, the first woman, tempts Adam into sinful disobedience. A variant story of the fall from Eden depicts two females, Eve, who was virtuous (except for the snake and the apple), and Lilith, who considered herself Adam's

It is amazing how little is written on the virtue of gentleness. We are afraid of the concept. As women we have struggled inordinately to dismantle the old shackles of how we ought to behave. We don't want to be taken advantage of; we don't want to be abused. Gentleness and strength are not opposites: They are complementary.
~ Adele Wilcox

equal. Because Lilith refused to allow Adam complete power over her, she was banished from the Garden of Eden well before the ultimate fall from grace. Lilith went off on her own and was rumored to have become a succubus (a demon assuming female form to have sexual intercourse with men in their sleep), forever giving strong women a bad name.

Those old tales continue to perpetuate WOMAN AS MYTH. They attempt to present woman as secondary to man—second in marriage, in business, and in life. But the idea of woman as the second sex is as much a myth as that old notion that pink is for girls and blue is for boys.

Lynn Peril, author of *Pink Think* (New York: W.W. Norton and Company, 2002) says, "Women from the 1940s to the 1970s were coaxed to 'think pink' by persuasive advertisements and meticulous (though often misguided) advice experts. Feminine perfection meant conforming to a mythical standard, one that would come wrapped in an adorable pink package, of course." (We will talk about more pink and blue, later on).

In recent years we have come to see the real power of women, or in the words of the old aphorism, "The hand that rocks the cradle rules the world."

> Infancy's the tender fountain,
> Power may with beauty flow,
> Mother's first to guide the streamlets,
> From them souls unresting grow.
> Grow on for the good or evil,
> Sunshine streamed or evil hurled;
> For the hand that rocks the cradle,
> Is the hand that rules the world.
> William Ross Wallace~ 1851

While the good news is that more men are rocking the cradle than ever before, the traditional view of that hand on the cradle still sees it as a woman's. From her status as mother, woman is perceived to have power over the whole world. Yet, when that phrase was first coined in 1851 women were not even allowed to own property! The term began to be used, over and over again, decade after decade, to offer women solace. As if Mom, waiting at home, diapering the new baby, pounding the dirt out of the rugs, checking on dinner in the oven, was a woman's due, and the respect accorded to it, her reward.

Never doubt that women who elect to be mothers are proud of it, and many women who don't elect it, grow into it. Never doubt that women are smug about this exclusive ability to bear children, something men will never know. It is so important that when we are denied the chance to procreate, we often go to great lengths, medically and socially—opting for artificial insemination or adoption—to repair that injustice. Even women who have chosen to remain childless often display as much nurturing and caring as any biological mother.

This ability to produce children should not be demeaned, however, by the continued recitation of a poem from centuries gone by, as if our contribution to business and politics should remain by the crib. You will learn later on that mom plays a big role in shopping online.

If we explore the woman as myth concept, delving into the psyche of what women want and why men have such a hard time figuring that out, we may begin to discover how to successfully market to women online. For reference sake, let's look at Woman as Myth in this story of King Arthur and the Knights of the Round Table. Perhaps it will help illuminate the first step in discovering how to market and sell to women online.

ଚ୍ଚ~ଚ୍ଚ~ଚ୍ଚ~ The story begins with King Arthur and his favorite nephew, Sir Gawain (the most handsome man in the kingdom) on an afternoon ride through the forest. King Arthur and Sir Gawain are accosted by a giant that bears a grudge against the king. Being a knight himself, and noticing that the King and his nephew are unarmed, the giant refrains from appeasing his need for revenge.

"I will not harm you," the giant tells King Arthur. "Instead, I challenge you to answer one question and the grudge I bear will be forgiven."

The King, being a man of virtue and courage, knows he cannot win in a physical fight with the giant, and since he certainly doesn't want to put his favorite nephew in harm's way, agrees to the challenge.

"I give you one year," the giant says, "to find the answer to this question: What do women really want?"

There is a moral dilemma here larger than the worry of physical defeat: How will it look to his kingdom if he cannot answer this question? So, Arthur, being the intelligent senior level manager that he is, delegates the responsibility of this task to Sir Gawain.

Gawain accepts the challenge—what choice does he have? And off he rides, resigned to the usual *noblesse oblige* of the day, confident that he will find the answer quickly and easily. After all, he's not only a knight—and an intelligent one at that—he's also very handsome. What woman would resist his charms, and in his arms, refuse his request?

Ah, if he'd only known—better men than he have tried and failed at this quest.

The story goes on to detail Sir Gawain's humiliating defeat at the bosoms of hundreds of women. A lot of unqualified responses, none of which inspired Sir Gawain to return to King Arthur in triumph, filled his head and left him as confused as the day he started. At long last (this is a myth, remember) Gawain enters the Forest of Inglewood where a female guardian attends to a magic well. This woman is purported to know all there is to know, leading Sir Gawain to boldly approach her despite advice from others that he will be sorely disappointed.

The guardian of the magic well is so ugly Sir Gawain cannot believe his eyes and topples from his horse in shock. The woman looks calmly into Gawain's eyes and tells him that, yes; she has the answer he seeks. But, to obtain it, he must promise to marry her.

Summoning his knightly courage—there are sacrifices one must make for one's king, after all—Sir Gawain agrees and they trot off to the chapel to be married. When the time comes to meet the giant and answer his question, Sir Gawain is prepared. Let us note that in the myth the marriage is working out well and to Sir Gawain's surprise, after a few weeks of marriage, he does not see his bride as ugly any longer.

To the giant, Sir Gawain offers this reply: "What women really want is...freedom." The giant lets out a bellow and stomps away muttering under his breath about "the state of things where even the deepest secrets are now available in the common folk." And how "England was surely going to the dogs since the glory days." ๛๛๛๛

In some versions of the myth, the answer is that women want sovereignty. For our purposes, we will accept that *one* of the answers to the question of what women want is that they want freedom; freedom to be who they are.

The challenge now becomes: How do you treat each woman as an individual, when your products exist to benefit ALL manner of women (and even some men)?

You take a page from companies the world over that have been successfully marketing to women for decades and are now online continuing their reign—companies such as Mary Kay, Avon, Wal-Mart, and Victoria's Secret. Then, you look at the successful online companies that sprung up out of the tech rush of the 1990s and are still around to talk about it: Amazon.com, AOL, iVillage, Hallmark, eBay and more. And—you lip stick'em.

WHAT WE LEARNED IN THIS CHAPTER:

- o Women have discretionary income and they are spending it online.
- o Women are different from men in many ways. It's in your best interest to learn and understand those differences.
- o The mythical image of a woman ruling the world by staying home "rocking the cradle" has no place in today's technological world.
- o As a whole, women want you to consider their interests and their needs in your marketing messages.
- o Women have more gray matter than men, but men have bigger heads.

2. Lip-Sticking

Be Clear and Honest in Your Sales Message

Jabberwocky
'Twas brillig, and the slithy toves
Did gyre and gimble in the wabe;
All mimsy were the borogoves,
And the mome raths outgrabe.
Lewis Carroll—*Through the Looking Glass*

Lewis Carroll was a creative and intelligent writer. More than a mere poet and the author of *Alice in Wonderland* and *Through the Looking Glass*, Carroll was also a scholar credited with mathematical writings that include *An Elementary Treatise on Determinants (1867), Euclid and His Modern Rivals (1879), and Curiosa Mathematica (1888).*

Jabberwocky is taken from *Through the Looking Glass*, written after *Alice in Wonderland.* Carroll combined words and phrases to create verse that seems nonsensical, but that exists to challenge traditional thinking and beliefs. Using language to get people's attention worked—Jabberwocky is quoted to this day in English literature classes, in business articles, and in books on marketing to women.

It's mentioned here because language is so important in marketing. To sell to women you need to do more with your lips than mouth platitudes. You need to make sure the words you use stick—like glue, in our conscious thoughts and our unconscious thoughts. Don't resort to words we have to decipher with a dictionary, and don't invent acronyms that look "cute" or jingles that insult our intelligence. Just be honest, tell us what you have to offer, and then stick to it.

BUT JANE SAID...

"I know you think you heard what I said, but what I said is not what you heard." Sounds like a case of miscommunication, to me. The point is: communication is more about *listening* than speaking. The listener owns the message. Can't you just hear your mother's voice in your ear, "Jane/Dick, say what you mean, and mean what you say." You are allowed to roll your eyes, but you have to admit now that your mother was right.

Words are more important today than ever before. The Internet and Web depend on your words to convey your message to the millions of women out there searching for your products.

Our favorite mode of communication today is e-mail. E-mail is one reason the post office wants to do away with Saturday delivery. The proliferation of e-mail messages across the global medium of the Internet—messages that don't require stamps, mail trucks or mailmen, excuse me, letter carriers—has considerably lightened the local letter carrier's bags.

But e-mail isn't perfect. Improper use of e-mail is a key example of how ambiguous words can be. The number of misunderstood e-mail messages floating through cyberspace could probably fill the Grand Canyon at this point, and I'm not talking about spam. Relying on short paragraphs, truncated sentences and bad punctuation is causing many e-mail messages to say things the writer didn't mean them to say.

It's all about word choice—about the missing voice of an e-mail message. I talked a bit about voice in the introduction; now you will begin to see how important it is and how, on the Internet, readers are actually listening to what you say. Your message is being read, yes, but there is a voice attached to every word. Every word conveys part of your marketing message.

This popular '60's saying seems to say it all:
"Telephone, telegraph... tell a girl!"

Voice goes beyond the text written on your Web site. Voice is the combination of words, design, and navigation that convey your intent. Since studies show that women are the experts at talking—and that girls typically have better reading and verbal skills than boys, starting in grade school and continuing throughout college—isn't it important that the voice you use on your Web site speaks to us in words we not only understand, but can also relate to?

ACCIDENTALLY ON PURPOSE

My clients hire me for my communication skills. I am most often sought out to rewrite the words on a Web site than any other task. When doing so, I have to pay close attention to the end-user's knowledge of the site's purpose. When the client is attempting to attract women as well as men, I know it's important to explain details without talking down to the customer!

Another vital task in developing good Web site copy is to write in active, not passive voice. Most people cannot separate themselves from writing the way they speak. This ends up with copy such as this request describing the perfect job applicant, which came off the career page of a technical Web site: *absent minded of long hours.*

Absentminded (no space) means: "lost in thought and unaware of one's surroundings or actions: *given to absence of mind.*"

I personally wouldn't do business with a company that hires people given to absence of mind, would you?

Using the wrong word tainted their meaning. They meant *unmindful of long hours*, which is what they should have said.

Examples of passive and active tense:

PASSIVE: "A2XYZ online is very respectful of you and your privacy. We will not sell or share your personal information with others. If you sign up to receive e-mailed updates from us, we will promise to only e-mail you once a month."

ACTIVE: "A2XYZ online respects you and your privacy. We do not sell, nor do we share, any of your personal information with others. Sign up to receive our monthly newsletter. A2XYZ delivers qualified information guaranteed to save you money."

Sometimes the trick is to read your text out loud. Read both of those sentences out loud and notice how much easier the active voice is to assimilate in your brain. Curt and to the point, it also contains a call to action that the passive voice lacks.

Pictures play an important role, also, but for this discussion we are concerned with how you put your words together, what the whole message communicates, and how it conveys your intentions. This is so vital to reaching the women's market, ignoring it is tantamount to committing business suicide.

Women are more verbal not because we're smarter. It's because we like words—they enable us to share; share stories about our lives with our friends and relatives; share information about our health and our children; share secrets, and—share bargains. We like talking about all of those things.

When we share a conversation on the bargain we just found online at your Web site, it means we are lip-sticking your message all over the Web. You can't buy better advertising than that—it will be tapped by the online power of your words and ours.

TRUST ME

Marketing in the dirt world is a challenge all of its own. It's slowly beginning to adjust to the new market realities of the 21st century. There are a few industry giants that seem to recognize the value of courting women—companies such as Ford, with an emphasis on the women's emerging market in car sales; McDonald's with an emphasis on nutrition (really, McDonald's is only copying Wendy's, which has been offering salads for years now); General Mills with its *Nutrition for Women Instant Oatmeal* (Golden Brown Sugar; mmmmmm!); and

Mom's Motrin® with its commercials depicting strong, active Moms who don't let aches and pains dictate their activities.

TV commercials aimed at the women's market are flourishing. This new orientation toward marketing to women is clearly illustrated in the recent change in commercials for Brawny® paper towels. The days of the little woman trying to cajole her husband or partner into helping with the cleaning have disappeared. The new brawny man is shown happily using the product to get the house ready for a romantic dinner with his female companion.

These are a few old-world companies entering the new millennium with an understanding that the women's market deserves serious attention. These companies understand that women are different from men. They know that using competition (I'm better than you) or hard-hitting tactics (car commercials showing men driving aggressively on empty roads) attract far more men than women. Women can be competitive, but we spend more time *helping each other* than trying to be better than each other. And, while some young women out there may get turned on by those fast cars speeding down long stretches of empty highway, the women with the money to spend are not in that market. Learn about them in Chapter 5, "S-E-X-Sarah-Ellen Xceptions."

Meanwhile, many established marketing companies rooted in the dirt world are still so clueless their experimentation with how to market to women effectively is having the same effect as throwing a water balloon at a barn. A lot of territory gets wet, but the message evaporates into nothingness in no time.

E-commerce and the clicks and mortar world have thrown the marketing industry into confusion. Everyone knows the first rule of sales is to build trust, but the dirt world can't quite figure out how to do that in a world increasingly connected through a computer cable.

Building trust online isn't that hard to do. It's a matter of challenging traditional thinking and discarding that old-fashioned thinking that Dick is where you should be putting your focus. Dick isn't spending as much time online, nor is he forking over the cash to buy your products. I'll tell you what Dick is doing online: he's reading news, he's playing games, he's checking the stock market and he's—well, looking at pretty pictures. If he does any shopping online, it's to get a last minute gift for a birthday, an anniversary, or some other special occasion that he doesn't have time to run off to the mall for. Online he can click the item into a shopping cart, have it wrapped and get it delivered overnight. What more could he want?

Men operate like this, on and off the Internet, because they are territorial, focused, and solitary by nature. Marano, in his *Psychology Today* article mentioned earlier, points out that men operate by seeing "a geometric system, taking directional cues in the layout of routes," while women "personalize space by finding landmarks."

Consequently, when Dick approaches the decision to buy something, whether he's considering new stocks, a new car, or a new chair for his office, he's thinking about getting the shopping experience *over with as soon as possible*. Most men make a beeline to the department or store they know has the item they want. They want to go in, get what they came for—new slacks, a new suit, a new shirt, a gift—and get out. They do not want to wander around window-shopping. Whether he's in the mall or on your Web site, Dick knows what he wants and he wants to buy it and be on his way.

Actually, if Dick is shopping online, he's as likely to be buying a gift for his wife, his mother, his girlfriend or his kids, as he is to be buying something for himself. Your site—built to attract women and offer advice on how to make them happy—is going to make his life so much easier he will bookmark it and come back again and again to let you make him look good! Offer him the kinds of things that will make the women in his life happy, and I promise you that those women will stop in to buy from you for their mothers, sisters, daughters, husbands, and all their friends!

What's not to like about that?

WRAPPED AND SHIPPED

Because Dick is generally in a hurry when it comes to shopping, he is sometimes too trusting and prone to take things at face value online. If you say you have the item he wants, and that you'll ship it, he believes you. As long as you have it wrapped and shipped to arrive on time, he's happy. If there's a glitch—the product is late or broken—he will chalk it up to experience and shop elsewhere next time.

He might shop by brand name, but if he does, it's likely because the brand name store is where his mother or his wife shops. He is **sooooo not interested** in the shopping experience! He considers it an ordeal and mostly just wants to get it over with as soon as possible!

Women, on the other hand, want *the shopping experience to do something for them.* We especially want it to go on and on! Like our friend, Dick, we value convenience. Unlike Dick, however, we enjoy taking time to make our selection, and we need to trust you before we will buy. Yes, even women have to rush their shopping, sometimes, and when that happens today, we're researching online in order to run in to the mall, get what we want, and get home.

Lip-sticking is building trust. It involves our having confidence that you will honor your two for one sale, or that you support your loyalty program with serious product offerings. We won't click that "buy now" button until you've lip-sticked us. A good way to start that process is by showing us that exchanges will be handled with a smile—and very little effort on our part.

Another way to show us you care is by offering something extra, something of added value. Wrapped and shipped is good, (free shipping counts more than sale price), but don't make us wait until the end of the buying cycle to learn about your shipping requirements. If the shipping cost causes sticker shock, you've lost us.

Early studies of how surfers view Web sites proved that when a visitor lands on your homepage, she gives it a quick review—less than two seconds worth of time—to orient herself. Her eyes immediately go for text, searching headlines and captions to see if she's in the right place, then her gaze fixes on the center of the page. Web usability experts call this area of your homepage "prime real estate." It's where you will succeed or fail in drawing the visitor in to buy your products or services. That prime real estate can look different on different monitors, and it will display differently in different browsers. This means if you aren't careful how you build your site, you may lose your visitor during those first few critical seconds.

If she hasn't clicked out of your site after those initial 8-10 seconds, your visitor has viewed your logo, decided to stay and is making a decision on what link she will click next.

While she is checking out your prime real estate, she is also noticing your navigation links and other important text using her peripheral vision. Put testimonials on the right or left, but most importantly, give her a reason to click into the catalog or product page. Offer choices such as different sizes, colors or variations right in the prime real estate section of your homepage. Don't say, "Click here for catalog." That does little to engage the reader.

Choose more compelling language for the prime real estate section of your homepage: "Summer Ts in Soft Pastels" is an eye-catcher for April/May sales; "Shimmering, Slinky Holiday Sweaters–Short and Long Sleeved" works great for Christmas.

Knowing the right power words may involve a bit of research, but it's worth it. Offer a feedback form on your site and ask women who visit your site what they like, what they don't like. Ask them how to improve your products or services—and be specific! Give them multiple-choice answers—and leave a space for comments. If you rely on preconceived notions of what women want, I guarantee you will be disappointed. Worse yet, if you're one of those businesses still buying into the women's myth as stated in Chapter 1, the only sale you will make online will be to your own mother.

Failing to address your core market properly is suicide. And it's not a male-only weakness. Many women-owned businesses are guilty of these mistakes, also.

Why? Because it's easier to go with the flow. The effort of changing your thinking and then your approach to selling can seem too difficult. I am here to tell you that it's a task that needs to be done, regardless of gender or product/service.

If you're a man, don't make the mistake of judging women's needs and desires based on your mother, your sister, your wife, or your grandmother. Use them as valuable informants, but don't limit yourself. Reaching the truly enormous women's market online requires talking to every woman who visits your site and some who don't. Put a link to your feedback form on every page, and ask the women who visit your site to share your URL with friends. Offer an incentive for their time. Free shipping is a no-brainer. Understand that the words you use will influence how the woman visiting reacts. "Honest Opinions Wanted" is a good introduction to your feedback form. "Free Product for Your Thoughts" is another.

If you're a woman doing business online, you may be relying on your intuitive understanding of marketing to women, and while *Dickless Marketing* supports that strategy—it does work—don't forget to follow up that intuition with careful research investigating how other women feel about your product.

> **Women make up slightly more than half of the population, but they control well over half of the spending.**

WHERE DID YOU GET THAT??

When a woman is shopping, she is often looking for gifts or personal items for *family and friends,* rather than shopping for herself. Before she ventures online, she may already have asked friends and family (other women) where to buy what she's looking for; what color is good; whether or not the style is right for the end-user; and numerous other questions—even if she's buying a refrigerator! It's when she gets to the store, physical or virtual, that she may let her gut (intuition) dictate her final purchase.

> **In a small, informal mouse-to-mouse survey I conducted, women said they were more likely to consider the opinion of family and friends when purchasing gifts. When purchasing items for themselves, the opinion of family and friends was rated second to price and quality, which received equal scores.**

Chapter 1 showed that **women make more than 85% of the buying decisions in this country** and influence even more. We love to report great bargains or a new product that catches our eye, but we are equally likely to circulate a bad-shopping experience. We will e-mail all of our friends almost as soon as we click off the site that insulted us. In this new media marketplace, we are just as likely to be Instant Messaging, sharing the information *at that moment*. If so, the bad news will get passed on to hundreds, maybe thousands, of other women in the loop in less than one hour.

Women are critical because our goal is to please the people we care about; people that include our relatives, friends, significant others, and even new acquaintances. We aren't thinking about how much thanks we're going to get, or whether this will get us into Heaven. When a woman is shopping for others, she is wondering, "Is this the right color? Is it the right size? Is it the right style?" And, "Will she or he (the receiver) be able to return it easily?"

This means your task is to show us that you understand our need to buy something that is *going to make someone else happy*. You need to dispense with the jabberwocky and offer a firm, warm handshake that conveys trust. In this country, a handshake is still a symbol of respect, acceptance, and trust. I challenge you to count the number of ads you see that depict people shaking hands. The act of sealing a deal with a handshake is firmly planted in our psyches as a solid promise. It's lip-sticking at its best.

Shaking hands online isn't as tricky as you may think. You do this by being truthful about your company and your products. You do this by displaying pictures that show the product details (design thumbnail graphics that, when clicked on, enlarge to show more detail), and you do it by addressing your Web visitor with the same courtesy and respect you would show your own mother or sister. That means using words like "Please" and "Thank you," and, where possible, addressing her by name.

Look at this example:

IVILLAGE.COM

iVillage, the largest women's community online provides an excellent example of how handshaking and personalization give the visitor the feeling of being part of a community. At iVillage, there is an immediate sense of familiarity. The words **Welcome Back!** in the prime real estate section of the page invite the visitor in to see what's new, as if you've been there before. This homepage gives numerous options with dozens of links, but the flow of the page is orderly, with the most important links in that prime real estate section of the page. In addition, the site uses white space effectively so the titles and links don't overwhelm the reader. It's easy for a woman to quickly and easily decide where she wants to click next.

Of course, if the visitor is already a member of the community, that welcome back note will greet her by name, the first step in personalizing your relationship—consider it the warmth in your handshake. "Welcome Back, Jane," makes her feel right at home, and ready to consider shopping. I will talk about personalization, and how it is becoming the marketing tool of the new age, in Chapter 5. What we're learning here is that personalization is as good as a handshake, and it helps lip-stick your sales message.

If you click over to www.womans-net.com, a woman's networking site, you will see a similar layout; clear navigation links at the top of the page, graphics that depict women in business or at home, and an invitation to *personalize the page.*

Women love the opportunity to add their personal touch to the places they visit online. Allowing us the option to choose our own color our own layout, and even to add our own "favorite links," will make us your friend for life.

Guess how we spell friend in *Dickless Marketing?* Try: S-A-L-E-S.

Another site that works well is www.flylady.net.

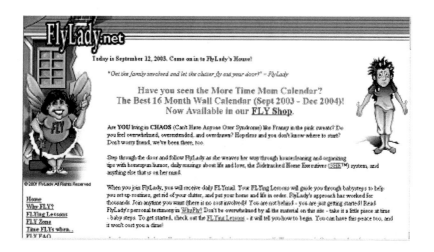

This site is designed to help women get more organized. Notice how the owner draws her visitor into the site with well-placed text and promises. She writes as if she is speaking directly to the visitor and this note helps us move down the page to see what goodies she has to offer: *"**Our home page is long.** You need to scroll to the bottom to see it all. We use it as a bulletin board to showcase the activities we are currently working on."*

She also posts notes from satisfied customers. Testimonials from real people who visit her site and buy her products. You cannot get better advertising than that anywhere in this universe! And it's free!

$14.3 BILLION AND COUNTING

The U.S. Census Bureau shows that retail e-commerce sales in fourth quarter 2002 were at $14.3 billion, up 28.2 percent from fourth quarter 2001. If you're online selling something, (and you have actually made sales) you are part of that statistic. But which part?

During the dot-bomb implosion, hundreds of new businesses opened up online. The Internet, eager entrepreneurs were told, was going to make them rich. Then—the bomb hit. Eyes no longer shining with the glow of instant riches, most of them crawled away to nurse their wounds. Some of them returned to corporate America, many of them tried again. Those that were determined to get it right the second time are the owners of small businesses who should be reading *Dickless Marketing* because selling to women is going to help you push that $14.3 billion higher and higher in the coming years.

Census Bureau reports also show that after the dot-bomb blast minority-owned businesses grew four times faster than the national average. As I mentioned in Chapter 1, despite the fact that there are more women than men in the U.S. and the world, women are still considered a minority. That means women started a lot of those businesses. In fact, women-owned businesses are predicted to spend more money on technology this year (2003) than traditionally male-dominated businesses.

Where are all of those new businesses? I say most of them are online. Even if they have an offline store or office, the women who left corporate America to pursue their dream of self-employment knew the Internet was the best place to begin their new venture.

Savvy businesspeople, male and female alike, understand the value of an Internet presence. All it takes is a Web site, which is easy enough to build. All you have to do is drive down to your favorite office supply store and buy some software and you're good to go. Right?

Not right.

IN WONDERLAND

Yes, you can choose a template from an HTML software package, or one from an online Web development company. You can install it on your PC and find yourself spending hours, days, weeks, trying to fit your company logo and products into *their* code, *their* design, *their* interface. I'm not saying this never works. I've known some small business owners who were moderately successful at it. Most of them knew some HTML code before they started. Or they took an afternoon seminar in Web design to learn how to "do it right."

I can tell immediately, as soon a new client shows me his or her homepage, whether or not the site was put together by a serious designer or by the client. Yes, indeed, I can tell the difference between homemade and professionally done right away. I bet many of your online visitors can, too.

There's no way around it. When you decide to tackle building an online presence, you are very much like Alice entering Wonderland.

Imagine there before you, on your dining room table or your kitchen table, or wherever you are jotting down ideas for your new business, a bottle labeled "Drink Me" and next to it, a round cake labeled "Eat me." Somewhere in your subconscious, your gut is telling you to do one or the other because the situation you're in requires action and you're sure if you eat or drink one of these tasty treats, the wonders of the universe will open up to you.

Careful. Careful. If you remember correctly, the drink me bottle in *Alice in Wonderland* shrunk her to the size of a pea. Hard to do business when you're that little—having your customers always looking down on you.

Eating the cake transformed her into a giant. Also, a difficult way to conduct business—with you always looking down on your customers.

Alice had a bit of a hard time getting around in Wonderland because she was unfamiliar with the territory and no one was being truthful with her. You are more fortunate. *Dickless Marketing* is here to show why you shouldn't drink everything the so-called experts give you, and why you shouldn't eat anything you either haven't baked yourself or doesn't come from a trusted friend. Isn't that something your own mother or your bossy big sister would tell you?

As time goes on, the Wonderland of the Internet is settling into a business arena with predictable outcomes. Professionals who care about how the Internet works are standardizing certain aspects of Web site development. One particular group is the W3C, the WWW Consortium, headed by the inventor of HTML, scientist Tim-Berners

Lee. For more detailed information on what the W3C is doing to set online standards, visit the Web site at http://w3.org .

At this time, the standardizations we're most familiar with breed a certain familiarity. When Jane goes online to shop, she isn't stuck in a strange world of Wonder, the way Alice was. She has certain expectations involving information design and Web site functionality. We know that words speak volumes in a shorter space on the Web; we understand that people read differently on a computer monitor than they do when viewing print material. We know that there is an expectation on the part of the end user that the Web site will *do something for her.* Not that SHE will have to do something for the Web site, although that's the reality. You want her to shop, right?

Getting her to shop at your site and buy from you can change the Internet you know from a Wonder-howland full of the unexpected, into a shopping extravaganza giving you the cha-ching shivers.

Here's why:

- o   More women than men are online.
- o   Women have discretionary income to spend.
- o   Women shop for a lot of other people.
- o   Women talk to each other about their shopping sprees.

Yes, slithy toves may still slink about like serpents, tempting the Alices you are plying your wares to, but Alice isn't listening to slithy toves or serpents. She's competent and informed. She knows a snake when she sees one.

TICK, TICK, TICK

The Internet has truly leveled the playing field for small business and for women. The WWW, the interactive, pop-up playground of the Internet, which is where most businesses reside, doesn't care if you're a one-woman shop, a group of four, or IBM. It offers the same opportunities for success to everyone.

That is patently untrue. You may still be reading it in marketing e-zines and in hundreds of other places both online and off but the Internet is not concerned with the playing field. What does it mean, anyway? Does it mean the SMBs (small and medium-sized businesses) have suddenly found the Holy Grail of *real-time communication?*

Excuse me, but what, exactly, is the telephone? Isn't that real-time communication? You dial, there is a ringing sound, the person you called picks up, and you speak—in real-time. So, why is the term *real-time* considered so closely attached to the Internet and perhaps less and less to the telephone?

It's because the telephone is no longer real time. Today you're more likely to get someone's answering machine than a real person—especially in business. If you don't get an answering machine directing you to voicemail, you get a computer-generated voice routing you through the company directory. Press 1 for Sue, press 2 for Joe, and so on. Moreover, on our newest mobile phones text messaging and Internet capabilities are just as important as sound quality. As the Verizon cell phone ads repeat, "Can you hear me now?"

On the Internet, *real-time* refers to an activity, an interactive process. It's the ability to shop, chat, or research on *the user's own time*, which may or may not be on the businesses' 9-5 schedule. That's what's real about it. Think of it this way: the end-user is in charge. When Jane is online she understands that TICK, TICK, TICK, THE WORLD IS HERS AT A MOUSE CLICK. That's far more practical than having her hung up on the phone, fuming over a tinny voice offering to connect her to everyone but the person she really wants to talk to!

Here is where Jabberwocky comes in. Trying to sell your products using nonsense words or gibberish won't work. Shopping online is a real time function (no hustling out to the car to drive 20 minutes to the mall), giving women the advantage. Playing fast and loose with your marketing message will send Jane clicking into a competitor's site as fast as she used to hang up that phone that refused to connect her to the party she wanted to talk to.

PUMPING IRON

Let's get serious. The Internet hasn't leveled the playing field. SMBs have owned the playing field for some time now. Small and mid-sized businesses account for more money and more payroll than the big boys, by a long shot. Think about it. One reason the world is courting small business today is because many people have lost faith in the Enrons, the Worldcoms, the Global Crossings, the Kodaks, and the Xeroxes of the world. Their only interest is in certain shades of green; Hamilton green, Ulysses S. Grant green, Benjamin Franklin green, colors that line their CEO's pockets, not their employees' pockets.

SMBs are entitled to a pat on the back. Most of them treat their employees well, meet payroll and offer benefit packages. Those who work from home manage to support themselves and pay their taxes, albeit with an extension now and then. When all is said and done, the workforce at those logo-touting corporate giants is made up of folks who spend much of their hard-earned income at small businesses— much like yours.

> **The Center for Women's Business Research reports that "women are active Internet users, yet women business owners are much more likely than any other woman to make personal purchases online — 57% to 40%."**

At the Small Business Administration reports show that small business was responsible for three-fourths of employment growth and 90% of new business in 2000. These are businesses with gross revenue under $5M, and generally with 100 or less employees. Some economic indicators allow companies with 1-500 employees to join the small business club, as long as their gross revenue is under $10M. Regardless of which definition you choose, small business has muscle. Muscle that is being pumped up by the tender sex.

The Center for Women's Business Research, notes: "as of 2002, there are an estimated 6.2 million majority-owned, privately held, **women-**

owned firms in the U.S., employing 9.2 million people and generating $1.15 TRILLION in sales."

There is nothing Jabberwocky about that! Small business rules, and women rule small business! We've come into our own. We only ask that you look us in the eye, speak to us in words we understand, and offer us incentives when we do repeat business with you. BTW (by the way), incentives are not coupons. Incentives are price breaks, product offerings, and lifetime guarantees.

I AM WOMAN, GIVE ME MORE

I have spent that last 10 years working with more than a dozen business professionals both in marketing and in sales. All but one was male.

At first meeting, these illustrious professionals all welcomed me with open arms. I was courted with promises and expectations that flattered my background and success in sales and communications. However, I soon found out in each case that my being hired was more a matter of adding lipstick, or typing skills, to the group than of adding a knowledgeable professional.

I worked hard to be included in management positions in those companies. After years of pounding on that glass ceiling, I'd finally put a crack in it and managed to crawl through with only a few cuts and bruises. I

> Whatever women do they must do twice as well as men to be thought half as good. Luckily, this is not difficult.
> ~ Charlotte Whitton

bought into the whole 20th century mentality that dictated I compete with the men in my workplace on their level. This meant wearing business suits in colors that were strong, appealing, but not provocative. It meant working as hard or harder than anyone else. It meant contributing openly, eagerly, and consistently to round table meetings. In short, I was wasting my time trying to prove Charlotte Whitton's popular feminist slogan.

Over time, I learned that the color of my business suit didn't matter. Coming in early and staying late didn't matter. I was relegated to the "myth" status given to most women, as mentioned in Chapter 1.

I'm not talking 19th century, here. I'm talking about the early days of the Internet, the technology boom and start-ups, where I was hired as part of management. My writing skill got me in the door and while I did a fair amount of that, I just as often ended up answering the phone, managing the supply room, or opening the mail.

These experiences were frustrating in more ways than I can count. My *magna cum laude* in English didn't matter. My credentials in English Honors and College Honors didn't matter. My successful sales background selling technology to senior level managers didn't matter.

My presence was a challenge to these men. Oh, they weren't worried that I would take their jobs; it was beyond them even to imagine that I could take their jobs. What I discovered was that they were playing a business version of king of the hill on a slope already crowded with males. They knew that the introduction of a woman changed the rules, making the game too complicated. It was easier to pretend I wasn't there. My efforts at trying to fit in were met with occasional pats on the back—literally—and requests to do filing or make coffee.

No matter how smart I was or how hard I worked, these men were only going to let me sit at the table. They were not going to let me play the game. What they didn't know is that their gender stereotyping only made me hunker down and grow stronger.

CONSTRUCTING OUR OWN POWER

Today we have women owning and/or working in many traditionally male dominated industries. Take construction; women own 9.1% of construction companies. We have women dentists, 26,000 as of the year 2000. Women research car prices, models, and options online and then go out and purchase more than 50% of all new vehicles.

There are now more women industrial engineers than men and more women in top public administration positions than men.

Naturally, we are moving into the online arena. "I am woman, hear me roar," resonates across the Internet with all the power of Eliza Doolittle singing "Just You Wait Henry Higgins!" (*My Fair Lady*, George Cukor Director 1964). Just as Eliza Doolittle rose up to take her rightful place in  Henry Higgins' household—by his side, not two steps behind—women today are partnering with the significant others in their lives and forging a strong Internet presence that warrants your attention.

The Internet is encouraging women to shout, "I am woman, give me more!" More attention, more products, more information, more of everything. We are driven to be proactive in the use of our power.

We have the power today to raise children on our own if we need to, and, for those of us without a significant other, our power allows us to flaunt our single status proudly, not with that old guilt-driven goal of fooling family and friends into thinking we're out there looking for Mr. Right when we're not.

Many of the Janes I'm telling you about in *Dickless Marketing* are comfortable living without Dick—in fact, the Census Bureau reports that between 1970 and 1990 the number of women living alone doubled from 7.3 million to 15.3 million. That is not to say we plan it that way. We like having men in our lives. It's just that today many of us are fixing our own appliances, mowing our own lawns, and changing the oil in our cars. The men in our lives are our companions, partners, and friends. There are few Eliza Dolittles waiting for modern day Henry Higgins to rescue them from the gutter, today.

> **More women than men have earned bachelor's degrees every year since 1982.**

Instead, Jane is active and involved, building a strong future by herself or with a supportive partner. She is using her power and courage to open new business in a new territory that she and her male peers don't yet fully understand—on the Internet.

MIGHTY JANE

The majority of women are using this power to make life better for their family, their friends, their significant others, and for the good of society.

Women do not want power for power's sake. Most of the new millennium Janes are allocating their power to others, in greater numbers than ever before. This sharing, the lip-sticking we use to communicate with each other, helps us share our hopes and dreams. We share advice and counsel. And even though many of us hold down full time jobs, we volunteer in record numbers.

We do this by building communities of like-minded individuals focused on getting things done.

Communities are what the Internet is all about. In Chapter 6 we will talk about communities in detail. Now it's important to understand that the original intent of the Internet was to bring people of like minds closer together, bridging the cosmic divide of space and time, in the kinds of communities woman have made their own all over the Web.

Online communities encompass everything from art to amphibians; from babies to bumper stickers; from moms to migraines. If there's an interest for it, it's online and if it's online, women are involved. Women have chosen the Internet as their global voice. That is why you need to understand lip-sticking before you try to market to the gender that uses it. Lip-sticking involves using your mouth for more than pretty descriptions of your products and services. It means understanding that wearing lipstick does not damage our brain or negatively influence our opinions.

Yes, women, as a gender, like to look nice, which is why we wear lipstick. But, we don't want our attractiveness to change the way you treat us. Don't make promises you don't intent to keep. We are big on commitment.

Women do more online than build businesses. They also shop, research, chat, and help their kids do their homework, online. Women are embracing the Internet to communicate with family members, with groups that belong to the same organizations they do, to locate old friends and find new ones. We even use it to find significant others. Women are all about communication and community and if you want to sell to them online, you need to get your mind firmly around that idea. It's this global voice that the inventor of the Internet imagined when he first began tinkering with computer cables and phone lines.

THE INTERGALACTIC NETWORK

To understand the concept of "community" as it applies to the Internet and Web, a short trip back in time may help. It may seem like a visit to Jabberwocky, but it's a necessary bend in the road to understanding how community fuels not only the Internet, but also women. And how it all goes back to lip-sticking.

Back in the day, (1960ish), when Dr. J.C.R. Licklidder was asked by the Department of Defense to work on ARPA (Advanced Research Projects Agency), he envisioned a brave new world that would change the future of mankind forever.

Licklidder's hope was to devise a computer network that would thrust mankind into a world of communication not limited by space or time. A world where people and machines formed a "symbiosis," allowing communication to be transformed beyond words into thoughts based on ordered protocols that were more effective—perhaps even more profound—than anything that had ever come before.

In his book, *Virtual Communities,* (New York: MIT Press, 2000) Howard Rheingold said this regarding the beginnings of the Internet, "The new generation of Camelot-era whiz kids from the think tanks, universities, and industry, assembled by Secretary McNamara in the rosier days before Vietnam, were determined to use the momentum of the post-Sputnik scare to bring the Defense Department's science and technology bureaucracy into the space age."

One answer was NASA, a government sub-agency that became a scientific and engineering force of its own. It was the Defense Department's creation of the Advanced Research Projects Agency to find and fund bold projects that would actually contribute to the meeting of minds between man and computer that drastically altered the human landscape. Suddenly, human information and communication became a thing of ones and zeros, forming a digital language that whispered along *inside of the machines.* It was silent and invisible, but oh so observable.

Licklider called it "interactive computing." This was the seed that grew into the vast tree-like universe of connections we all know today as the Internet. When Tim Berners-Lee started constructing HTML code to allow graphics and color to be added to the Internet, he imagined the addition of all of this data as a gigantic spider Web, connected through invisible threads, all over the world. The World Wide Web was born and information became a shared medium between countries, universities, government agencies, and also between real people.

A SHARING UNIVERSE

It began with *time-sharing.* As the first, most important step to the threshold of personal computing (i.e., one person to one machine), *time-sharing* consisted of creating computer systems capable of interacting with many programmers at the same time, instead of forcing them to wait in line with their digital cards or tapes.

We need look no further than the science fiction tomes of forward thinkers such as Arthur C. Clarke, Isaac Asimov, and H.G.Wells, to recognize the inherent desire of man's need for community. Many of their science fiction novels revolve around man's desire to communicate with machines—

> The more one does and sees and feels, the more one is able to do, the more genuine may be one's appreciation of fundamental things like home, and love, and understanding companionship.
> ~Amelia Earhart

hoping to make life easier and better for people. Machines were meant to do the labor, people were then supposed to while away the hours communing with each other.

This is how the Internet began, with *time-sharing communities.* Communities populated with groups of like-minded people throughout the world; people connected mind-to-mind, idea-to-idea, hope-to-hope. Far beyond the computer programmers, time-sharing communities reached the thinkers, artists, and business people of the new millennium.

Remember that women like to share? We are at the forefront of this vast sharing community. Women are embracing the Internet the way men embraced the automobile. "Ah, at last, a bona fide vehicle that will get me where I want to go!" Could that, perhaps, be shopping?

COMMUNITY SPIRIT

Women don't see the wires and electrodes in the computers that control our Internet connection. We don't worry about the ones and zeros that make up our digital world. We are part of, yet separate from, the business arena the other gender has spent centuries building into that good old boys network. A place consumed by the need to fill itself with the nonsense of jabberwocky—please, save us from another useless acronym, we are tired of them!

> **The letters ACRONYM are NOT an acronym.**
> **Folklore abounds saying the name "acronym" is itself an**
> **acronym from Abbreviated Coded Rendition Of Name**
> **Yielding Meaning but dictionaries show that it actually**
> **comes from the Greek *akros*, meaning point, and *onuma*,**
> **meaning name.**

Rather than worry about how the technology works, women are forging ahead, using the technology to build communities online, communities that exist to benefit the whole of society, successful, robust, supportive communities designed with specific purposes in mind. What may seem like idle chat to you is really a gathering of great minds struggling to deal with family, friends, business, careers, politics, world affairs, and, of course, where to buy the best shoes. It is within these communities and portals that the Internet really functions to bring storeowner and customer together. If you want to sell to the women who visit your Web site, you will do well to show some community spirit.

Do not waste our time with false promises laced with marketing jabberwocky. If you are using your lips to attract us, make sure you get your message to stick by selling to our strengths and our needs.

WAL-MART ONLINE

Examples of successful companies who understand women are companies like Avon, Mary Kay, Victoria's Secret. But they also include the not-so-obviously female companies like Wal-Mart and Hallmark. These are companies that treat women like goddesses, companies that organize their offline stores to make shopping not only easy and pleasant, but very much like visiting a trusted friend. These are companies that have put a lot of time and effort into making their online stores just as pleasant and easy to shop at.

Consider Wal-Mart.

The outstanding success of this retail store is a direct result of its appeal to its core market—women. When trying to duplicate that success online in 1996, Wal-Mart didn't quite hit the mark. By 1999, the company knew it had to do something to boost sales. They hired Jeanne Jackson, the 48-year-old former president and CEO of the Gap's Banana Republic division as well as CEO of Gap's e-commerce unit. Jackson faced a daunting challenge, but if anyone was up to it, she was. After all, she represented the store's core market. Her first act as CEO was to take the Web site back to start-up status.

It worked. In 2001, Mike Troy, writing in *Retailing Online* said that Wal-Mart "has shown visible improvement the past two years with a noticeable emphasis on seasonal promotions. The prominence of Walmart.com within the retailer's monthly circular has also stepped up." In his estimation:

> **"The best recent example was the pre-Thanksgiving weekend circular. It featured a page devoted to jewelry and an ad encouraging customers to 'learn how to buy a diamond at Walmart.com.' A jewelry learning center was prominently featured on the Walmart.com home page."**

Although Jackson stepped down from her position as CEO in December of 2001, she had set the retail giant off on the right e-commerce track. Taking the site back to start-up status, and focusing on the way shoppers use the Internet, helped improve Wal-Mart's design and navigation, encouraging offline customers to conduct business online—shopping from home in their pajamas. As a final, shining touch, personalization was added and the rest is history.

Wal-Mart is a true user-friendly, female-friendly Web site. At the end of 2001, it ranked as one of the top five Internet shopping Web sites in terms of visitors, after eBay, Amazon, Yahoo! Shopping, and MSN Shopping.

AVON.COM

Another female-friendly Web site is Avon.com. This mega-successful personal care company knows how to keep up with the times. The tagline tells it all (which, by the way, is all in pink on the site):

the company for women

Notice how Avon announces (as if we need an announcement) that it's not just a woman-focused company—it's **THE** company for women. A visit to its Web site reveals what that really means.

Shop Online is one of the first links I saw when the homepage downloaded. The pictures of glowing women do not overwhelm here. Their glowing good looks and diversity imply that the products offered here are for all women, not merely for celebrities, or women who want to be celebrities. On the top left of the homepage there is a *Newsflash* which, when clicked on, takes the visitor to a page discussing Avon's walk for breast cancer.

They are not only showing community involvement, they are lip-sticking to the highest degree: "You've just taken the first step towards making an incredible difference in the fight against breast cancer. The Avon Walk for Breast Cancer will bring together thousands of people to share their stories and to celebrate life while making an enormous contribution toward funding access to care and finding a cure."

Meanwhile, back at the homepage, the visitor is not overwhelmed with options, there is plenty of white space, but all of the ingredients of marketing to a predominantly female audience are evident, including a privacy policy and a login link for returning shoppers. While I am not fond of the color pink as it continues to apply to women, it's become a marketing standard and you will find it here and at many other female-focused Web sites, including the Queen of Pink's site, **MaryKay.com**. So, I bow to the greater minds of these mega-successful companies.

HALLMARK.COM

A click over to Hallmark shows a similar layout to the Avon site. It's simple, direct, and engaging. The colors are for fall at the moment, but I expect they change with the seasons. You will probably see red and green, come Christmas, fireworks for New Years and more pastels come Easter next year.

Hallmark puts everything in the prime real estate section, from the "your account" button, to the headline, "September birthday fun!" and the offer of "party ideas, birthday quotes and more" for anyone stuck for special touches to a loved one's celebration.

This site is designed to make shopping quick and easy for visitors. Not only can you purchase gifts online, you can develop a wish list. Clearly, this company knows how its customers shop, and the lip-sticking shows in the descriptions beneath the links; such as:

FREE September Desktop Calendar
Download our interactive calendar for a month of facts and fun!

Anyone taking advantage of this free offer will have the Hallmark name on their PC or MAC desktop EVERY DAY for the month of September. Can you think of a better way to continually remind customers you're there for them? A click on that link opens a calendar that is decidedly feminine, by the way. Plus, the download instructions cover all the pitfalls anyone unfamiliar with downloading programs might encounter.

These successful companies spend millions of dollars every year asking questions until they get it right. They know their core market is women. They know women have control of the family finances and influence what gets purchased at work. They practice lip-sticking to the nth degree. You could learn a great deal by spending a few hours reviewing how they do what they do, so well.

It comes down to knowledge. Building a strategy to sell to women online means asking questions, questions such as:

o What can we do to make your shopping experience more pleasant?

o How can we improve our products to make your life easier?

o What do you like best about us?

o What do you like least about us?

o What is your favorite thing to do on your day off?

o What can our Web site do to help you check out faster?

o If we gave you a million dollars to spend on improvements at our Web site, how would you spend it?

o Do you have anything you would like to say to the CEO of our company?

Questions are guaranteed to get you answers. Lots of answers! In Chapter 10, "Was will eine Frau eigentlich?" I'll share the answers to my questionnaire on what women want when they're shopping online. Meanwhile, read on to discover how to make friends with the F word: f as in female, of course!

WHAT WE LEARNED IN THIS CHAPTER:

o   Lip-stick your women customers by using an honest, friendly voice when you speak to them.

o   Study what other successful online companies are doing to get women to their sites.

o   Don't talk down to women. We like details and explanation but it doesn't mean we're stupid.

o   The Web isn't TV, radio, or print. Stop writing copy as if it were. Hire a Web copywriter.

o   Slithy toves are not a new deodorant or skin crème. They are nonsense words. Avoid them in your advertising.

3. Making friends with the F Word

Female-friendly Web sites

Anne Morrow Lindbergh once said that good
communication was as "stimulating as black coffee,
and just as hard to sleep after."

Females account for 51% of the U.S. population. While not technically a minority, we are often given special consideration normally associated with minorities. The Equal Employment Opportunity Council (EEOC) includes us as "women and minorities" in their section on "disadvantaged groups." In some respects this can be helpful; in other respects, it causes a whole set of problems.

This sometimes-privileged status can be helpful when it makes us eligible for government funding that might not be available otherwise. It causes problems when it becomes a label with negative connotations. As members of a group singled out for help by the government there is a perception by some people that women don't have to work as hard as others for our opportunities.

Yes, government funding is available—see information at the Minority Business Development Agency (http://www.mbda.gov), and women use it to help build their businesses into successful enterprises, just as any small business owner would. But being a woman does not guarantee funding will be awarded.

Like any other business owner, women have to prove business viability and need for funding. Also, regardless of gender, certain specifications have to be met before government funding is made available. In addition, understand that government funding is money that needs to be paid back. It's a loan, not a gift.

I will concede that females—there's the F word in the title of this chapter—in the U.S. as a group, are assigned some privileged status by the EEOC. Women themselves, however, have other, more personal, titles we like to use. The words and numbers compiled by researchers who jumble charts and graphs all day long may call us what they like; in our minds we are mothers, sisters, wives, and girlfriends. Those labels suit us well.

There are business labels we are proud of, also. Some of us are Fortune 500 females. The Carly Fiorina's of the world (CEO of Hewlett Packard), the Ann Mulcahey's of the world (CEO of Xerox), and the Meg Whitman's of the world (CEO of eBay), are as much a part of our sisterhood as the checkout girl at the grocery store or the sales clerk down at the mall. We look up to them because they have entered that old boys network and made their presence felt, and they are setting new standards for business success.

On the other hand, some of us don't even know what the Fortune 500 is. We're stay-at-home mothers, or part-time workers and we don't often follow the stock market, although we do read the business section of the paper. It's enough to be taking care of our families, cleaning, cooking, doing laundry, and seeing to it that the kids get to soccer practice or gymnastics on time. We're no less important than the women who are pounding on the glass ceiling; in fact, we may be more important. Because we're part of a select group of women supporting the women in power by offering time and energy to be there when they need us.

Some of us are dedicated to a full-time career outside of the home. That career may propel us to Fortune 500 status; it may give us satisfaction because it's part of a non-profit; it may be the extension of a hobby or just something we enjoy so much we do it because we can.

The many women who are part-time workers are usually putting in time just to add a few dollars to the family income to buy kids ballet shoes or hockey sticks. Because we want to contribute to the household income, and because many of us are entrepreneurs at heart, we are looking to this new millennium and its ability to offer us home-based business opportunities. Author Sandy Botkin, in his book *Lower Your Taxes—Big Time* (New York: McGraw-Hill, 2003) says, "This [home-based businesses] has become and will continue to become one of the greatest mass movements in the U.S."

CARING IS THE BETTER PART OF PERCEPTION

In a traditional sense, as mentioned in Chapter 1, women are the guardians of hearth and home. We embody nurturing and caring, although the last half of the 20th century saw men rise to the challenge by showing us they could nurture and care for their children with the best of Moms—traits they learned from their mothers and/or sisters, I warrant.

Looking at women from the late 19th century through the 20th century, we can see how our role in society grew and changed dramatically. We went from being protected figures in the kitchen and playroom, out to factories (think Rosie the Riveter) and, with the invention of the typewriter, into business offices. This change in status had an enormous affect on many preconceived notions about rearing children,  housekeeping, cooking and even education, not only for us, but also for the men in our lives.

The statistic that "women [today] still shoulder 70% of traditional household duties in addition to their day jobs" is still being printed in newspapers from Seattle, Washington, to Boise, Idaho, to Punxatawney, Pennsylvania. I'm not sure what that statistic is supposed to prove, but it presents a narrow view of the American woman. In general, it tends to denigrate men and leave women feeling either smug or enslaved.

In the end, it refers to women in middle-income families who shoulder the responsibility of work and household duties in a matter-of-fact manner that supports but doesn't endorse that quote.

Women take care of things because we can, or because we have to, or because we think we have to. We often shoulder 70% of the workload at home because we find it easier to do so. While some women resent being in charge of all household duties, including childcare, others give it a resigned shrug.

Yes, we would like the men in our lives to pitch in more, and many of the younger women I spoke with are accomplishing that goal, but it's helpful to understand that women are used to this home/career multi-tasking. The organized among us plaster the refrigerator with project charts, outlining tasks and carpooling duties by the day and hour. The unorganized among us scurry along with those charts and duties stuck into the cubbyholes of a mental cabinet in our brains.

In his famous '70's comedy skit, Bill Cosby joked that he'd "lost control" of his house to his wife. When left to care for the children, his wrinkled nose and boyish whine, "Where is your mother?" always put the audience in tears of laughter. This skit is still funny today— my own children get a huge kick out of it. Why? Because nothing has changed! In fact, in a recent JCPenney television ad, a tired father, left home to care for his two-year old, a toddler clearly unhappy about being stuck in his high chair while his father tries to read the paper, is seen shaking his head, lamenting out loud, "Where is your mother?"

The suggestion is that she's out shopping. It's a good bet she was out shopping in Bill Cosby's case, also! When women aren't at home, or at work, we're probably shopping. Usually in groups of two or more.

The fact that it's humorous to depict men as clueless about childcare isn't something we invented. The new millennium continues that old millennium fallacy, the same way it continues to refuse women credit for knowing how to change the oil in their cars. Obviously women give men credit for knowing how to take care of the kids. We leave the children with them all the time! And many men accept that women know how to take care of their cars. My local Jiffy Lube employs a woman to do just that.

> You can't get spoiled if you do your own ironing.
> Meryl Streep

Some things never change. Just as we still depict men as poor at child care, and women as clueless about car care, we also still expect Mom to be the "finder of all things" and the one who keeps the refrigerator full. While the majority of women today are breaking out of this cage to run free, they still carry the "May I help you?" gene in their genetic make-up. It's what makes them roll their eyes every time their boyfriend or husband asks where his favorite shirt is.

NATURAL ADVANTAGES

In her book and audiotape, *Natural Advantages of Women* (Texas: Wizard Publishing, 2003), Michele Miller writes, "There are approximately one billion nerve cells in the human brain. Not only do women have significantly more connections between these cells than men, they also have an advantage in the region known at the *corpus callosum*, the main tissue bridge that links the two hemispheres of the brain." Miller goes on to note that; "Researchers believe that this combination of size and connectivity makes women perceptive, articulate, and verbally fluent." As one aware of the way women have flocked to the Internet, I was not surprised by the image Miller used to describe the brain's function. One comment struck me so forcefully, I had to include it here: "Our brains are virtual superhighways of whole-thought processing!"

In fact, research uncovered in recent studies done at Stanford University, Emory University (Atlanta), and Ghent University in Belgium reveals interesting facts about the way women think. None of this is brand new, by the way, but it does bear repeating. The research confirms previous statements that women are programmed to operate on a verbal level while men are programmed to operate on a spatial level.

> **From NBC late night talk show host, Conan O'Brien,**
> **"A study in *The Washington Post* says that women have**
> **better verbal skills than men. I just want to say to the**
> **authors of that study: 'Duh.' "**

Another female trait that flows along with our verbal acuity is the way we argue with the men in our lives. Men and women react differently to "heated discussions," as we call them at our house. But the lyrics of a popular Country Western song sung by Terri Clark in mid-2003 makes my point so much better than anything I might try to compose, I have to include it here. This song shot up the charts in record time, supported by hundreds of women calling in to radio stations asking DJs to play it again and again.

The song is, "I Just Wanna Be Mad for Awhile" (written by Kelly Lovelace and Lee Thomas Miller). In it, Clark sings about her anger at her husband of seven years using these words, "I think I'm right, I think you're wrong," then admitting that she'll give in, in awhile.

The song really hits home to women when Terri croons about being mad but still putting the coffee on in the morning and still loving her man. Then she says, "Yes, I'm being stubborn," and, *"No, I don't wanna go back upstairs."* (my italics)

I spoke with over a dozen women and several men about this line and while some think it's too broad—not all men want to solve problems in the bedroom—most of the people I spoke with laughed and nodded their heads in agreement. Men do want to fix arguments by "going back upstairs," because they need that physical contact to reassure them all is well. Women just want to be left alone—for a while.

This is a part of the female psyche many men can't get their synapses around. Don't feel bad if you're one of them. You're in good company. Women are complicated creatures; sometimes we even confuse ourselves. What I'm attempting to illustrate to business owners is that when we think we're right,  it's in your best interest to let us be right. As a business owner selling to women, especially online, letting us be right gets you more sales than arguing with us. Learning to build a rapport that doesn't demean us, even when we really are wrong, can be the start of a beautiful friendship.

At *Dickless Marketing* friendship = S-A-L-E-S.

ALL THE COMFORTS OF HOME

When you think of a woman-owned business think home and family. Fully 60% of women-owned businesses are operated out of the home, *because we want it that way*. We are *family-oriented* and for every man who is boasting househusband status in this brave new world of gender bending, there are thousands of women who are juggling the role of wife, mother, and business professional, quite successfully. Some of them have been doing it for many more years than the very first househusband out there.

We want to be surrounded by reminders of why we need this business to succeed (home and family), and we learn very quickly to parlay our sensitive nature into the kind of multi-tasking that enables us to cope with a temper tantrum from our two-year old, while fielding a phone call from an unhappy client, at the same time we're jotting down items for our grocery list.

We feel the two-year-old's angst; we relate to the client's concerns; and we know that having dinner on the table at 5:30 is as much for our own good as it is for the family's good. If there is one-thing women are definitely sensitive to, it's the food we feed our families. Women who trot their kids to fast food restaurants because they didn't have time to prepare dinner will make sure those kids get some fruit for dessert, or have a glass of milk with a granola bar.

Running a home business is a time consuming task. It can overwhelm even the strongest, most professional individual out there, man or woman. The reason women are embracing this option in increasing numbers today is because we are not less family oriented in the new millennium, we are *more* family oriented. We want control of our lives. We want to be with our kids when they get home from school. We want to be appreciated for our skills and capabilities.

What better way to do that than to start our own business, out of our home? We're well suited for it, and we make it a success because we multi-task better than men.

In *Megatrends for Women* (New York: Villard Books, 1992), Patricia Aburdene and John Naisbitt note that the latter part of the 20th century opened the door for what they called the "Women's Leadership Style." Woman use their intuition and their sensitivity to be strong, successful managers. Because women are social beings and because we trust our "gut", some men may believe women are less fit for senior management positions. Men tend to shy away from the emotional aspect of intuition. In their world, being social and relying on intuition makes for bad business. In the real world, those two qualities make for great business.

Why? Because being social and following intuition opens doors. Women know how to listen, a skill that endears us to our clients and customers. Women can read faces and tell at a glance whether the client we're dealing with is ready for the close. We even do it over the phone. For a short while in a previous incarnation, I worked on the phone selling DSL. Out of a team of over 60, I was one of the top five producers every month. When I left, I had a pipeline all the other salespeople were bidding on! Everyone wanted my leads because they were more than tips, **they were people prepped for close.**

Like most women, my telemarketing skill was in the ability to form a relationship with the people I spoke to on the phone—long before I tried to sell them anything.

Where have you heard the term *relationship* lately?

On the Internet, of course. The Internet is all about relationship building. CRM, customer relationship management, is a major portion of doing business online today. In the old days they called it customer service, but it still means the same thing—keeping the customer happy. Being online gives you the ability to reach thousands of people, no, millions of people, all over the nation and the world. This makes CRM vital to your business success.

As far as the gender most represented in customer service roles, you already know it's women. And it's not just because we like to talk. Women relate well to other people; it's in our nature to commiserate and use patience to defuse a customer who may be a ticking bomb. This is why you see so many minority—think women-owned— businesses popping up on the Internet.

GAINING CONTROL THROUGH CHANGE

In management roles, women often outperform men. In *Megatrends for Women,* the differences between men's management style (traditional management) and women's management style (women's leadership) are showcased in a lengthy chart, which includes differences, such as:

MEN: Goal: Control		WOMEN: Goal: Change
Limits and Defines	vs.	Empowers
Punishment	vs.	Reward
Rigid	vs.	Flexible
Knows all the answers	vs.	Asks the right questions

Some men I know wear these traits like a royal cloak. Others object strenuously to the criticism of males that they see implicit in those comparisons. I can only say that the facts speak for themselves. Men are territorial. They want to fix things, regardless of whether or not the other person wants it fixed. Once again, their brains are wired to be analytical and focused on a solution.

Women's brains are wired to be empathetic and social. We listen because we want to understand. Generally, we offer to help only when asked.

The qualities listed in Aburdene's and Naisbitt's book continue to exist, at home and in the workplace but there are changes afoot; the new millennium is teaching men how to be more flexible, and it is also producing some women with the "queen bee" syndrome, wanting to control the situation much the way those good old boys did in the last century.

Be aware of how these character traits influence your thinking and that of your potential customers. The ability to recognize their existence will help you build a stronger Web success. It's because women are empowering themselves and others for success—with a little help from their friends, both male and female—that you truly do need to address these differences. A continued focus on men alone will leave you without any customer relationships to manage!

It's time to step out of the old world way of thinking where marketing was aimed exclusively at DICK because he was the alpha male. I invite you to enter the new millennium where JANE isn't concerned with alpha status because she's busy typing in her credit card number to buy your products!

Aburdene and Naisbitt wrote *Megatrends for Women* in 1992, with many predictions for the 21st century, some of which have come true already, some of which never will. Their view of management styles demonstrated the reasons women often make better managers than men. Nonetheless, their conclusions show the old world style of reasoning. What we don't see in their writings is the recognition that today's women are smart, savvy, and can handle business deals with the best of them.

BRINGING IT HOME

An interesting fact about women and shopping is that women use the same products at home that they use at work. In her role as the office manager in charge of supplies making sure the company bathrooms are cleaned and well-stocked, or as a manager influencing which supplier to use for company cell phones, computers, or software, a woman is more likely than a man to *take the items she uses at work home with her.*

As a gender, women like to have our favorite things around us, no matter where we are. We get fond of certain things, items that make our day-to-day life easier or better, and we surround ourselves with these items, both at work and at home. It's in our nature.

> According to a "Shopping 2000" study done by Greenfield Online, the Internet has overtaken the mall and catalogs as the point of purchase for computer software and books.

This means that if you sell one or more of the products and/or services we buy, personal or otherwise, you have a chance to get double the sales from us. It doesn't matter where we are when we buy; if we find you while we are surfing online at home, we'll end up taking you to work with us. If we find you while we're researching products online at work, we'll take you home with us. Either way, you win.

Men are not quite so loyal. Men may like a certain product at work, and use a completely different product at home. In my experience, if a man runs out of a favorite product, let's say he prefers a certain brand of razor to shave with, he will not return home empty-handed if the store he normally shops at is out of that brand. Nor will he drive to another store to find it. He will merely substitute something of similar, sometimes inferior quality and cart it home proudly, as if to say, "Mission accomplished."

As we've discussed, this is because most men operate in that *command and control mode,* as Aburdene and Naisbitt say. They have little room in their lives for developing brand loyalty. (Except where it comes to cars, I think. I've seen men argue for hours over whether a certain brand of car is better than another brand.)

Command and control mode has served the status quo well for hundreds of years. But things have changed in the complex computer-supported society of today's consumer. Today, Jane invites you to join her in the new millennium where, since Dick is intelligent and goal-oriented, you may find that he's designated Jane as his shopper. He is not giving up his role as CEO or President or whatever title suits in this age of job-title invention, but he has accepted the fact that Jane is often more organized, more balanced, and better able to handle Internet shopping than he. This frees him to handle tasks he is better suited to.

I am not suggesting you stop selling to Dick! On the contrary, I'm introducing a new age truth to you: **If you really want Dick to get your message, get it in front of Jane first.** It's guaranteed that she will share it with Dick, and all of the other people in her life. Sharing is what she does, after all.

SHOPPING WITH SUSAN

Let's use an example of how different men and women are, especially when it comes to shopping. We will observe how Susan buys a bookcase for her home office. And, then we will observe how Susan's husband, Jay, buys ice cream for the evening's dessert. Again, this scenario is only an example; to those who pooh-pooh it, I say kudos to you! But, in the real world, it often works this way.

Susan isn't buying a bookcase on impulse. Impulse buying is a whole separate issue, which we cover on our Web site www.dicklessmarketing.com. Susan is an office manager at a local car dealership, and two afternoons a week, she works at home. Because she likes the bookcase in her office at the car dealership, Susan already knows she wants one just like it at home.

In addition to her job as a full-time office manager, Susan is a Mom with two children, 7 and 9 years old. Once she gets out of the office, she is too tired to trot off to the mall to look at bookcases. Instead, she logs online  and decides to surf around a bit to see what's out there. She already knows where her office bookshelf was purchased. It's a local furniture store, but she wants to see what deals are out there at Amazon.com or Dealtime.com two sites where she often comparison shops.

This time, Amazon and Dealtime don't do it for her. Their listings don't include the local store her office bookshelf was bought in and she doesn't want to pay shipping costs for an out-of-state furniture store. She does a quick search in her favorite search engine on the store name she wants to shop in, and waits for it to show up.

> **If you are that store, and your Web site is not listed in the search engines, Susan will not find you and she will be forced to shop at a competitor's site.**

The store is listed and Susan has a broadband connection, so she reaches it quickly and easily. Clicking into the homepage, she immediately sees a link to product choices. When she clicks on it, it opens a list that includes "Solid Wood Bookcases." She clicks on that link and there's her bookcase, complete with picture. To her surprise and delight, it's on sale!

But wait; there are three other styles that look very nice, and two sizes: a four-shelf size and a six-shelf size. Her office bookcase has five shelves. Susan spends a few minutes considering the shelving options, and then makes a decision. She chooses a four-shelf bookcase in a similar but slightly different style than the one at work. She clicks the BUY button, is immediately taken to a page that shows her product in her shopping cart and asks if she would like to check out or keep shopping. She clicks the check out button.

Before typing in her credit card number and the personal information needed to ship the item to her home, she checks for security, including a privacy statement. She immediately finds the two signs of a secure site: the browser shows **https://,** where the extra S indicates the checkout area of the site is secure, and the site has a lock at the bottom right, also showing it's a secure site. At the bottom of the page there is a link called "Terms of Use." Susan clicks the link and spends a moment skimming the site's privacy statement. Satisfied it has the right software to protect her credit card and that it won't sell or share her personal information with third party partners, she goes back to her shopping cart.

Now she's ready to click the submit button and complete the buying process. When she does this, the Web site generates a screen shot not only thanking her for her business, but also informing her that she will be receiving an e-mail confirmation of her purchase and a tracking number. Happy with her shopping experience, she now has time to help the children with their homework.

Meanwhile, as Jay is driving home from his job as a manager in a computer store, he feels a need—call it a craving—for chocolate ice cream. This is a staple in his home and as he cruises along Route 555, he begins to lick his lips in anticipation. It doesn't matter what's for dinner, Jay is already focused on dessert and he can't wait for that rich, creamy ice cream to make its way around his tonsils! Once at home, Jay checks the freezer for the carton of chocolate ice cream usually sitting right there in front of everything else.

Panic attack! They are out of chocolate ice cream!

All through dinner a downcast Jay emits sigh after sigh. Susan finally laughs and tells him to go out and get some chocolate ice cream, if it will make him happy. Jay heads off to their favorite supermarket, six miles away.

Once at the supermarket, Jay wanders up and down the freezer aisle not sure where the ice cream is kept (Susan usually does the grocery shopping), finally coming to the coolers where there are at least five different bins. Each bin is full of different brands of ice cream, in more than a dozen different flavors. But—no chocolate. Jay goes up and down the freezer aisle again and again. He's sure there has to be chocolate in one of those bins.

After approximately five minutes of searching, Jay heaves a sigh and accepts defeat. The store is out of chocolate ice cream. He knows this because there is no chocolate to be seen in any of the ice cream freezer bins. Of course, he does not ask a clerk to check out back— even in the new millennium, men don't like to ask for directions. At this point he is desperate for ice cream. He decides vanilla fudge will do just fine. The kids like it, he thinks Susan likes it, so, he buys it.

Mission accomplished.

SHOPPING WITH JAY

Now, let's reverse roles. Let's send Susan to buy Jay's ice cream and Jay to buy Susan's bookcase.

Jay calls Susan at work to ask her to stop by the supermarket on her way home to pick up some chocolate ice cream. He has a sudden craving for it and remembers they ate the last of the carton at home, last week. Susan agrees to do this for Jay, if he will research bookcases for her. She tells him about the bookcase in her office, specifically says she wants one just like it to put in her office at home, and then tells him the name of the store her office purchased its bookcase at. No problem, Jay says. He knows all about bookcases. He'll make sure she gets what she wants.

Susan pulls into the supermarket and heads for the ice cream aisle. She doesn't hesitate at bin number one or bin number two; chocolate ice cream, as she well knows, is in bin number three. Well, it usually is. Reaching bin number three and seeing no chocolate there, Susan begins looking for a store clerk. Noticing a clerk stocking shelves in the soup aisle, she heads over and asks if the store is out of chocolate ice cream or if maybe there isn't some out back? The clerk agrees to check, returning a moment later shaking her head. No chocolate. They may be getting a delivery tomorrow, she says, but, for tonight, Susan is out of luck.

Susan's shoulders slump momentarily. Jay really likes chocolate. And the kids love it. Even though Susan is dead tired, she goes out to the car and drives to another supermarket farther away, and finds a good stock of chocolate ice cream there. She purchases two gallons, just to be safe, and feels satisfied that she was able to get just what Jay wanted. On the way home, she wonders how Jay did with her bookcase.

After hanging up the phone with Susan, Jay glances at his watch and sees that he has six minutes before his afternoon sales meeting. "Bookcase," he says to himself. "Piece of cake." He is already logged on to the Internet—the company has a T1 line—so he clicks his mouse over to his favorite search engine, Yahoo! (Yahoo! is a directory, but functions as a search engine to many people) or maybe he uses Google, the most popular search engine online today, and types in the words "office bookcases."

"Piece of cake," he thinks again, tapping his pen on his desk in tempo to the music playing on his office radio.

"Office bookcases" offers him 11,400 possibilities. The first link is a company in the UK. In the middle of his result's page, he sees three links to Amazon.com. Ah, pay dirt! He clicks on an Amazon.com link that mentions office furniture and gives his watch a quick glance while the page downloads. Time is a wasting!

The link to Amazon.com is perfect! Jay is ecstatic! This site is a partner site to Amazon, so it must be good. Jay chooses a four shelf bookcase that looks like mahogany or maybe it's maple, certainly not pine, stopping for a second or two to try and remember what Susan said about the particular bookcase she wanted. He can't quite remember, but he's confident that Amazon.com, a well-known and respected shopping site, would not partner with crooks, so he clicks on the BUY button and proceeds to checkout.

The Web site in question opens a window that tells him it is taking him to a secure site. Jay begins moving nervously in his chair. That meeting is almost ready to start. Finally, the page opens up. Jay fills out the form, has to reenter his credit card number twice because in his hurry he types it in wrong, then he clicks "submit." The site congratulates him on his fine purchase and asks him for his e-mail address to send a confirmation note. Jay types in Susan's e-mail address, since the bookcase is for her, but...he remembers at the last minute that she recently changed e-mail addresses. He isn't sure this is the right one. But, since he has to type in something, he leaves well enough alone.

He isn't thinking about receiving a confirmation e-mail describing the purchase, complete with item price and shipping cost. He also isn't worried about tracking the purchase. All he knows is that Susan asked him to get her a bookcase, and he did.

Mission accomplished.

UH-OH

What happened here? Jay got the ice cream he wanted because Susan considered his needs above her own. She traveled out of her way to get what Jay wanted because she didn't want to disappoint him with another flavor of ice cream, even though she probably knows one or two flavors he likes, as well as chocolate. She feels good about completing her task, albeit now she is even more tired and there is dinner to prepare and the children to deal with and a report from work that she needs to go over before bedtime.

Jay thinks he did what Susan asked him to do. He found her a bookcase. Was it the bookcase she asked for? No. Does it matter? Not to Jay. A bookcase is a piece of furniture and that's what he bought (many men I shared this story with looked at me with lopsided frowns; they didn't think Jay did anything wrong, either). When Susan expresses her disappointment to him later that night, he will be totally clueless. Susan will most likely go online and cancel Jay's order, find the correct bookcase herself and buy it—because the type and the style of bookcase matter to her.

While Jay's bookcase may be similar and it may even be close in price, it isn't the bookcase Susan asked for. She specifically filled Jay's request for ice cream. Jay took Susan's request, processed it as "need bookcase" and promptly fulfilled that request. However, he did not consider her specific request because to him a bookcase is just a bookcase. Not only that, Jay was in such a hurry, he wasn't sure the e-mail confirmation address he typed in was correct. This could mean no confirmation of the order, no tracking information, and a lot of headaches down the road if the bookcase never shows up.

There are several important distinctions here. First of all, neither Susan nor Jay went online to buy the ice cream. Can we all agree that at this time and place in the world, buying ice cream online is not an option? Even if your local supermarket participates in online shopping, the cost of having it ship you one gallon of ice cream would be ridiculous. This is not pizza we're talking about.

So, ice cream needs to be bought in person from your local supermarket. Back to Jay and Susan and the second item, the bookcase. Both of them went online to buy the bookcase. Why? Because it was faster and easier than shopping offline. Both of them did a search, yet only one of them was specific in her language. Both of them had other things to do and wanted to get this task done quickly, but only one was concerned with actively checking how the Web site in question was handling her personal information and her credit card information. And Susan, more than Jay, was concerned with the ability to track her purchase.

You have now learned that making friends with the F word means understanding that females are loyal and dedicated shoppers. We like options and we will consider new products or services if they fulfill a void in our lives. Had Susan not known exactly what make and style of bookcase she wanted, she would have done the same thing Jay did; she would have searched using Google, MSN, AOL, or any one of several other search engines. And, she may have ended up at Amazon.com, also.

It's unlikely, however, that she would have purchased just any bookcase, as Jay did. No matter whom she was doing the shopping for—herself, a family member, or a friend—Susan would have *shopped around until she got exactly what was requested.* Unless you give her a compelling reason to stay on your site, be prepared to see her take ownership of the experience by clicking into a competitor's site.

This is just an example. In reality, women like Susan and Jane are willing to go online and buy whatever they need. Sometimes we like researching your products first, but the main reason we're clicking that mouse is for the convenience it gives us. That means, no matter what you sell, we'll look for it online at some point in the purchasing process.

> **Women are responsible for more than 50% of the traditional male purchases such as automobiles, electronics, and PCs.**

Susan's shopping experience showed us that females are particular about their purchases. As we get more savvy with Web shopping, and as we open up more and more of our own businesses online, you have the opportunity to sell more than underwear, perfume, or jewelry to us. And please, don't think we have to go ask a man every time we want to buy electronics or tools or furniture. We like having a man's advice, but every year we get less and less dependent on it. In my survey, only a few women said they liked having a man around for large ticket item purchases. The rest of the women reported that they were quite comfortable shopping for these things on their own, thank you very much.

CHOICES ABOUND

It should be clear by now that women are particular about their purchases, and they shop around. The Internet is attracting them more and more as a shopping venue because:

- o It's convenient; they can access it any time, day or night.
- o It's faster than driving to the mall and wandering through store after store.
- o It's often cheaper. Buying online can save money, especially if the Web site offers free shipping.

In Chapter 6, "Ties that Bind," I'll be showing you how to use e-mail to get us to buy from you. E-mail is proving to be both more personal and more relaxing than anyone imagined it could be. Getting to know your clients by offering deals through e-mail marketing or through an informative newsletter allows you to share personal experiences with them. It also gives them a way to respond in kind. We like to know the person behind the product. Using e-mail to connect to us makes you more human.

Shopping is more than obtaining goods and services. A woman considers shopping as a means to make life easier for herself and her family. As an online merchant, you have the ability to influence every woman who logs on to the Internet today. You have the tool—your Web site; you have the opportunity—daily, weekly or monthly updates of your products and services; and you have our attention—we like to shop online.

PLAYING BY THE NUMBERS

Ignoring women's financial resources can cost you plenty. Eighty to ninety per cent of women today handle their own finances. Recognize the power of the baby boom generation where women are part of a demographic called the "sandwich generation." These are women caught between raising children and caring for aging parents. Help us cope with that issue; it's directly related to our need for financial advice, comfort, assistance, and empathy.

Some Internet statistics still show women lagging behind men in utilizing the Internet for financial services. But as more and more women start their own businesses and become savvy about money, they will be reaching out online for help. If you ignore them, or treat them as arm candy to your male clients, you will lose out on a great deal of profit.

> By 2010, it's estimated that women will control 60% of this nation's wealth.

Internet studies show that for now, women log online most often for healthcare information and health services. Following an interest in health, we like shopping for specialty products such as clothing, toys, and athletic gear. These are products that are family oriented, making them important items to women. If you have the opportunity—and you do if you have your own Web site—to HELP women find answers to issues surrounding these topics, do it; do it now!

Here are some suggestions worth exploring:

- o Start a newsletter that includes health information and relate it to yourself or your product or service.
- o Develop a monthly tip sheet on the latest and greatest in athletic gear for that over 40 hiker or biker.

- ○ Show us how to design a deck, a rock garden, or a dormer.
- ○ Think outside the box. Give us information on new computer equipment or the latest cell phone.
- ○ Get personal. Relate a personal experience we can empathize with, or report on a local community event.
- ○ Explain the stock market to us. I, like many women, get cross-eyed trying to understand numbers. If you know an easy way to get us to deal with our finances and our 401K, do it now!
- ○ Don't forget, we buy for all the members of our family; kids, husbands, dads, moms, aunts, uncles, cousins...

Don't treat us like kindergarteners; instruct us, but treat us like adults.

BE SPORTING

Speaking of sports; females are participating in sports in record numbers today. We're very proud of Annika Sorenstam's showing at the American Colonial in May of 2003. Those of us who are over 40 remember Billy Jean King's trumping of Bobby Riggs in 1973, proving that women can play in a man's world. Women are champions in almost all sports, these days. We're learning the rules of competitive play, and some of us are finding that we like it a lot.

In fact, we like sports so much, many women are learning to play golf at the tender age of 45 or 50. Some of us are taking up rock climbing and hiking instead of giving in to that usual mid-life slump. Seniors and baby boomers are a viable, rich market, as you will learn in detail in Chapter 5, "S-E-X. Sarah-Ellen Xceptions."

Because women are remaining healthy and active well into their seventies today, this market is wide-open for online sales. The seniors of the new millennium aren't sitting on porches knitting baby bonnets all day long.

They're biking and hiking and swimming. If they can't do those things, they're encouraging their daughters and sons to do them. Can't you hear them now, encouraging their kids to get outside and "Breathe that great mountain air!"? This is a prime target for any company selling sports gear, camping gear, athletic wear, vitamins, health food, personal care products, and so much more.

Mature Marketing online http://www.maturemarketing.com/ says, "too many marketers—and advertising and public relations agencies as well—are focused on the 25-49 age group. They 'confidently' expect that by communicating to these younger consumers, their message will rub off on the Boomers. Or they might use a stereotypical 'Senior Citizen' (lots of gray hair!) to represent the age 46+consumer spectrum. ***They are wrong—in their philosophy and their approach!"***

The bold type is from their Web site, not from my keyboard. The message is clear. Baby boomers and seniors have the cash and the incentive to spend it but too many marketers are chasing the youth culture to notice. The site goes on to report that *female boomers* are more likely to make purchases online than males. It's easy to see why that is true. The U.S. Department of Health and Human Services Administration on Aging puts the current life expectancy of women at approximately 80 years, six years longer than men.

> **"Online buyers, ages 50 and over, will account for almost one-quarter of all online retail spending by 2007, and older users are more likely to make an Internet purchase due to an online ad, with 30 percent claiming to have done so versus only 19 percent of the overall online adult population."**
> http://Web.jupiterresearch.com/bin/item.pl/home

These are women who can afford to be generous to their children and grandchildren, and to themselves.

The old saying, "You're not getting older, you're getting better," rings truer than a lover's promise. Women today are remaining sharp in body and mind. All of us, men and women alike, have certain nostalgia for our youth. Those of us over 40 hanker for hot August afternoons when the only relief from the heat was to hop in the car on Sunday afternoon and ride out to the country to get ice cream at a real dairy. This is the stuff of successful marketing. Use those memories to your advantage when trying to attract women. Draw us in to your site by building on that fond memory, that nostalgia we are so reluctant to give up.

Learn how to break out of traditional thinking that links women with the kitchen, diapers, laundry, taking messages, and the color pink. Those women were strong leaders in their own right, but today's woman will not be forced into that old mold. Yes, in the old century Dick was the favored child because of his gender. Yes, baby boomers grew up in a time when that was an accepted practice. Females today are standing behind Jane, and we expect you to line up with us.

The baby boomers and seniors who invented the tools that power the world today are crowded with both genders and we all applaud the direction the new millennium is taking us. Never doubt that we know how to use this new tool, or will learn what we need to know.

The generations that begat computers and network connections, understand the force of progress. For example, Nancy Reagan tells this story in her memoirs; when then President Reagan was challenged by a college student who said Reagan could never understand his (the student's) generation because, "We have television, jet planes, space travel, nuclear energy, computers," the President replied, "You're right. We didn't have those things when we were young. We invented them."

> **In 1984 Geraldine Ferraro, Chief of the Democratic Committee in Washington, was asked by Presidential candidate, Walter Mondale, to be his running mate.**

Yep. It was seniors and boomers who brought home appliances into the kitchen to make women's work easier. They are also the generations that began actively using credit cards, and they begat the *me generation*, sometimes known as hippies. They're also directly responsible for the first woman to run for Vice President of the United States. Today they are turning their title over to the latest marketing craze, the MSP generation, which I will talk about in Chapter 6.

By now, you should be asking one question: Out of the millions of other Web sites in cyberspace, how do you attract women—of all ages—to yours?

So glad you asked. I expect you have been told at least once in your life that some women are high maintenance. Just for the record, all women are high maintenance. The ones who say they aren't, are only fooling you. We like compliments. We like presents. We like lots of attention. We like having our opinion respected. If you do all of those things, you have a happy woman on your hands. Making us happy requires maintenance, high maintenance.

Think you know about high maintenance? Well, personally, I don't think you know Dick about it. Read on.

WHAT WE LEARNED IN THIS CHAPTER:
- o   Being female is not a minority status symbol.
- o   Females may be members of the Fortune 500, or not. In fact, most females who shop online come from middle-income families.
- o   Females in the U.S. work hard for their money. They are particular about how they spend it. Make shopping on your site easy for them.
- o   Forget the Alamo! Remember the baby boomers and seniors! They have money to spend at your Web site!
- o   Never send a man to do a woman's job.

4.   You Don't Know Dick

Getting Jane (and Dick) to your Web site to Shop, Shop, Shop

Learning is not attained by chance; it must be sought
for with ardor and attended to with diligence.
~Abigail Adams, 1780

Jack and Jill went up the hill, to fetch a pail of water. We all
know what happened next. Jack fell down and broke his crown,
and Jill came tumbling after. One of my sisters maintains that
the reason Jill came tumbling after is because she was so worried
about Jack she tripped and tumbled head over heels, just to get to the
bottom of that hill and administer first aid to her friend!

Whether you subscribe to this thinking or not, it reveals the mindset
of many women in the U.S. We hate to see our friends suffer. Maybe
that's because we, ourselves, hate to suffer. If you have a Web site
that is designed with crayons and filled with jargon, you are causing
untold suffering for us.

"You don't know Dick" is going to help you build a better site to ease
our suffering and, in turn, show you some ways to influence us to
shop at your site. Be prepared—building a Web site women will love
to visit and spend their money at involves the high maintenance I
spoke about in the previous chapter.

GETTING TO KNOW DICK

The reason I opened this chapter with Jack and Jill, two fond and
well-known 20th century nursery rhyme characters I advise you to
leave behind in your playroom at home, is because once again we see
the boy placed before the girl. In this new century, it's time to start
thinking Jill and Jack, and Jane and Dick, the same way many of you

may think "Mom and Dad." For those who have a Dad and Mom household, start practicing the "Mom and Dad" phrase right now!

While marketing to Jane involves understanding how to build and maintain a Web site that attracts women, we don't want you to alienate Dick in your quest to be female-friendly. A visit to the *Dickless Marketing* Web site at www.dicklessmarketing.com to check out the Dick-e-meter will give you an idea of some sites that pass the test for successful online marketing, both to Jane and to Dick. The results of our Dick-e-meter will eventually include comments and votes from visitors to the site. Voting will be done anonymously. The Dick-e-meter is designed to give visitors a glimpse of what's working online, and what isn't in regards to selling to women.

This Chapter is where you learn to build a great Web site, one that works for you, not against you. You will also learn what women want from e-commerce. Remember, if you give us what we want, we'll tell the whole world—including Dick!

HITTING THE BULL'S EYE

Targeted marketing is the current buzz phrase describing the core group you should be selling to. Anyone in business, on or off line, who doesn't recognize the value of target marketing please visit your local small business association and take a class on uncovering your target market. This is a task you need to perform before you can understand how to approach your *core market*.

Your core market, as mentioned earlier, is that hungry group of shoppers eagerly looking for your products or services. Within that core market, our friend Dick counts a great deal. He shops online, occasionally, and he also likes things easy and simple. However, my research has uncovered an interesting trait in Dick; Dick often lets Jane do his shopping for him. In many partner relationships between men and women, it's the woman who does the majority of shopping for the household goods, food, and family gifts. Even if those gifts are for her husband's (partner's) family. On those occasions when she isn't making his purchases for him, she is influencing what he purchases, regardless of its male or female quality.

This is why you need to get women to your Web site and make it easy for them to buy from you. Selling to Jane will improve your sales to Dick.

FROM DICK TO DILLER

In this century, I look to Barry Diller as my representative Dick. I mentioned him in Chapter 1. Let's look at why this media mogul is important.

Diller is best known for being the head of Paramount movie studios, starting in the lowly mailroom and gradually moving up to head honcho status at the ripe old age of 32. He is a legend in his own time, at least in Hollywood. The world likes to name-drop celebrities such as Bill Gates (my favorite Harry Potter look alike), Jeff Bezos (my favorite Tom Hanks look alike) and Michael Dell (who resembles an Oscar winning, supporting actor in a '40's B movie), in news stories almost every day. Yet the average citizen would only recognize Barry Diller if s/he reads the *New York Times,* or *The Wall Street Journal.*

Barry Diller is an exciting character because he is always on the leading edge. He attained billionaire status by climbing the corporate ladder at Paramount, but that achievement didn't result in his putting his feet up on his desk and leaning back to smoke a cigar. Not Barry. Ever the astute business professional, he spent the last years of the 20th century buying and selling companies for sport, so it seemed. At this moment in time, his name is popping up all over the place; at business publications such as *Business 2.0; The Wall Street Journal; PRIMEDIA Business Magazines & Media;* and more.

Why is *Dickless Marketing* interested in Barry Diller?

First of all, he's extremely successful. Second, he knows the value of moving forward, out of the 20th century and into the new millennium. Third, he has defined the Internet as the next big thing in business.

ANYTIME, ANYPLACE

In May 2003, *The Wall Street Journal* conducted a lengthy interview with Diller. A striking comment in the interview has Diller admitting he is not tied to his bricks and mortar office. These days, he's more likely to be managing his employees from the deck of his yacht. "We have high speed communications and all of that. It used to be that we'd do a lot of meeting stuff, but I'm not on the phone anywhere like I used to be. E-mail is very much our life and you can do that at anytime from anyplace." Thank you for making my point, Mr. Diller.

The Diller interview gives readers insight into how Diller became a cyber success, moving away from television and those old couch potatoes, to adopt the Internet. Calling the Internet "magic," he says, "The reason I've been so fascinated by interactivity, the reason I still refer to the box [the PC] as magic, is because it does things that still defy your imagining them." Here is where I part company with Mr. Diller because I say the magic of the Internet is precisely in the way it can deliver exactly what you imagine.

He also says, "The Internet is all about interactivity." I couldn't put it better, myself. We would all do well to follow his lead, given his outstanding success in the business world of both the old century and the new one. At present, Diller is watching specific activities online, predicting that these are areas of great promise. I agree with him. Since the Internet is, as he so eloquently says, all about interactivity, paying close attention to how Internet users tend to surf through your site can help you build a solid online presence that is sure to get women interested in you. Here are the specific online activities Diller, and *Dickless Marketing,* is watching for increased activity:

- ○ **PERSONALS:** Women like to get personal. We're very gregarious.
- ○ **DATING:** Women like to date. We're staying single longer, so dating is a lengthier and more involved process. We're looking for Mr. Right online.
- ○ **TRAVEL:** Women like to travel, and if they are traveling with a companion, they are going to go online to at least research the trip arrangements.
- ○ **INFORMATION ABOUT CITIES:** Men driving around in circles until the next millennium rather than stopping to ask directions is a popular joke founded in reality. Jane is not prone to driving around wasting time. She likes to be prepared. She is the one who is going to go online and get the latest information on what's happening, where it's happening, when it's happening, and how to get there.

THERE'S THAT MOVIE, AGAIN!

Building your *Field of Dreams* does not guarantee success online, despite what others may have told you. As we have mentioned before, "If you build it, they will come" only happens in the movies. A local Rochester, New York, Web design company, Biznetix.net, says, "Good Web sites aren't cheap, and cheap Web sites aren't good." We can see the truth of this in the hundreds of sites littering the Web with dated copy, poor design, or—horrified shudder—both.

These sites are usually built by the owner's fifteen-year-old neighbor or by novice computer users who sauntered out of their local business supply store with a box of Web-design software tucked under their arm, confident and cocky because they were going to build a killer site all on their own.

> Web professionals have years of experience and training in Web design, usability, navigation, and marketing online. Not many teenagers can compete with that.

It also includes sites built by serious business professionals who hired a good design firm to do what they knew they couldn't and ended up with the equivalent of a white elephant.

Don't make these mistakes. If you think you have already made them, learn how to correct them now. Let's go through each mistake one at a time.

You hired a teenager (or a college student) to build your Web site.

This teenager wowed you with his or her knowledge of HTML. Now you have a Web site built by a teenager, or a college student, who is wowed by his or her own work.

"So what's the big deal," I think I hear some of you muttering. "Jason…Jamie…Julie (whomever) is a smart kid. S/he knew what s/he was doing. There is nothing wrong with my site."

Think again. Would you hire this student to scout out a good bricks and mortar location for your physical store? Would you depend on this student's knowledge of what's hip to write copy and design your brochure or sales literature? Teenagers and college kids, even talented ones, cannot give you the skilled results a qualified professional in the business of Web design and development can give you. You want experience as much as talent, and those teens don't have it.

Yes, teenagers and college kids know HTML; it's as familiar to them as comic books were to their boomer parents. Some of them design killer Web sites, too. But in the end, you risk sacrificing success because every visitor to your site will judge it by the quality of what your competition offers. If your competition spent time and money hiring Internet business consultants with knowledge not only of the design aspect of building a Web site, but also the business aspect of the Internet, your "killer" Web site with its neat front end design but invisible back-end functionality will lose you credibility and sales.

Yes, I know out-of-the-box Web design software is popular.

No doubt about it; those software packages offer some mighty fine programming. All of them include a WSIWYG—pronounced, *wisi-wig* a "What you see is what you get," format to build your Web site. Think about how word-processing works; as you type, it formats according to the style you've set (or the default if you don't use styles), and magically you have a letter with an opening, a body, and a closing. Point and click, and you're done.

"And what's wrong with that?" I hear a few of you mumbling. Why, the site you built using that out-of-the box solution is just as good as Charlie's down the road. You know Charlie—he owns the bait shop. His Web site has a big red worm on a yellow banner at the top and it shouts, "BEND ME, TWIRL ME, SLICE AND DICE ME: I WILL BAIT THE FISHES NICELY."

I think Charlie wrote the verse above while under the influence—of bad judgment. If you are comparing your site—the site you want Web surfers (especially women) to visit and purchase products or services at—to a site that sports bad poetry in conjunction with bad design (a RED worm on a YELLOW banner is not eye-pleasing on a computer monitor) it's time to review and reconsider some of your design elements.

A good Web site is in the same category as an architectural marvel: a building not only beautiful to look at (good design), but filled with designer furniture (good content) and stunning artwork (great images).

Sites built with out-of-the-box programs can be professional, but they too often suffer from the PICNIC syndrome— "problem in chair not in computer." Using them is not as intuitive as the software companies would have you believe. In reality, the computer programming part of building a good Web site is only half the job. If you've seriously studied Web design within the last six months, if you have a degree in English and know how to craft good Web copy, if you're good with image editing software, go ahead, build your own Web site.

The question is, who's going to rescue you when you want to build forms, or design interactive concepts? It's rather like asking someone to build a house without the proper tools. Professional architects and construction firms build houses. But they don't fill the houses with furniture and lighting fixtures. You have to hire other professionals to do that.

Professional Web design firms build Web sites. A firm will also have access to a good copywriter and a search engine optimization expert. Use an out-of-the-box solution only if you are prepared to be not only the Web designer, but also the Web master.

Being a Webmaster is a full-time job. It requires constant attention to your Web site. Webmasters fix broken links. Webmasters update content regularly. Webmasters build forms and monitor traffic. If you are doing all of this for your Web site, whom, may I ask, is running your business?

Your Web site was built by a respected professional with a degree in design.

For those of you who recognize the value of hiring Web professionals to design and construct your Web presence, leaving you time to focus on your business, I offer you an extended round of applause. This includes hiring a one-person designer who works out of her home, or hiring a large firm with on-staff designers. However—you knew there was going to be a *However*, didn't you?—did you hire a Web design firm that:

o   Has a solid portfolio and was proud to show it off, complete with glowing testimonials?

o Was willing to answer all your questions up front without confusing you with technicalese? (too much technical jargon)

o Understands the difference between surfing the Web and:

- Watching TV
- Listening to the radio.
- Reading a magazine or newspaper.
- Has studied usability, navigation, and Web copy writing.
- Has a search engine optimization expert on staff.
- Is staying in contact to make sure you update regularly?

If your Web design company knows Web design but doesn't understand how the Web works, it won't matter how beautiful your site is. Lack of professional work in any of the points above makes you eligible for mention at: www.webpagesthatsuck.com

A good Web design professional, or firm, is one that understands the Internet. Understanding the Internet involves knowing how surfers surf and how they buy online.

FRAMING FOOLISHNESS

Frames continue to be a big no-no when it comes to building a strong, user-focused Web site. Most Web designers will tell you so, but there are many designers who prefer frames. Understanding what a framed site is, and the issues to the end-users, will help you decide if this is an option you should use.

Framed Web sites have a static left-hand or top-navigation bar. The content on the page changes with each click, but the sides and top (the frame) of the site remain the same throughout. This is a neat way to keep the visitor focused on you because your look and feel is always constant. But danger lies ahead for those who would use frames.

Framed sites often have scrollbars on the right requiring users to scroll down to read information at the bottom of the page. Sites using frames make it difficult for the reader to print the page—generally the right-hand text gets truncated, or cropped off. In many computer monitor settings, a framed site will have copy that takes up most of the screen, requiring the user to scroll from left to right. Ask anyone you know how much he or she likes scrolling from left to right.

Hint: NO ONE does. Which is why frames are so unpopular.

Good Web designers know how to develop a framed site that is seamless and easy to navigate. Let me say this again, **good Web designers** know how to develop a framed site that is seamless and easy to navigate. I know a bit of HTML, I know how to put a Web site together, but I am not a good Web designer; I would never attempt to build a framed Web site for myself. If you are building your own site, whether using HTML you learned at a four-hour class or using an out-of-the-box solution, my advice is to avoid using frames.

Framed sites put together by amateurs often have faulty navigation. A user may click her back button to return to a previous page and end up on a completely different page—one she hasn't even visited yet. If your frames put her in a maze she can't get out of, she will go away and never come back.

If you are considering a Web designer, make sure his or her portfolio includes well-done framed sites that do not scroll to the Atlantic Ocean but do offer easy linking to inner pages and back.

Framed sites can also be e-commerce unfriendly. When frames are not coded properly, surfers may get caught in that maze I mentioned above; one wrong turn and she will find herself going round in circles, without a clue to where the exit is. Women shoppers like to use that back button on their browser to recheck the color or size of an item they are about to purchase. If your framed site sends her off somewhere other than the page she wants, her shopping experience becomes a chore and she will abandon her shopping cart without a second thought.

For the brave among you, test your would-be designer's examples. Use your own experience navigating one or more of your designer's framed sites and record the experiences of a few trusted friends—preferably one or two who are Internet newbies (still learning how to navigate around the Web). Once satisfied that your designer knows how to build a framed site, one that will be easy to use and get around in, ask the Web designer how the search engines are going to find it.

As of the writing of this paragraph, search engines do not recognize frames. The search spiders will only see a blank page if you use frames. Blank pages do not get added to search engine databases. A **good Web designer** knows how to code a framed site to make it visible to the search engine spiders. Search engine optimization experts also know how to do this. Failure to comply with this step when building a framed site puts you in the Internet library, but you will not show up in the e-catalog.

IN THE BEGINNING

Now that we have the issue of how NOT to build your Web site out of the way, let's talk about how you go about building not only a good Web site but also one that will attract and wow the largest consumer market online. The market that includes your Mom, your sisters; your sisters' girlfriends and your sisters' girlfriends' Moms; your Aunts, your grandmother, their friends and their friends' friends.

Our example is a site in the Rochester, New York, area. Notice how all the necessary information is offered in a first-glance scenario:

http://www.welkerproperty.com

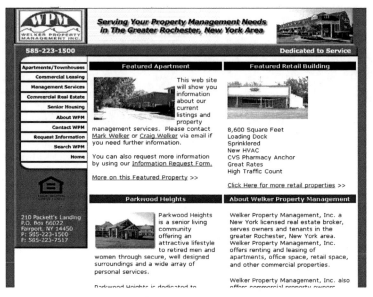

- **WHO** they are: www.welkerproperty.com; a property management company.
- **WHY** they exist on the Web; "This Web site will show you information about our current listings and property management services."
- **WHAT** they do; "Serving property management needs in the greater Rochester, New York, area."

Using Welker Property as the standard, those readers who already believe they have a decent Web site do not get to sit back and relax. Women are particular and your site may pass the who, the why, and the what listed above, but it how does it perform in the other important areas of Web design and functionality?

THERE IS NO PLACE LIKE HOME

Creative writing students are told to start their story at the beginning. The beginning is the place the story actually has its origin. Many successful writers begin their story or novel with a flashback. This is an attempt to build suspense. A good example of how successful this can be is the Star Wars series of movies. We are only now seeing the actual starting point of the saga, including the true backgrounds of the main characters.

On the Web, the place most visitors will get to first is your homepage. As you will see when we discuss search engine marketing and search engine optimization, it's entirely possible for a Web visitor to find you via a search engine and be offered a link to an inner page of your site, bypassing the homepage altogether. It's like opening in a flashback and while that's not bad if the

> "Begin at the beginning and go on till you come to the end, then stop." King of Hearts' advice to Alice in *Alice in Wonderland.*

page she lands on is your product page or your catalog page, it can be disconcerting.

Inner pages of your site may not give the reader the information she wants about you, YOU the Web site owner. Getting to know you is an important part of gaining a woman's trust. We like to see your front room. This means we want to see your homepage. If we have landed on a page removed from the homepage, and you have no link back to it, you risk losing us before we ever get started.

> **Therefore, when building a site to attract women, remember the 3-click rule: Web visitors must always be able to get from one area of your Web site to another in no more than three clicks.**

You may be tired of hearing the advice above—I am certainly not the first person nor will I be the last—to say it, but it's important because more sales are lost through poor navigation than through bad design or poor copy writing.

It's on your homepage that your Web visitor learns the who, the why and the what of your business.

Notice the WHAT part of Welker Properties' homepage. A designer who knows the value of stating upfront not only what the business does, but also the exact area it serves, built this site. I cannot stress strongly enough that no matter how far you want your Web site to reach, from across town to across the world, if you do not announce your locale in your copy and in your source code, you stand to lose a great deal of possible local business (we will get into source code later on).

GETTING THERE FROM HERE

*The most important aspect and function of your Web site, after your **homepage** is the navigation.* Let me restate that—*the most important aspect and function of your Web site after the **design** is the navigation.* Something must be wrong with this computer. It won't type what I want it to. *The most important aspect and function of your Web site after the **content** is the navigation.*

Have I thoroughly confused you? Good. You were depending on me to get you from point A to point B in the paragraph above and I purposely misled you. Why? To show you how frustrating it is when you follow a link on a Web site and end up in a corner you can't back out of.

I also want you to understand why the links on your site should be in understandable text format, not in pictures that require a mouse-over to explain what's hiding behind it. You also need to understand why those links should provide a direct path to the correct inner pages, while also providing a way back.

Approaching the women's market requires understanding that many members of your core market are still on dial-up. "As of April 2003, most users in the U.S. connect to the Internet using dial-up modems of 56Kbps or less. 51.13% use 56Kbps modems, 9.47% use 28/33.3Kbps, and 3.95% use 14.4Kbps modems. All told, 64.55% of home users in the U.S. connect to the Internet at 56Kbps or less." http://www.websiteoptimization.com/bw/0305/

Expect broadband to overtake dial-up in the next year or so—pushed by the Yetties, those young, entrepreneurial, tech-based, twentysomethings who often seem to have less patience than a three-year-old at Toys R Us.

Face it—no one wants to wait around for your Web site to download. You have *approximately* 20 seconds to allow that to happen. Most women admit to waiting only 8-10 seconds.

Optimizing your images is the first step to shortening Web page download time. Images are the first elements of a site to load. Since they load one at a time, if you have several images (your logo, a product picture, any text links your Web designer fashioned into images, etc.) keeping their size to a respectable limit will help keep your download in the acceptable range. If image editing is not your forte, find an image expert who can help out with this crucial task.

WORD OF CAUTION: Don't use images as links to other pages! Use text in another color or font to attract the visitor's eye. Text downloads much faster than pictures. Women appreciate this as it lets them quickly and easily read what's what on your site. Copy (text) gives them clear options they can assimilate at a glance. Remember my mentioning in Chapter 1 that women are verbally inclined? We like words. Humor us. It's to your advantage.

Sites rife with images that require mouse-over, or worse, substitute the image for the text (a shovel and rake for gardening tools, for instance), risk alienating your Web visitor before she even gets a chance to see what you have on page three, or in your catalog—which you have hiding

> A heartbeat is about how long it takes to click a mouse button and open a window to your competition's Web site.

behind that thumbnail picture that looks like a book with your company name on it. Never make the Web visitor guess where a link will lead her. In Web design, it's called the "don't make me think" function.

MAPPING WITH WORDS

Long before you open that box of Web design software your cousin told you to buy; long before you decide what color you want to make your background; long before you choose placement of the navigation bar—left, right, or across the top—spend some time developing a site map to get a clear sense of the "information architecture" of your site. A site map flows downward from your homepage.

It looks something like this:

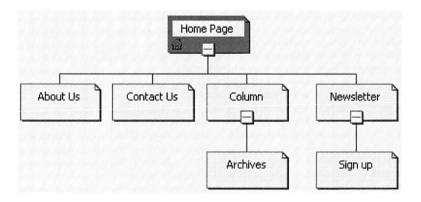

Notice the clear labels showing the names of each page. Work on developing a clear navigation flow; connect the pages in a simple, straightforward manner. Be sure to show site visitors how to get from here to there with a maximum of those three clicks we talked about. This often requires you to have the homepage button on **every page**.

It's not a bad idea to list all of the major links on every page, also. Many successful sites have their navigation links at the top of the page, and a duplicate set at the bottom. This works well for sites that require scrolling beyond one or two page levels. No one, especially a busy woman trying to save time and money, wants to scroll back up to the header of your page to access a link to the next page, or your catalog, or your "About Us" section.

Many sites today utilize a user-friendly navigation bar at the TOP of the Web page, instead of along the left or right side, allowing more space for page content. Without a need to scroll down, links to other parts of your site are always in clear view.

Sites that have a more complicated layout or structure, such as Continental Airlines' site which has links to Programs and Services, flight arrivals and departures, specials, and more, may require more than three clicks to get around in, but your site, if you're mainly selling products and services, should not ask a visitor to remember all of the pages she visits, in the order she visits them.

Your navigation should do that for her.

Scrolling down is not as big an issue as scrolling from left to right. Studies show that Web visitors will scroll for one and a half or two page lengths without complaining. More than that and they get a bit ornery. Again, **NO ONE** wants to scroll from left to right.

Keep your copy centered on the screen so all of the text is viewable at once. The only way to be sure this will hold true for all visitors to your site is to view each page in all the browsers available: Internet Explorer, Netscape, Opera, and Konqueor.

Monitor settings—how your monitor is set to display information— are another issue. The default monitor setting is still 600x800. I know Gen Xers who have practically grown up with the Internet who are still using this outdated setting. Web surfers who have been online for more than three or four years may be using 1024x768, which allows more content to be shown on the screen. Don't rely on what you think is popular. View your site in several monitor settings to gauge how it will appear to the end user.

WEB PAGE ETIQUETTE

A functional, female-friendly site includes the following pages to assure reliable contact and service:

An **About Us** page—Women like to know who you are. If you're inviting us in to your showroom, or your parlor show us your picture. Use professional pictures that are friendly and open, or snapshots that have been optimized by an image expert. Include a short bio assuring us you are knowledgeable in your craft or service.

A **Contact Us** page is required, perhaps with a map to your physical location, or a tidbit of information on your city or state. A Contact Us page is required even if you are not looking for local business. Customers wanting to contact companies that have a national or international presence often look for a local connection first. If you have neglected to include a Contact Us page that shows where your headquarters or home base is, you will lose out on that business.

Include a **News** page to update visitors on what's happening at your company, even if it's only a note saying you've exceeded sales goals this month or that the receptionist had a baby boy last week. Women like personal news. It makes you our friend. If you are not comfortable sharing personal information, just be friendly. Women like daily inspirational quotes, or jokes. Include original information that sets you apart from others.

This should go without saying: don't forget the **Products/Services** page. On that page, offers us links to your catalog or to pages with pictures and further information on the products you sell. Images should always include alt text: a short note saying what the image represents. Search engine spiders cannot see images; your alt text gives them something to read. You can be creative with "alt-text." Write it so it includes a call to action: "This item on sale today only!" Use thumbnail images that when clicked on open up a larger view of the product.

One of the most important issues I would like you to learn from this Chapter is that time is of the essence. Women go online to research and buy because their lives are so busy they no longer have time to jump in the car and drive the 20-30 minutes to the mall, then window shop and, finally, fight with the crowds at the checkout counter. Women I spoke to about their online shopping habits were adamant in this. They shop online because they are too busy to shop offline. Sometimes they want to see the sales or the choices, and then go to the offline store. Again, they are saving time and energy.

The difference online is in the fact that your Web pages, not your sales staff, are your personal introduction and handshake. Those pictures of yourself and your staff provide a sense of comfort to us. Value-added content such as maps, local weather, inspirational quotes, and historical information on your city or town—impresses women and shows them you care. Caring is a good thing.

Having navigation links that connect quickly and easily to inner pages and back again will keep us smiling and willing to spend our time and money with you.

BUY NOW!

Be very careful not to make us guess where your shopping cart is. Put a link to it where we can't miss it, along with a submit button that is big enough to see from across a crowded room. When we're ready to buy, make it as easy as boiling water; get a pot (product), fill it with water (purchasing information), set it on the stove (credit card number and address form) and light the fire (submit button.) Then clean up for us—send us an e-mail telling us when the item will ship.

These are the critical points so far:

- o Web visitors follow text links better than graphic images depicting products.
- o Female-friendly means up front shopping cart and sales information.
- o Convenience is a major consideration; product quality and price follow in close order.
- o Words are important, but keep them simple; your Web visitor will not read them, she will scan them.

Ask your visitors to help you make their experience at your site pleasurable. Give them a chance to make comments and then take their advice! More than one woman who took my survey commented on this. "Read your feedback!" they said.

THE MONA LISA AND THE GRAND CANYON

This brings us to content. Content experts deal not only with the words and images on your site, but the overall design, layout and usability. I am not going to delve deeply into the realm of usability here. I suggest you visit the IBM Accessibility site (see below). IBM has taken usability and accessibility to heart, especially for folks who have vision problems, or other disabilities that make using a mouse or keyboard difficult. They have developed an excellent chart to help you check on how effective your content is.

http://www-106.ibm.com/developerworks/web/library/w-mertz.html

Let's consider the old adage that a picture is worth a thousand words. Take the Mona Lisa or the Grand Canyon. My familiarity with the Mona Lisa is only through articles and photographs, but she is known the world over for her smile—a smile described as enigmatic by art experts. I would say enigmatic is a $50 word, as opposed to sly or shy, which sound like $10 words to me.

If we accept the experts' opinions and agree the Mona Lisa has an enigmatic smile, we should then thank those experts for putting our thoughts into word(s) and for using the right word(s). In this instance, a painting as famous and beautiful as the Mona Lisa almost *requires* a $50 word, merely looking at the picture is not enough. We want someone to articulate the experience.

If we consider the Grand Canyon, we have a similar issue. This magnificent natural wonder defies description, so people say. Yet visitors to the Grand Canyon do describe it—all the time. I have yet to see it for myself, therefore I rely on the words of others who have visited it to regale me with its breathtaking majesty. I've found that few people, if any, can describe it without using gold-plated $50 words.

The Grand Canyon and the Mona Lisa are only two of the world's great wonders that beg for description. I could go on and on, other wonders are the Sphinx, Niagara Falls, and Mt. Everest, but the point is—words are the carriers of the message.

The price attached to words isn't the issue. The fact that we *want to use* $50 words to convey our meaning of these wonders is the point. The Mona Lisa and the Grand Canyon both beg for extraordinary comment. The words become the connections that allow the viewer to share the experience! You are advised, however, to keep your Web copy simple and direct, *except where it can handle those $50 words*, such as in sales copy.

> **SPECTACULAR SALE—TODAY ONLY!**
>
> **STUPENDOUS CLOSE OUT—BUY NOW!**
>
> **UNIQUE GIFTS AND ANTIQUES FOR THOSE WITH**
>
> **DISCERNING TASTES!**

For your call to action, $50 words work great! For your Web copy, use them sparingly or you will dilute their effect. Be powerful, but keep it short and sweet.

Not convinced yet that words count, and good words count double? Take this phrase: **WOMAN WITHOUT HER MAN IS NOTHING.**

> **Men often punctuate it like this: "Woman, without her man, is nothing."**

> **Women look at it and tend to write it this way, "Woman, without her, man is nothing."**

It's the same sentence with the commas set in different places. Each sentence is grammatically correct, but each one conveys a distinctly different meaning.

As mentioned earlier, another goal and a marker of good copy is to write in active tense; *Our company performs reviews in-house,* **NOT** *Our company will perform in-house reviews.* I refer back to the KISS principle—keep it supremely simple. Remember to ask the reader to do something. This call to action is a must—"click here for today's specials," "sign up for our newsletter and receive our free e-book," or "sign up for free monthly coupons." Don't forget the feedback form. As a last measure of interactivity, ask visitors to share their experience on your site, or refer a friend and give them the means to do so; this means software that allows the visitor to send your URL or contact information to a friend using e-mail.

TRACKING EYEBALLS

People don't read online text the same way they read text in print. The human eye tracks words on a computer monitor in a totally different manner than on the printed page, or on a television screen. Early studies done in the 1990s by the Poynter Institute, followed subjects' eyes as they surfed Web pages. The results showed that people scan, or skim, text online. The goal of the online reader is to gather as much relevant information as possible, in the shortest amount of time. Once the reader has determined the basic meaning of what you've written, she will often go back and read the complete text. Or she will print the page to read it at a later time. http://www.poynter.org/

Roger Black, in his book *Web sites that Work* (Adobe Press, 1997) says, "The only person who will ever read every word on your Web site is your mother."

This is why I advise you to consider your Web copy as vital information. Its purpose is to provide the reader with information about who you are and what you can offer her. It should also lead her to perform an action: for instance, click into another page for product information or sign up for a newsletter. Since online readers will only skim the copy at the onset, break it up into small paragraphs, with bold headings followed by bullets with targeted news.

The scanning, skimming behavior of your Web site readers is also why you need to be selective with color. The blend of your color and your design, in partnership with your text, is a marriage of convenience, not love. The convenience is to the reader, not to you.

A note of caution on homepages that open with complex animation and/or Macromedia Flash: this continues to be a no-no. It is especially true for the women's market. The designer who developed that loud, riotous movie shown as the introduction to your Web site is not doing you any favors. Your homepage is not part of a movie trailer, nor is it a commercial in between television shows. Get your logo in front of us, give us a precise tagline—a sentence about who you are and what you can do for us—and let us take it from there.

If you're tempted to have blaring music or a Macromedia Flash opening, ask yourself one question first: How much do YOU like the pop-ups that interrupt your Web surfing on a minute-to-minute basis each day? That's how that movie you want to build will impress first time visitors to your site. If you haven't figured it out yet—it isn't about YOU—it's about THEM!

> Quotes from ClickZ.com show over and over that macromedia flash and elaborate animation can be death to online success. http://www.clickz.com/feedback /reader/article.php/1023261

For example:

The following Web sites have good navigation and good homepage content. The web owners obviously gave thought to the words they used and to the way those words direct the reader what to do next.

http://www.justgiftbaskets.com

As the domain name states, this site sells gift baskets. The homepage does not need to waste space describing the company products and/or services; they are right there for the visitor to judge. A visit to the actual site will show you that the most important part of it is the text in white on a red background, located at the top right of the page.

That is an 800 number. Women are slaves to that 800 number. Every woman I interviewed or chatted casually with about shopping online volunteered the statement that she is leery of buying at a site without an 800 number. My mouse-to-mouse survey supported this, also. Be aware, however, that the 800 number needs to connect with a real person, not a phone tree. If you route her through numerous departments to get an answer to her question, she will check you off of her shopping list.

At JustGiftBaskets.com the "login" and a "help" link are in easy view of our eyes and in easy reach of our mouse. This header is not only easy to read, it directs the eye upward by using color to guide Web site visitors who may be members and want to login right away, or who may have a question warranting a phone call.

Remember when I cautioned: don't make women search for that submit button? Here, having the cart link set in the header is a perfect way to show new visitors where they need to go to start their shopping. Clicking it takes you immediately to a page that offers several payment options and is quite clear about what is in the cart and what is not.

Below the link header and the well-designed logo, there are images of a few of the site's products. Each image has alt-text attached to it. Not only can the search engine spiders catalog this page because the alt-text is content it can read, the Web visitor uses the alt-text to reassure herself that the image is, indeed, exactly what it depicts. Seems simple enough, but you cannot read the visitor's mind. Don't make her "think." Let your site content, images and navigation do that for her.

Below the pictures here are links, which give the reader more information on what the site has to offer. These text links also satisfy the search engine spiders by giving them relevant content to read.

At the very bottom of the page this company shows how much it values its customers by providing security and privacy statements, a business guarantee, and delivery information. All of these are value-added content assuring visitors that privacy is respected and that the site owners have taken the worry out of shipping. A business guarantee tells shoppers the company respects their business. The site then goes the next step and offers a reminder service! Admit it, we all need reminders to keep track of whose birthday is when, or what date Mom and Dad's anniversary is!

In general, navigating through this site is a breeze. As visitors scroll down this homepage, they are treated to visual clues and text links to inner pages. As the page scrolls very little, most of what the visitor sees is immediately visible on almost any monitor setting. When they reach the bottom of the page they come to two menu boxes allowing them to choose their next move. Above the menu boxes is a prominent call to action: "Find the perfect gift."

What's not to like about that?

The only issue I have with this site is that they do not have a home button on every page. I clicked through to buy a basket but wanted to see something back on the homepage and had to click my back button several times. Otherwise, this site is a shining success as a place I can go to purchase a gift for a friend, relative or colleague. This site receives a B+ on the Dick-e-meter for:

- o   Easy navigation.
- o   Using color and images to direct the eye to key parts of the page.
- o   Offering a Help option and an 800 number.
- o   Assuring the visitor the information she shares will be kept private and will be protected.
- o   Allowing the visitor to personalize her account by offering a reminder service.
- o   Using value-added content in a reminders page and in a page detailing how to care for flowers.

THE FARMER IN THE DELL

http://www.almanac.com

Yankee Publishing has been in the customer service business for more years than I have candles coming on my next birthday cake. Their Farmer's Almanac Web site is a stunning example of the give to get principle. Anyone familiar with Zig Ziglar, the motivational speaker, knows he promotes the "give to get" principle; give to get states that the more you are willing to give others, the more you will get back in return.

This site is designed to evoke an old-fashioned, rural American mood and it works! The homepage background is faded yellow, with the logo set across the top, white lettering on a red background.

Along the top is a sales banner flashing unobtrusively, alternately selling seeds, garden tools, fund raising or subscriptions to the print edition of the almanac. It all helps set a certain mood, which is carried throughout the site.

The Farmer's Almanac does not need to explain its purpose—anyone who does not recognize this logo has been out of the country too long and needs to get in touch with family right away!

From a female perspective, the homepage gains my trust immediately because it remains true to the idea I already have of this trusted magazine. The yellow background is true to the design and color of the magazine, and while some visitors may find it taxing on the eye, that is offset here by the font color and flow of the text.

But, wait—the fun and delight has just begun! Right in front of my face is a bright yellow sun and, **above the fold,** a calendar. The sun face is a nice touch, but the calendar is what caught my eye. It offers not only the days of the week, but a note saying how close we are to…summer, spring, Memorial Day, Christmas, whatever happens to be coming up that month. To a woman, this is a great way to be reminded that every month holds a birthday or a holiday requiring us to shop.

Our busy lives often let those important dates and holidays creep up on us, or slip away without recognition. This site can save us from our own forgetfulness! But it gets better—just below the calendar is a link in red that warms my heart: "Personalize the items on this page." Did I do it? You bet I did! Now, when I login, it addresses me by name, gives me my local weather report, and offers me sale items.

Online research marketing firm, Marketing Sherpa, noted in a summer of 2003 report that readers might ignore sales copy and links on the right hand side of your Web page since we have all been conditioned to recognize the content on the right hand border as a sales pitch. The Farmer's Almanac site uses this consumer predisposition with a bright white box on the right showing several tempting links to articles, tips and tales. These links are an invitation to venture farther into the site–no purchase necessary.

In printing, the best copy—headlines and content—is positioned **above the fold** of the newspaper; hence, when putting things at the top of the page on a Web site, refer to it as positioning *above the fold.*

Interesting headlines to articles and value-added content, offered before the sales pitch, softens the copy running below. The reader can quickly peruse the offers and make a decision on whether or not to click on them. Women like being offered free advice and information. On this site, getting it in front of us before the sales speak is a great way to draw us in to do some shopping.

This site doesn't hold anything back. It's not only a welcome respite at the end of a troubled day, filled with great product offerings and information on the weather or what holiday is upon us, it also gives a history of the Almanac that oozes with nostalgia. Where else can you learn that in 1942 a German spy, apprehended by the FBI on Long Island, New York, was found to be carrying a copy of *The Old Farmer's Almanac* in his coat pocket!

While you may not be able to top that on your site, you can supply value-added content about your local area and include it either on your homepage, or on an inner page. You will learn in Chapter 5, "S.E.X. Sarah-Ellen Xceptions," why this can help you make sales in the women's market. What's not to like about that?

This site gets a Dick-e-meter rating of A. Try as I could, I could not find any negative issues with this site. Some may find it overly busy, but I find that it succeeds on all levels, marketing well to women, by offering us:

- o   User-friendly layout and design
- o   Easy, simple navigation
- o   Value-added content
- o   Products that come with an age-old guarantee
- o   Personalization

BRAIN MYSTERIES CURED

Didn't your mother always admonish you to study hard and get good grades in history class? If she didn't, I'm sure your teacher did. There is an old saying that everything old is new again, and Sean D'Souza proves it on his business marketing Web site:

http://psychotactics.com

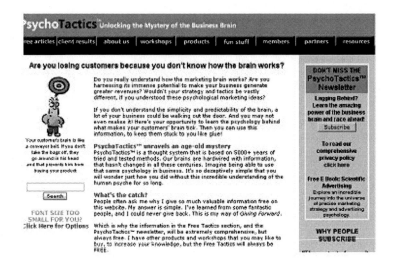

D'Souza promises to unlock the age-old mysteries of the brain that control spending habits. From his homepage he states that: "PsychoTactics™ is a thought system based on 5000+ years of tried and tested methods. Our brains are hardwired with information that hasn't changed in all these centuries."

There is a lot of information on this site, information that works because D'Souza has a focused format and he keeps it fun. Especially endearing to women are the cartoon characters throughout the site— characters that are cute enough to bring a smile to your face, but not so cartoonish that you feel as if the site owner is treating you like a child.

D'Souza's homepage introduces these characters right away with a funny looking little guy in a green T-shirt showing the caption: "Your customer's brain is like a conveyor belt. If you don't take the bags off, they go around in his head and that prevents him from buying your product." This immediate teaser is a psychological call to action. It makes the reader pause, think a bit, then begin to read more.

Everything on the PsychoTactics™ homepage and site beckons the reader to explore.

Valuable content and information, free advice, and/or free giveaways combined with ease of navigation, and simple design, give the visitor a pleasant Web visit. D'Souza has more than one call to action on his homepage; he offers visitors advice on how to change the font, how to subscribe to his newsletter, and more.

A good Web site, as shown in all of our examples, has clear, upfront information that gives the reader an immediate sense of where she's landed. On this site, you see the trademarked logo and the tagline, "Unlocking the mystery of the business brain," presented in white text on a green background. The color may be a different shade of green on your monitor but the effect of using white text on a dark background works well to direct the eye where the good stuff is. D'Souza then does

Love at first sight? Not our clients, says Sean D'Souza

something even more eye-catching—he shows the eye-grabber word TACTICS in bolded black.

Directly below the attention-grabbing header are links to all the inner pages of this site. One of the things that makes this site Female-friendly is the obvious humor displayed throughout. D'Souza's marketing is invigorated with jokes, cartoons and personalization—another Female-friendly tactic. For instance, on an inner branding page there is a list of mistakes many people make when trying to brand their new business. It's free, it's useful, and it has a friendly tone, as if D'Souza is speaking directly to the reader.

On PsychoTactics D'Souza uses the right hand sales copy section to offer his free newsletter at the top of the right side banner, followed by his free e-book, then cleverly adding testimonials.

We haven't mentioned testimonials yet, but these are very much like the stars your grade school teacher used to put on the papers you took home to Mom and Dad.

Testimonials tell visitors your company and its Web site can be trusted! Women feel more comfortable on a site that lists testimonials—especially from other women—than on a site that merely spends six pages touting its impressive background and showing off the list of letters after each senior manager's name.

In an interview about how the sexes differ in their shopping habits, I asked Sean how he made his site so Female-friendly. He admits it was sort of by default; since he is comfortable in the company of women he succeeded in building a presence online that women would flock to because he used his own advice and chose to focus on friendly text, easy formatting, and helpful links. Check out the "font too small for you" link. It opens a new screen that instructs users on how to increase the font size not only for this site, but also for their entire system! The ability to change the font size on D'Souza's site is value-added content that does more than educate—it shows that this Web site owner cares about the people who visit his site.

"People who are primarily women," he says.

D'Souza is smart to include the font instructional. Font size is a crucial element of your site. The IBM Accessibility site is a good resource for information on how to address this issue for people with vision problems. For the rest of us, remember that not all visitors are under 30 years old. If you're selling to women, and to the baby boomers in particular, make your copy easy to read by using a font size larger than 10-point. Also, use dark colors that show up well on a white background. Light font colors on a dark background are not as effective, unless you know a great deal about color combinations.

D'Souza has a number of other insights into the differences between men and women as shoppers. He believes women like the Internet because of its non-threatening nature.

"On the Internet," he says, "a woman can shop and not have to worry about a salesperson bothering her. Men just get bored with shopping," he chuckles. "They like gadgets." In fact, D'Souza offers this nugget of marketing information, "Studies have shown that women's stores are smart to add a section with electronic gadgets for men to hang out in while their wives shop."

Sean goes on to note that men are territorial, much more so than women. This puts men in negotiation mode when shopping. Sean says women are motivated by trust. He's seen it on his site time and time again; women come to get good marketing advice and go away with a sense of trust. He not only hears from them with positive testimonials, but they send their friends to check him out.

"One of the most popular items on my site," he shared, "is the '*What Bugs You?*' bug. This gives visitors permission to complain about anything they don't like on the site." Sean feels that women "seem to need that permission more than men do."

It may seem like a generalization, but it fits. It's because we don't like to hurt anyone's feelings. Offering us a place to voice our opinion, good or bad, is like inviting us in for coffee. Do that, and we will want to look around at what you're selling in order to offer advice on that, too! Even if we don't buy anything, you gain important information that can help improve both your Web site and your product sales.

A proper review of D'Souza's site would not be complete without mention of his recipes page. Here is PsychoTactics' unique value-added content and personalization. There is no reason for D'Souza to include recipes on his marketing site, but he does. Instead of giving visitors the ability to create a personal page of their own, his approach is to open himself up to us, showing a fun photo of himself on his "About Us" page and including some favorite recipes from his homeland of New Zealand.

He also uses his signature, in his own handwriting, on his site. "Another trust builder," he says.

What's not to like about that?

My only issue with D'Souza's site was that I could not find a homepage link. Within 24 hours of our discussion, he had one added to the bottom of every page.

Ah, the power of the Web. Imagine trying to fix your Yellow Pages ad if it contained a printed error. I worked at a company where our phone number was incorrect—we were stuck with that error for an entire year! A supplement to the Yellow Pages was printed to *make nice,* but it was added after the fact. It couldn't change the mistake that cost us many clients, no doubt.

Do not take the issue of having a link to your homepage throughout your site lightly. Many, many Web sites make this error. Going back home is a woman's prerogative—exactly like changing her mind. Make it easy for us, and we will reward you with sales.

PsychoTactics™ gets an A+ on the Dick-e-meter for:

- o Building a site that is easy on the eyes.
- o Providing good navigation.
- o Encouraging visitors to provide feedback.
- o Offering qualified advice—for free!
- o Opening himself up to the reader with value-added content in the form of recipes and a freewheeling photo of himself that makes him look like a fun guy we would like to get to know better.

WHISTLING ALL THE WAY TO THE BANK

Remember that everything about your Web site resonates with your voice; it speaks for you and for everything you offer both on your Web site and in your offline store. When you make it easy for us to see who you are, what you do, and go that further step to make buying easy for us, we will do so.

> **Maya Draisin, Executive Director International Academy of Digital Arts & Sciences, and President of Webby Awards, Inc. says, "The trend this year [2003] is toward using the Web to connect people online to mobilize them offline."**

Wow us at your site, and we'll visit your store. It's as simple as that.

Women have placed our pink flag in the virtual dirt of the digital world and we are proudly standing over it. But, we don't want to stand there alone; we're bringing everyone we know with us. And that includes husbands, partners, brothers, and sons. Come and join us. We won't make you wear pink—unless you want to.

FAVORITE COLORS

Speaking of pink. Who remembers this ditty from days gone by? "I never saw a purple cow, I never hope to see one. But I can tell you anyhow, I'd rather see than be one." (Wouldn't you?)

Gelett Burgess wrote that silly poem in 1895. He never expected it to be his defining work, but that's what happened. The world took to the silly poem and never let him forget it. In his own defense, he wrote this follow up:

"Ah, Yes! I wrote the *Purple Cow*. I'm sorry, now, I wrote it! But I can tell you anyhow; I'll kill you if you quote it!"

Amazing true fact: Once upon a time in America, pink was for boys and blue was for girls.

You are going to discover that color can do for you what the purple cow did for Burgess—define your Web presence incorrectly. You have two choices; one is to be distinctive in a positive way by understanding how color works; the other one is to end up with a purple cow you just want to get rid of, like our friend Gelett Burgess.

In 1914, *The Sunday Sentinel* advised mothers that, "If you like the color note (in an earlier article, we assume) on the little one's garments, use pink for the boy and blue for the girl, if you are a follower of convention."

In 1918, the *Ladies Home Journal* had this to say about dressing our babies in pink or blue: "There has been a great diversity of opinion on the subject, but the generally accepted rule is pink for the boy and blue for the girl. The reason is that pink being a more decided and stronger color is more suitable for the boy, while blue, which is more delicate and dainty, is pertier for the girl."

Pink for men was popular throughout the 1920s. In that era, it was clothier Brooks Brothers openly offering men's shirts in pink. In the '40s and '50s, during his reign as King of rock and roll, icon Elvis Presley was seen more than once in pink pants and pink shirts, often with a pink scarf thrown around his neck for good measure.

I am sure this is blasphemy to some. The idea of pink for girls and blue for boys has been so ingrained in our psyches that we rebel against any notion that it was ever different. In some defense, I remind readers fond of fairy tales that in the Western version of Cinderella, based on the popular 1950 Disney cartoon, Cinderella's pink ball gown was torn to shreds by the cruel stepsisters. Her fairy godmother made her a new ball gown in sparkling blue.

My research shows that pink was considered a watered-down red, and as late at the 18th century it was recommended for boys not girls precisely because red was considered a color that was too strong and fiery for little girls.

How the reverse ended up for us in the 20th century is the subject for another book, another time. That it prevails today is reason enough to start you thinking about the colors you will use, or are using, on your Web site.

FLIRTING WITH SUCCESS

Should you be using pink on your site to attract women? Maybe, maybe not. Color studies show that the color pink is often used to "show childish innocence, or characters with child-like personalities." The present day world often considers pink flirtatious, or depicting the freshness of good health; i.e., being "in the pink." At other times, pink is used to indicate purity.

Since we do know that people scan pages online and seldom read every word, you have an opportunity to use color to your advantage. Work with your Web designer to make sure the colors on your site do something—draw the eye to a particular product or link; give the reader a sense of warmth and closeness (as the Farmer's Almanac site does by using yellow to portray a sense of nostalgia), or to create a mood. Mood is also a part of voice, of course.

Pink may work in some areas of your site, and not in others. If the meaning of the color you choose is in transition, as pink was in the early 20th century, some of your visitors may have associations with it that are not flattering. When considering color understand that your choices are related to subjective interpretation. What you perceive as a result of the colors you choose may not be what the visitor to your Web site sees. Be careful how you approach this element of your design. Ask friends and family to view several different color schemes before you actually lock yourself into one.

Many Web sites aimed at women use the color pink generously. Some of the sites we will talk about in Chapter 7, "Meeting at the Well," are predominantly pink. Women's communities and partnerships, as well as non-profits, seem fond of the color pink. Additionally, there is no escaping the pink ribbon depicting the fight against breast cancer worn by both women and men the world over.

Be thoughtful about the colors you choose. The colors that you feel best suit your products and services, including the colors of your logo, may appear very different once you get them up on the Web. Since color is as important as navigation and Web copy because it works in conjunction with those two elements of Web design, I advise you to build and view your Web site in several different color schemes before locking into a final choice.

WOW! Winning Over Women

There is no indication that in order to make friends with women, you need to dress yourself up in pink! Marketing online is moving away from the winning of an eyeball war—those who attract the most traffic, get the most sales—to an issue of personalization—those who make the most friends online, get the most sales.

Remember, at *Dickless Marketing*, friend = S-A-L-E-S.

COLOR MINE CLEAR

The issue of color leaves gender behind and becomes something of a functionality issue online. Different Web browsers display colors differently. It's your job to find out exactly how that bright blue-green scarf you're promoting this month looks in all the different browsers, including Netscape and Opera, two popular browsers used by folks who do not care to use Internet Explorer.

Also, remember that the monitor setting being used by your Web visitor is her choice, not yours. Is the baby boomer sitting at home in her dining room looking at you on her monitor using a 600x800 standard display setting or the popular 1024x768? Is she viewing your site on a 13-inch monitor a 15-inch monitor or something larger? How is that thumbnail picture of your latest, greatest product coming through?

Color Matters, a Web site dealing with the issues of color in many mediums, including the Web, has detailed information on how we view different colors on a computer monitor. Understand that much of the sharpness and contrast of color is created by the individual computer operating system, the monitor and the browser accessing the Web. Color mutation is a given.

At Color Matters http://www.colormatters.com/chameleon.html they write: "The most common effect can be compared to viewing an image through dark sunglasses. In addition to this, each computer will be operating within its own color space. Earthy brick tones created in one color environment may shift into cosmetic pinks in another. A corporation's teal green logo is guaranteed to be any number of variations of blues and greens on the Web."

Your color choice can result in a global catastrophe if you choose a tint or combination that has bad vibes outside of the United States. Whether or not you are actively marketing worldwide, America is still a melting pot. Many of your potential visitors have not been born and bred here. If they come to like you, you may well find yourself serving their relatives in Europe, Asia, or the Far East. The following are common current color associations in Western culture:

Red: passion, romance, fire, violence, and aggression. Think of stoplights or signal warnings.

Purple: creative, or mysterious; it holds a hint of royalty, mysticism, and rarity. In some cultures, this color is associated with death.

Blue: the color of loyalty—think: "the men in blue;" it is also the color of security and tranquility, but it can depict coldness or sadness. It is also not a good color to use if you are a food-related company; blue is a natural appetite suppressant.

Green: go! It also depicts nature, fertility, growth, and envy. In the U.S. green is often associated with environmental awareness, (Greenpeace) and is often linked to fiscal matters.

Yellow: the sun; use it for brightness, illumination, but understand that it can depict illness or cowardice. At the Farmer's Almanac site the use of yellow was shown as cheerful by using a cartoon of a smiling sun.

Black: power; for those boomers out there, black is a memory of tough, disappointing times but in the new millennium, this strong color can also be used to show sophistication and contemporary style. Be aware, however, that it will never fully lose its closeness to death, morbidity, and evil. (Darth Vader)

White: purity, innocence, cleanliness, truth, and peace. On the other hand, it can also indicate coldness or sterility. In China, white is the color of death. White space on a Web page is a good thing, even on the homepage.

TIIINK BRAND

Color can also be used to brand yourself. Think Big Blue (IBM), the Yellow Box (Kodak), or Pink Cadillacs (Mary Kay) and the red of the Target bull's eye. We will talk more about that in Chapter 6, but for now let's end this short Web development tutorial with some tips and tricks on how to make sure your Web site passes the usability, readability, and eye-appeal test not only for women, but for all of your Web visitors:

- o Use color to reinforce your brand. Follow the guidelines above.

- o Use high contrast for readability. Don't make your readers squint. Text is skimmed online; keep it short and sweet with bullets or different-colored text to show emphasis.

- o If you are trying to be trendy, be aware that next year you will be outdated. If you can afford the redesign, go for it. Otherwise, forget trends.

- o Be true to your audience. A technology company does not want to fall victim to colors that look frivolous, yet, with many women in the market for technology products and services, don't limit your design process to colors attractive only to men. A craft site may want to use a blend of primary colors to show off their wares. Sites that sell financial services should use green, but soften it with blue that shows your loyalty to personal attention.

No matter who you are or what you're selling, test, test, test: how does the site look; how does it work; how does it appeal to end users.

Check with your audience; teens, young mothers, Moms, Grandmoms, all have varying tastes for color design and functionality. Ask your family and friends to surf your site more than once before you launch, and record their experiences.

Remember to view the site in different browsers. The most popular browsers at the moment are Internet Explorer, Netscape, AOL, and Opera or the Linux browser, Konqueror.

Other important issues about design and functionality that are critical to your online business success will be covered in succeeding chapters. As

> Run your business, lest your business run you.
> ~ Benjamin Franklin

you read on you will learn the importance of a privacy statement; ways to assure your customer her credit card is protected (getting and using a merchant account); and how to make the buying process seamless and easy to complete.

Cha-ching!

Coming next in Chapter 5, "S-E-X Sarah-Ellen Xceptions: Baby Boomers vs Gen Xers & Gen Ys," we will be looking at the shopping differences between the baby boomers and their close siblings, the seniors, as well as the online shopping habits of the Gen Xers (twentysomethings) and Gen Ys (echo boomers).

Who can say MSP marketing?

WHAT WE LEARNED IN THIS CHAPTER:

o Like most Web surfers, women like text to lead them through your site. Don't confuse us with graphic links that are supposed to represent text.

o Keep your navigation simple—show her the shopping cart!

o Some women like pink, some don't.

o Have a clear call to action: Ask the visitor to **DO** something.

o Offer value-added content; a free newsletter, information about your local community, recipes, anything that sets you apart from the competition.

o Accessibility and usability count.

o It isn't about **YOU**—it's about **US**—keep the animation and **loud music** to yourself or take it out back!

Dickless Marketing

5. S-E-X Sarah-Ellen Xceptions

Baby Boomers vs Gen Xers & Gen Ys

> "Never doubt that a small group of thoughtful, committed citizens can change the world. Indeed, it is the only way that ever has." ~ Margaret Mead

"The past has taken over the present. Nostalgia is all the rage. Everywhere you look, something points to the past. Pop culture has become a living museum of the good old days."

These sentences, quoted from an article in *Direct Marketing Business Intelligence* magazine, June 2003, show that nostalgia is thriving throughout the U.S. today. This chapter of *Dickless Marketing* is going to show you how to use nostalgia to your advantage. I will also open the door to the future of online shopping, when today will be the nostalgic focus.

PUSHING THE ENVELOPE

The baby boomers just won't let go of those rock and roll days of the '50s, '60s, and '70s. Their collective influence on media advertising and production is coming through loud and clear. It's apparent on radio stations devoted to playing oldies but goodies. We see it on television where "American Dreams" and "That '70s Show" have their basis in yesteryear. There seems to be no end in sight—nostalgia's reach is even touching the 2003 television fall line-up, giving viewers new shows with music from the boomers' teen years playing in the background.

Direct Marketing Business Intelligence is not the only magazine touting the power of "remember when." *Business 2.0* showcased the reappearance of baby boomer products such as Breck Shampoo and Ovaltine in one of its early 2003 issues, and in August of 2002 the

Wall Street Journal ran an article titled "Small Town, USA," touting the national hankering to revisit the good old days.

Even more conspicuously, the movie industry is embracing nostalgia, resurrecting those comic book heroes of yesteryear; Spiderman, The Incredible Hulk, and Superman. Clearly, the baby boomer market is pulsing with possibility.

Research and statistics divide the baby boomers into groups—aging boomers, those 56 and over, and younger boomers, those 55 and under. Other reports lump boomers in with their younger brothers and sisters, labeling those over 30 years of age but still under the age of 50 as boomers. The truth is much simpler. It's so popular to call yourself a baby boomer today that anyone born between 1946 and 1964 happily harkens to that label. I will call my representative boomer shopper Sarah.

Information regarding Sarah's online spending will show you why the boomers and seniors are so important. It will also show you who has the most spending power, and what will get her to spend it on your Web site.

The twentysomethings and late teenagers, the Gen Xers and Gen Ys, comprise another group that it's difficult to separate successfully. They are the up and coming consumers who have been shopping online for much of their adult lives. They also spur online spending in the baby boomer group. I will call my representative for this group of shoppers, Ellen.

I will show you not only what impresses the Ellens, but I will help you understand why your focus should include them, but not be centered on them. You will learn that they shop differently from their moms, but that they also mimic their mothers' values when it comes to shopping online.

The tweens and teens pretty much still depend on Mom and Dad for money. You will get their business if you attract Sarah and Ellen to your site (Sarah may be the one paying for their purchases; Ellen may be the one influencing their purchases).

Each of these generational communal groups encompasses a unique and special place in the American social order. Together they make a powerful market that could be shopping on your Web site—if you take the time to learn how they think and how they spend.

> **I simply contend that the middle-class ideal, which demands that people be affectionate, respectable, honest and content, that they avoid excitements and cultivate serenity is the ideal that appeals to me, it is in short the ideal of affectionate family life, of honorable business methods. ~Gertrude Stein**

DORMANDISE, PASS GO, COLLECT $200

The Buzzwhack dictionary at http://web.buzzwhack.com/ calls *dormandise* "the act of bringing back brand names from collective *consumer conscience* such as Ovaltine, Breck Shampoo, and the Care Bears." Any online small business disputing the value of dormandise marketing is doomed to watch others succeed, much the way the unfortunate holder of a *go to jail* card in the game of Monopoly cannot proceed past GO and will not collect $200.

We might consider the game Monopoly, marketed by Hasbro®, Inc., a product worthy of dormandizing except that it has never gone out of favor. Considered "the quintessential American game, as it provides players with the opportunity to make their fortune," http://www.hasbro.com, this board game was a household standard for the baby boomers.

Candy Land, a favorite boomer board game, was invented by Eleanor Abbot in 1949, as she spent many weeks in a hospital bed recovering from polio.

The boomers contributed a great deal to building the game's popularity in the U.S. *Do not pass go and do not collect $200* has become an adage in its own right, used to taunt unsuccessful relatives, friends, or enemies. It's often spoken with bravado if the speaker has managed to get past GO and collect his or her $200. Paying attention to this chapter of *Dickless Marketing* will give you the chance to use that phrase with confidence.

Growing up in the '50s, '60s, and '70s was a unique experience many Americans continue to cherish. No child growing up in this century will ever experience anything like it. Boomers enjoyed the benefit of a childhood full of inventive play with games and toys built from their imagination. They made dolls out of popsicle sticks, devised moving vehicles—called them wagons—out of old tires and pieces of discarded wood, and built forts constructed with old blankets and broken chairs.

Summer vacation to the boomer kid meant rolling out of bed at seven a.m., grabbing a mouthful of Cheerios® before running out the door. Play lasted until we collapsed onto unmade beds after the street lights came on. Store-bought toys were simple things like Lincoln Logs™, pogo sticks, and board games. It may shock some readers to learn that as children, boomers were seldom supervised. Our days were spent meandering about our neighborhoods, with almost complete abandon.

Boomer children enjoyed their playful, carefree world wrapped in the freedom of a society at peace. In those early years of the last century, America enjoyed a positive world image bolstered by its clear victory in WWII. Those post-war years led to a prosperity that has yet to be matched. Many early baby boomers listened to the radio on rainy days, having no television to watch. Many early boomers I spoke with said they were disappointed with television when it came to their house. Somehow, "The Lone Ranger" and "Hop-a-Long Cassidy" on the small screen didn't measure up to the mental picture they had conjured up while listening to these heroes on the family radio.

"Trust no one over thirty!" was the boomer battle cry of the young boomers and they began to shape our society in '50s and '60s. They embraced rock and roll with all the eagerness of teenagers on a first date, much to the dismay of their staid and respectable parents. They spent hours playing board games. (Scrabble™ and Chutes and Ladders™, two popular children's board games, were invented during the boomer years). Boomers introduced the world to the mini-skirt, go-go boots, and free love.

Reminders of those happy years are popping up in advertising everywhere you look today, and not necessarily prompted by ad executives over the age of 45. Indeed, commercials on television hyping baby boomer music or memorabilia (think Old Navy and the Gap) are being developed by Gen Xers. Only a year or so ago the Gap was promoting khakis in a commercial with Gen X and Gen Y kids doing the swing, a dance straight out of the '40s!

Direct magazine delves into the benefits of nostalgia and notes that in reality, it's "nothing more than what's in vogue." Could it be that today's nostalgia is no different from the longing our own parents had for their version of *the good old days*?

Whatever it means, nostalgia influences marketing at all levels, especially online. It's especially important in *Dickless Marketing* because baby boomer and senior women are the fastest growing group of Internet users in the U.S. A look at the Better Homes and

Knowledge Networks (May/2003) reports that 48% of boomers have bought something online. http://www.statisticalresearch.com/

Gardens Web site gives us a look into the boomer influence:

http://www.bhg.com

When I interviewed Dottie Enrico, the site director of *Better Homes and Gardens* online, I learned some interesting things about women and the Internet.

Better Homes and Gardens is a print magazine that has been around at least as long as the baby boomers. BHG's online presence reflects its commitment to both genders, but you can see from the screen shot above, it appeals more to women than men.

As the manager in charge of this Web site, Dottie Enrico needs to know women, she needs to understand how to approach men, and she can't let age and gender differences get in the way of her ultimate goal: to attract visitors to the BHG Web site.

"We use the magazine to drive traffic to the Web site," she said. At the time of our conversation, she couldn't give specific stats on unique visits, but she offered a guesstimate: "I'd say three-quarters of our visitor numbers are women. One-quarter of them are men."

The women come for crafts, recipes, holiday ideas, communing, and sharing ideas. The men come for home improvement advice, remodeling articles, and to buy books. With over 40 million page views per month, this site has the how-to of marketing to women online down pat. Much of the credit has to go to Dottie, not only for her professional work on the site, but because she knows and understands women and how they use the Internet.

Like many women, Dottie admitted that her first venture online wasn't to surf aimlessly; it wasn't even to e-mail family or friends. She went online to connect with a select group of adults. She wanted to locate families adopting children from Korea because she was adopting a child from Korea. Her search offline hadn't turned up anything close to home. But she needed information, and a way to connect with others who understood what she was going through. She found that online, through an AOL group. It convinced her this new "mobile society" was a powerful tool that would change the way people communicate.

Eventually her interest in the Internet led her to her present job as site director at http://www.BHG.com. The real-time communication of the Internet, the "mobile society" as she calls it, became her means of reaching out to share a specific personal experience with other women and men, and to hear their stories.

Her advice to small businesses trying to find their niche online is to "Find groups with an interest level that matches your products."

At BHG, Enrico says traffic is dictated by the end-user. The magazine and the e-zine keep visitors happy by giving them information that's useful, requested, and applicable to their lives. As a mother site to other successful Web ventures, such as *American Baby* and *Ladies Home Journal*, BHG attracts a majority of females. The site sells to women on a daily basis. They know how because they get it. They get it because Enrico looks beyond the technology—beyond those computer cables and monitors, all the way into the hearts of the women who make up the core market of BHG.com.

Dottie Enrico looks at the Internet as a way people can share personal information they might not have access to otherwise. Sharing, she agrees, is a major reason women go online. What's not to like about that, I ask you?

SARAH IS READY TO BUY ONLINE!

It may surprise some readers to learn that boomer women are avid Internet users. This group of Internet users, the 45-to-64-year olds, are also more likely to own fax and copy machines, large-screen TVs, and satellite dishes. They are so technically savvy that new retirement communities today include broadband Internet access. Virginia Reinhold of the *Baywinde Senior Living Community* in Rochester, New York, told me, "All the senior living facilities today are including Internet access. It's the seniors who want it, not their kids, as some people assume."

Market research online confirms Reinhold's statement.

> **Charts show that in the 50-54 year old age group,
> 52% are online.
> In the 55-59 year old age group, 43% are online.**

More than 47% of the entire group own cell phones and show incomes ranging from $50,000/year to in excess of $100,000/year. Clearly these Internet shoppers are, as we say in sales, low-hanging fruit—ripe for the picking!

It doesn't end there. Census reports tell us that the number of Americans over 50 years of age is expected to grow by 40 million in the next 20 years. Within this booming market, women are the gender projected to have the money to spend. Online, they are spending it with companies that "get it." In other words, with companies that understand their needs and wants.

Cyberatlas, the Web marketer's guide to online facts, reports that 26% of boomers are expecting an inheritance from their parents, making them prime markets for financial advisors. This bodes well for other smart marketers who understand the value of this potentially cash-rich group.

Within the baby boomers themselves, 49.1% are male, 50.9% are female. Together they represent annual spending power at an estimated $1.1 trillion. As the boomers move into senior citizenship, you can expect the percentage of females to grow, while the percentage of males will shrink. It's a fact of life. Women live longer. The latest reports from the U.S. Department of Health and Human Services show that the life expectancy for men is to age 72. For women, it's approaching 80 years.

CAUTION!!! Don't qualify Sarah as aging (no one likes to be reminded she is getting older). And don't refer to her as "younger" (she probably got enough of that at home—we in the U.S. always think of the baby of the family as being pampered, but I know many family babies who are caring for aging parents because their older siblings live too far away to help out). Labels that refer to her age will only make Sarah bristle with disdain.

ADOPTING AND ADAPTING

The leading edge boomers, those in the 55 and under age group, were early adopters of this fun new technology, seizing it with the same enthusiasm they continue to show for sports, traveling, jazz clubs and gathering in large groups rather than pairing off.

The novice computer users—boomers who may be retired and may not have used computers at work as much as their younger buddies— are showing increased interest in the Internet every year. They are logging on and learning the ropes from both their children and from friends and relatives who are years ahead of them in computer-speak.

These are what I call "the garage sale boomers." Most summer weekends you can find them hopping from one garage sale to the next. It gets them out of the house, they find quaint, interesting stuff, and they love finding those bargains—sheets, toys,

games, secondhand clothes—that they can share with their kids and sisters or brothers. Sarah is eager to visit Web sites that offer this service—think eBay. And she's showing her delight by opening her wallet to spend, spend, spend!

A visit to this Web site: http://www.wiredseniors.com, a portal for seniors who have embraced online communities, reveals a world of matchmaking, discussion forums, mall shopping, travel advice and more. This note on the site's homepage is indicative of the power and reach of this group: "Seniors Search would like to thank the Web Sites included below for their support in making the Internet more Senior Friendly to the 50 Million Internet Users who are over 50 years of age." Remember, Sarah is both a boomer and a senior and may be a bit touchy about one label or the other. Some women over 50 will not answer to the "senior" label. Others will.

WiredSeniors.com is talking to the Sarah who is a leading edge baby boomer, somewhere between 40-50. She's comfortable on the net— she uses e-mail every day to keep in touch with family and friends, she's healthier than her mother was at her age, and she is often caught in the *sandwich* generation—between children still living at home and aging parents who need her care. If she has no children at home, and is not caring for aging parents, she may be an *empty nester.* When marketing your products and services to her, use language she identifies with and never promise her something you can't deliver.

Look at this site and how it successfully approaches its core market:

http://www.emptynestmoms.com

A click on a link at WiredSeniors took me to EmptyNestMoms.com. This site uses an easy-to-view top page navigation and puts great content in the prime real estate section of the homepage. I discussed the prime real estate section of your homepage in Chapter 4, "You Don't Know Dick."

At EmptyNestMoms.com there is a bold Welcome note on the top right. Just below this introduction is an "ENM link" which leads to "Empty Nest Moms stories." Travel links, a message board, and an events calendar follow the ENM link. A short scroll down leads to the bookstore and—a pink link that says, "Let's go shopping!"

Clicking on that link opens a page with an invitation to a lingerie site, complete with plus-size items. Someone at Empty Nest Moms realized that women over 40 are still lively, sexy, and full of fun! If you mistake them for that ancient 20th century stereotype of a woman over 40, known to schlep around the house in floppy slippers and an old flannel shirt, you will lose out on the tremendous buying power she possesses.

Wired Seniors, the site that led us to the Empty Nest Moms site, is one of hundreds of sites aimed at marketing to baby boomers and senior citizens. I found the Empty Nest Moms site in two clicks, and from there I was treated to a shopping spree that took me all of 20 minutes. Try doing that by going to the mall!

NOSTALGIA WORKS

A MarketingSherpa report, "E-mailing Aging Baby Boomers vs. Seniors" encourages marketers to use nostalgia to their advantage. Because she enjoys reminiscing, Sarah responds to language straight from the '60s era of free love; Woodstock, Barbie, GI Joe, flower children, mini skirts, and hippies.

Sarah likes a personal touch. It doesn't hurt to use "Please" and "Thank you." Politeness never goes out of fashion. However, don't overdo it. Women in this age group are casual enough to call their maternal parent, "Mom," not "Mother."

Frank Feather's book *Futureconsumer.com* (Warwick Publishing 2000) spends over 300 pages outlining the e-commerce world of 2005-2010, showing that "Webolution makes the home again central to society." We need look no further than Wal-Mart for an excellent example of marketing to Sarah. She's been shopping at Wal-Mart for most of her adult life.

Wal-Mart, already a worldwide player in consumer goods, is among author Feather's top five Web sites poised for domination in the next eight years. Wal-Mart is also mentioned in *The Myth of Excellence* (New York: Crown Business, 2001), where authors Fred Crawford & Ryan Mathews cite Wal-Mart as the standard bearer of customer service and consumer sales. Wal-Mart's *every day low prices* (EDLP) philosophy allows the company to "sell in large enough volume to have firm control over supplies, keep prices low, and still clear a sizable profit." The EDLP sales process, as shown across the top of the Wal-Mart Web site in this screen shot, makes a committed promise to shoppers that the company will offer quality goods at prices that are better than sale prices, they are "Every Day Low Prices."

http://www.walmart.com

Over the years Wal-Mart has gained Sarah's trust by proving itself again and again. We discussed Wal-Mart and the difficulty the company had moving onto the Web, earlier. The superstore finally succeeded online only when Jeanne Jackson was hired to revamp the entire Web site in 2001, taking it back to true start-up status. When Sarah sees the Wal-Mart smiley cartoon face on television dropping prices all over the store, she expects to see those dropped prices reflected on the Web site, also. She is not disappointed. Notice the calls to action on this homepage.

On the right, where visitors are already tuned to expect sales copy, we see a header that shouts, "Splash into savings." This is a come-on for pool supplies and hot tubs, specifically designed for the summer season. The rest of the page is designed to direct the eye to the center of the screen—that prime real estate area—where "Summer Savings" is displayed in big letters.

Across the top of the page are the major links to inner pages of the site, pages for specific items Wal-Mart sells. Also, notice how there are links along the left. The left-hand links open pages that correspond to aisles in a Wal-Mart bricks and mortar store. If you scroll down to the bottom of the page—and Wal-Mart makes sure it's a short scroll—you see a search box offering to locate a Wal-Mart store near you. Sarah can find whatever she wants or needs almost at a glance.

What's not to like about that?

SLICING UP THE PIE

Mary Lou Quinlan, author of *Just Ask a Woman—Cracking the Code of What Women Want and How They Buy,* (New Jersey: John Wiley & Sons, Inc., 2003) conducted research with nearly 4,000 women who ultimately revealed that they consider the Internet a useful tool for browsing and research. Sarah, always on the lookout for bargains, chooses the Internet first when looking for information about products and services.

> **In her chapter discussing women's burgeoning affair with technology, Quinlan says, "...if your brand has no Web presence as late as 2002, you should know that many women might question your legitimacy as a modern marketer."**

Don't be lulled into the belief that Wal-Mart's EDLP is the only thing Sarah cares about. Wal-Mart has built a reputation on its EDLP, very much as Amazon.com has built its reputation on how well it personalizes your Web shopping experience. But price has its place, and my mouse-to-mouse survey showed that price is second to quality and customer service.

In *Myth of Excellence,* Crawford and Mathews are quick to note that price is only "a fraction of the whole." Sarah, who represents the majority of women I talked to, wanted quality goods at reasonable prices. As for shopping online, she was very concerned with the ability to *easily* return a product.

Crawford and Mathews say that shoppers on the Internet are predisposed to surf through several sites before choosing the one where they will spend their money. I've discussed that before; the ability to click in and out of one Web site after another gives Sarah power she does not have offline. Sarah likes the benefit of being able to pick out what she wants, at her leisure, without a sales clerk hanging around watching her every move.

To her advantage, not yours, Sarah can fill her online shopping cart and, at the last minute, click out of the sale without making her purchase. We will discuss how to keep her from leaving her cart before cashing out in Chapter 6, "Ties that Bind."

Equally important is the fact that if Sarah still has children at home, and many boomers Sarah's age do have pre-teens or teens still at home, or they are babysitting grandchildren, she doesn't have to worry about what to do with the children if she needs to run to the store.

Shopping online allows Sarah to relax, take her time, sip a cup of coffee or an iced tea, and browse to her heart's content. The children are playing somewhere in the other room or outside, not at Sarah's elbow whining for candy, gum, or some

> The average age of today's first time grandparent is 47 years.

poorly constructed toy deliberately hung at the checkout counter to attract little eyes and hands! (Yes, even the teens grab them when they're shopping with Mom!)

Shopping online is even more worthwhile since everything Sarah buys is shipped directly to her door or to the door of the person she's shopping for. With free shipping for many, many purchases, this is convenience to the max!

SIGNIFICANT LIVING

If you haven't gotten the message yet, let me spell it out for you: it isn't about YOU, it's about her; it's about Sarah. Sarah has full control of her shopping experience online. She is clicking the mouse; she rules what goes in and out of her shopping cart. She also engages in a new golden rule; **the one with the gold, rules.** Sarah is a Queen online. She has the gold.

In many cases, Sarah is single and loving it. As we will see below, Sarah is so much in control she is clicking that mouse, ruling that gold, without having to worry about asking permission.

Both leading edge boomers and novice computer users may be living solo—without a significant other. Statistics from the 1999 U.S. Census Bureau show that 25.1% of the women in the U.S. were living alone because they had never married. Almost 13% of women were divorced or separated, and 10% were widowed.

The same report shows that men were more likely to be married and living with their spouses, with divorced or separated men equal in number to women. Only 2.5% were likely to be widowed.

These statistics should help you understand the dynamics and lifestyle of the boomer women. As I mentioned in earlier chapters, women are the keepers of the house and as such, they spend the money and purchase the products that keep the family in shoes, socks, and soup. As time goes on, the stats presented here show that Sarah continues on this path of household power. She may be widowed, or remarried, but in either case, she is the one holding or controlling the checkbook.

Families without a male presence rose from 10.7% of all families in 1970, to 17.8% in 1998. These are families where the woman is the head of household and she's looking for easy lessons on how to fix a toilet, install a faucet, build a deck, or buy a computer. If you can tap into her willingness for *Do it Yourself*—DIY—products or books, you have a chance to connect and begin building a relationship that will turn into sales.

Studies indicate that many of the Sarahs enjoy the reality HGTV cable shows "Trading Spaces" and "While You Were Out," both focused on home redecorating. The DIY concept, done in humorous but helpful demonstrations, works well for those shows. Sarah's interest in them may easily lead her to the Internet to learn more—at your Web site.

Sarah likes those shows because they offer insight into cost-effective ways to decorate or otherwise change her home environment. Since slightly more than 60% of adult women in this country are employed outside of the home, Sarah likes changing her home furnishings or wallpaper or pictures, but she won't spend money on it unless she knows what she's getting.

> **The jobs women hold range from administrative support, at 23.7%, to professional specialty at 17.8%, service workers (except private households) at 16.7%, and executive, administrators, managerial positions at 14.3%.**

As the baby boomer women contemplate retirement, they are realizing there is no time like the present to finally—yes, finally!—do some of the things they've always wanted to do. Boomer women who spent 25 years in traditional working jobs are now going back to school to get that college degree they never completed back in the '60s or '70s. Others are splurging on cosmetic surgery; still others are learning how to make quilts, redecorate their kitchens, or they're taking time to travel to places they once thought they would never see.

Many others are doing the unthinkable—they're starting their own businesses! These are businesses that need supplies, capital, employees, and advice. If you have advice in one area or another to give, you should be offering it on your Web site.

"Retirement, more often than not, reduces household income, but that may not diminish buying power. If their (seniors) home is paid for and their kids are gone, they will have significant buying power even though their incomes are less than those of younger adults." (CyberAtlas June/2003)A boomer site which is a contender for high marks on the Dick-e-meter is:

http://www.oldtimecandy.com.

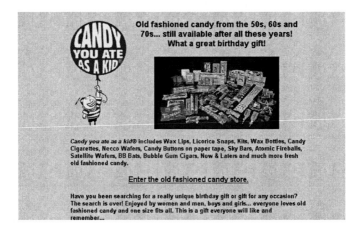

Old Time Candy seems particularly designed for Sarah. Since we know Sarah does most of the shopping for family and friends, this site qualifies as female-friendly for several reasons:

- o The "Candy You Ate as a Kid" graphic is informative and eye-catching—and downloads quickly. It is also a homepage link.
- o The description and product picture immediately identify what the site is selling.
- o The link to get into the site and start shopping is centered prominently in the prime real estate area.
- o The entire homepage is simple, straightforward, and focused. Once you click into the site, you enter Web-land where the familiar navigation shows left-handed links, while the instructive part of the page is centered for fast focusing.

o The shopping cart link for viewing or check out is located at the bottom of the page and is large enough to hit with a pie.

Sarah visits this site to buy familiar favorites for herself, or to purchase gifts for family and friends. There is value-added information, including a history of some of the candy sold, and a "Top 21 Favorites" list. Last, but certainly not least, the site gives a history on the "About Us" page that introduces Sarah to the owners of the site, complete with pictures of them *as kids*. The caption next to one picture says, "We have a lot of fun eating and selling the candy we ate as kids."

What's not to like about that?

Remember, women in general but especially in Sarah's generation, are motivated by community. We are going to get into the power of community and women in Chapter 7, "Meeting at the Well," but if you understand that baby boomer and senior women go online to communicate with family and friends first, then to do research on products and services, you are a step ahead of your competition.

Sarah's generation is also very interested in health issues. Providing an easy route to women's health studies or information on family health, including issues that affect men and children, is a winning strategy. Approach Sarah with respect and consideration, and give her a reason to stick with you. Then knock her socks off with your great products and services. She'll buy. Not only does she have someone with a birthday, an anniversary or a wedding almost every month of the year, she might be the partner in a business that needs computer networking services, or financial advice. Beyond that, she wants hints on how to remain vital and rejuvenated throughout the rest of her life.

~ 93 million Americans were "health-seekers," Internet users searching online for information on health topics whether they are acting as consumers, caregivers, or e-patients-2002.

FAST MARKETING TO A DIGITAL YOUTH

Broadband is the *in thing* for the Gen Xers and Gen Ys, also called Echo Boomers. These two groups experience technology as a plaything. They are video game enthusiasts, Instant Messaging experts, and hunger for a wide-screen plasma TV.

Ellen is our model for these age groups. She sees nothing wrong with paying $3.00 for a cup of coffee. She doesn't cringe when she pays more than $1.50 to fill her car up at the gas station. And she wants things her own way—today, not tomorrow. Her life has been built on the now-factor where a broadband Internet connection is a must-have in her life.

According to the September 2003 issue of *Demographics* magazine, "Many more women in this segment are economically independent. When these women marry, and the vast majority will by age 30, their families will have substantially higher incomes and spending power."

> **"Boomers are finally growing up, and we don't hold it against them that they forced us to beat them to it."**
> **Quote from Kate Fillion in *13th GEN: Abort, Retry, Ignore, Fail?* New York: Vintage Books, 1993**

Ellen and her younger siblings, the teens and tweens, are pushing the broadband industry hard. We can see this from research showing that the number of broadband households is expected to increase from 21.4 million in 2003 to 40.7 million in 2007. Broadband use across the board is indicative of the clout Ellen wields. Her generation does not want to wait around for anything—certainly not for your Web site to download. And, while her broadband connection can handle movie clips, animation, and/or Macromedia Flash, be careful how you use these bandwidth intense tools. Keep in mind that Ellen, like her mother, is shopping online for convenience first. Save the entertainment for your newsletter or e-zine.

With Ellen, you do have more leeway in your Web site design and performance. Ellen grew up with Sesame Street; she is used to fast, colorful, loud bites of information delivered in short spurts. It worked then, and continues to work now. The grown-up versions of the Sesame Street kids want their information relevant and current. And they like it loud and in their face, but not overpowering.

On the higher end of the Ellen scale, composed of those women who are out of college and have joined the workforce, you would do well to recognize that many of them are now wives and mothers. They are interested in finding out how to do those things better. Value-added content works for them.

Advice, tips, and links to information that is going to make both their working lives and their home lives easier, is sure to impress them. A large portion of them no longer live close enough to Mom to run over and get her sage advice. They might use Instant Messaging to do that, but if Mom isn't available at the same time they are, they will search online for answers.

Ellen is also actively involved in environmental issues. Her generation wants to take care of the Earth, not necessarily *the world.* Ellen is taking up the reigns her parents dropped when they exchanged flower power for paycheck power and joined corporate America. With lofty, admirable goals, the Ellens want to know that you care, too. A good way to approach Ellen is to support Earth Day, which usually occurs in April. Visit http://www.earthday.net and find out more information on Earth Day. Sites that show Ellen they're part of the "solution to pollution" and not part of the problem are geared for success with her and her friends.

HIGHER EDUCATION ONLINE

Within the college age market, a February 2002 report from *Harris Interactive and Youth 360* showed that college kids were responsible for $210 billion in sales during 2002. The study showed that 94% of them are choosey shoppers—a varied selection is their first requirement, followed closely by price. Branding came in last; only 27% cared what brand they bought. In Ellen's world, brand is only important if the company gives her choices: what style, what color, what design, what length, the list goes on and on.

Ellen is becoming the major consumer influence for the coming decade.

Michelle Conlin's article, "The New Gender Gap," *Businessweek* (May, 2003), showed that young women are "rapidly closing the M.D. and Ph.D. gap and are on the verge of making up the majority of law students." The article showed that girls are leaders in all areas. Senior class presidents? Girls. Vice-Presidents? Girls. Head of student government? Girls. Captain of the math team? Girls.

James Garbarino, professor of human development at Cornell University, is quoted in Conlin's article saying, "Girls are better able to deliver in terms of what modern society requires of people—paying attention, abiding by rules, being verbally competent, and dealing with interpersonal relationships in offices."

This is not a put-down of Dick. Indeed, it merely shows that gender roles are making that 180° turn the baby boomer women were fighting for in the previous century. We aren't leaving Dick out; no matter what other studies or reports you read might propose. Dick is a valuable partner, a friend, and a lover; he's so much a part of our lives that women today bristle at the thought that we want to replace him with sperm banks!

In Ellen's case, she may end up earning more than the man in her life, but it's a mutually accepted decision—she wants to be a doctor or a lawyer, he's willing to support her in that goal. The term househusband will be far more acceptable in this millennium than it was in the last one. However, expect that along with their increased earning potential, the Ellens will still be expected to fill the role of family caretaker. Relate to their needs: career, family, and self, (not necessarily in that order). With more money in their wallets but less time to drive to the mall, park and cruise the crowded store aisles, Ellen and her friends will be relying on the Internet and your Web site to keep their families in jeans, jackets, and jelly.

BLURRING NOW AND THEN

Ellen and her friends are masters at Instant Messaging. While the boomer adults in Ellen's life are only gradually learning this new form of communication, Ellen and her group are moving their fingers so fast over their keyboards, they create a blur. Many of them are using their cell phones for text messaging, instead of talking! This talented crowd has even invented its own language for communicating across their high-speed digital connections.

Text messaging consists of letters and numbers; i.e., "CUL8R" for "See you later." Other examples of this unique text-speak are "FDOFLOL," for "Falling Down on the Floor Laughing Out Loud." And, "IMHO," for "In My Humble Opinion." The text messaging language has grown far beyond my capabilities to keep up with it, but I know it's out there, and so should you. It's indicative of the way this group shares information and keeps in touch with one another.

Want more? Visit these sites and have some fun!

www.randomhouse.com/features/davebarry/emotion.html

www.cknow.com/ckinfo/emoticons.htm

www.netlingo.com/smiley.cfm

Ellen wants your Web site to relate to her in ways her parents don't. While she is community oriented as much as her mother is—using the Internet as a gathering spot—she is also fiercely independent and individualistic. Her brain is wired for the "sharing gene," but Ellen probably isn't sharing recipes and home decorating ideas, unless she was recently married. She's sharing stories on dating, on career options, on technology, and on how to find more time in her life for leisure activities.

Approach her with information on how your product or service is specifically designed to enhance her life. If your product isn't designed to do that, include links to places that will do that. Give her motivational sayings to start her day; offer headlines from her local area that show real people—people her age—accomplishing noteworthy tasks.

Let's touch upon that preconceived notion that young women are obsessed with their appearance. Ellen can be flamboyant and outrageous, or she can be simple and serene. She may be dedicated to a hobby or career and not at all interested in the latest Paris fashions, or she may be experimenting with her identity, sporting numerous piercings, with or without tattoos. Don't try to predict her moods.

> Sell to Ellen by understanding what she uses the WEB for: Communication, Entertainment, & Information, in that order.

Like her mother and grandmother, she is multi-faceted. The way she looks is important to her only in relation to where she is at the moment. Appeal to her sense of individuality, not to any predetermined notion that as a woman she wants longer eyelashes or redder lips.

Ellen is also using the Internet to research and understand her technical world. She may or may not be at ease with electronic gadgets and/or toys. Either way, if she wants to buy a PC, a laptop, or a PlayStation, she will research her options online before going offline to actually make that purchase. If you sell electronics and have a physical location, you can close a sale to Ellen using an 800 number on your Web site. A live voice, a real person, with the knowledge to answer her questions without making her feel silly, is a first step in getting her to buy.

Many members of Ellen's generation are in the early stages of their careers, while some are still college students. This means Ellen may have limited cash flow. She is already a wise spender, often shopping at her mother's favorite stores—Wal-Mart, Target, K-Mart, or browsing online sites as Amazon.com and/or Half.com, where she can compare and contrast pricing. This is why it's important to understand and research your competition. If your competition is successfully selling to Ellen, mimic their methods. Sometimes it pays to build a partnership with a competitor to get more traffic and better leads. For example, if you sell shoes, partner with a site that sells socks. If you sell gourmet food, partner with a site that sells dishes. If you sell pet care supplies, partner with a veterinarian's site.

DRESSING UP WITH ELLEN

Contrary to popular belief, women do buy clothes online. Cyberatlas showed that during the 2002 holiday season (Christmas), "online clothing sales experienced a 6% increase." The heaviest traffic was at the catalog sites.

Women of all ages want to look nice, and we live in a society that continues to promote products using drop-dead gorgeous models, but "looking nice" means different things to different women. For Sarah, acceptance of her maturity gives her time to explore new hobbies and activities. She may be clinging to nostalgia and memories of a riotous youth, but her focus is to dress nicely and show the world a well-groomed appearance. That means using make-up to enhance her best facial features, not to lengthen her eyelashes, or redden her lips.

A favorite site of both Sarah's and Ellen's groups is Coldwater Creek which has a customer base of 512,000. With a selection that is not too old-fashioned, and not too youth-oriented, chances are Ellen shops at Coldwater Creek **because her mother introduced her to it!**

http://www.coldwatercreek.com

A screen shot of the Coldwater Creek Web site shows why it's a favorite of both Sarah and Ellen. The layout and navigation is clearly displayed across the top of the page. I'm noticing a pattern here, how about you? The logo is not overpowering, but clearly represented, to assure the surfer she has arrived at the right place. Visible in the header area of flowers—a nice warm touch—is an "instant help" button that opens a live chat. This is a step beyond that 800 number I've been telling you is so important. Using live chat removes the chore of dialing and possibly being put on hold.

Notice the prime real estate section of this homepage. The title "It's all about summer" is a come-on that works. It promises clothing that will make the wearer look and feel great. Prominently displayed on the right, in the ad placement area, is a large blue ad sporting the invitation "Summer Clearance, up to 60% off wear-now styles." Notice the words "wear now." This is a call to action reminding visitors that summer is not going to last forever. Below this sales pitch is the personalization I've been touting as so important to women of all ages: "Just for you."

What's not to like about that?

Let's look at another favorite of both Ellen and Sarah; Old Navy, a sub-store of The Gap. Television spots for this store are big on nostalgia, attracting Ellen's mom and grandmother, while offering value to a large youth culture. The goal is to get Ellen's Mom in to buy for the kids and grandkids, while at the same time having Ellen accompany her to buy for herself. This store attracted over 300,000 shoppers in March of 2003, beating out The Gap, Victoria's Secret, and Lands End.

http://www.oldnavy.com

Again, the company logo is apparent but not overpowering. The site gets to the important stuff right away. Prime real estate shows several clothing styles and options, complete with descriptive phrases such as "Get casual cargos and comfy tees," and "Plenty of pockets."

Pricing is shown in the large red star, "Starting at $10.50." This store is known for offering low-cost clothing that lasts. On the lower right is an invitation to parents and teachers that says, "Help support arts education in public schools." Later on, in Chapter 7, "Meeting at the Well," we are going to talk about the value of community involvement. This prominent invitation on the Old Navy site is an eye-grabber that both Sarah and Ellen will notice. Sarah is more apt to click on it, but if Ellen is married, pregnant, or has younger siblings left at home, she, too, may want to check out this information.

Old Navy is successful online because the company has learned how to sell to Sarah and Ellen by being focused, specific, and offering options in price ranges these women can live with.

What's not to like about that?

The only minus to this store is that the company puts the Old Navy logo on almost everything. Ellen is not into that. She is the leading edge of the MPS marketing group.

MSP, NOT MSG!

MSG is an acronym for monosodium glutamate. It's a crystalline salt used to enhance the flavor of food. I know from personal experience that many people are allergic to it.

> "In the late 90s, LEGO achieved cult status among teenagers. They proclaimed their admiration on T-shirts, homemade when they couldn't get their hands on old, original LEGO shirts."
> This is true MSP. Martin Lindstrom, ClickZ 2003

What does MSG have to do with marketing to women online? Not much—except that I don't want you to confuse MSG with MSP because MSP has everything to do with marketing to women online, especially Ellen and her friends. MSP stands for "Me Selling Proposition." Coined by Martin Lindstrom at ClickZ online, a part of Internet.com, MSP marketing is focused on the consumer, not the corporation.

Ellen's generation has grown up with mind-boggling special effects at the movies, and with the World Wide Web. She is so in control of her environment—the world around her that includes not only her **place** but how that **place** impacts her life—that she is immune to the old-fashioned USP, unique selling proposition, used on her mother. Marketing articles and books still tout the necessity of USP, and I'm not suggesting we leave it behind completely. But when it comes to the Ellens of the world, MSP rocks.

Essentially, Ellen wants more than different colors, styles, or designs. She wants *control* over the actual product. If she can't *own* the experience, she is left unsatisfied. Sites that have the ability to allow Ellen flexibility in how her product is put together, from choosing how many pockets to put in her jeans, to designing her own jewelry, are better positioned to sell to her than sites locked into the ancient 20th century Dick and Jane world of taking polls, compiling the results, and designing products according to majority interest. An example of MSP can be found at:

http://www.polo.com.

The prime real estate section of the page grabs reader attention right away: **Midsummer SALE**. Next to it, a stack of colorful shirts is topped with another dynamic, enticing sales pitch: "Our classic shirt is new again, in incredible colors and fits." By approaching the Web visitor with proven buzzwords and sincere product offerings, Polo sets the scene for further investigation.

Polo puts their connecting links at the top of the page. As we learned in Chapter 4, links across the top of the site open the page up for content. Here, the links offer information the reader can assimilate quickly and efficiently before she sets her gaze on the sales come-on.

Polo knows its customer-base well; the pony continues to be important, as demonstrated in the bottom banner "Pink Pony New Arrivals."

I found the pop-up window that invited me **to design my own shirt** far more compelling. Interaction is the future of sales, especially online to Ellen's generation: MSP—giving the end-user control over product design.

Over the next few years, watch for the concept of MSP to dramatically affect e-commerce in many areas, especially those sales to Ellen's Mom and Grandmom. Once the business community catches on to this dynamic and profitable way to make sales, the results will spill over into other age/gender groups and go beyond the clothing, perfume, or shoe industry. Cars, electronics, toys, the list of possible markets willing to adopt MSP is endless.

I'LL TAKE MINE IN GRORANGE

The epitome of this marketing strategy is Dell computers. CEO Michael Dell recognized early on that the computer lends itself to personalization. It's not the ability to etch your name in the PC cover that counts, although I'm sure you're welcome to do so—no, the goal is to produce a PC constructed in pieces **according to end-user requirements.**

Dell has taken this concept to the pinnacle of success. Not only do they do 100% of their sales online, but Michael Dell understands that the "knowledge of all participants in a global market far exceeds that of any expert." Ellen, the end-user, is the one who determines what she buys from Dell, not Michael Dell. Ellen prefers control of product design and

> The MSP model operates on a Democratic decision- making process. Ellen and her friends are rejecting the old authoritarian/ hierarchal decision-making process.

use, and will eagerly shop at Web sites that understand and support her need for this option.

Do I hear some of you moaning that your products and services don't lend themselves to an MSP model? Think again. There are ways to build interaction into your e-commerce offering. Remember the advice in Chapter 4, "You Don't Know Dick," which said to ASK your Web visitor what she wants—and then give it to her? Building an MSP business model into your existing e-commerce structure can be as easy as getting specific in the questions you ask in your feedback form. What does the customer want that she isn't getting now? What options are most important? Would she recommend you to her friends? If not, why not?

Next, review the actual development of your product or service to determine how it serves the end-user. Where can it be tweaked or altered, according to customer satisfaction? There are jewelry sites and perfume sites that are already offering this option to their visitors. When Ellen shops at them, she is in complete control of the jewelry she buys or the fragrance she orders.

As a closing thought, think Burger King. Long before Dell computers recognized the value of providing customized PCs, Burger King's slogan was, "Have it your way." For their entire teen years, my children would not let me buy fast food burgers from anywhere else. They wanted it their way. That didn't put them ahead of the curve; it put Burger King ahead of the curve.

While Ellen may still be working towards that six-figure salary, she, like her mother before her, is often juggling home, family, and career. She will shop at your Web site if you give her good reason to. Get personal and she will grow to love you.

Remember that she is part of the overall shopping community we are discussing and that first and foremost, she is a woman. She values friendship and commitment. She talks to other women daily, exchanging thoughts on career, family, shopping, wellness issues and the environment. The principal difference between Ellen and Sarah is that Ellen is a product of technology. Ellen was comfortable with the computer long before Sarah decided to let it creep into her life.

Ellen wants her shopping done quickly, she wants choices in color and style, and she wants it her way; let her choose how many pockets, how many buttons, whether or not the item is round or square; let her have a hand in designing what you are selling and she will be happy.

Sarah wants convenience, quality, and choices. The Sarahs of the U.S. are NOT size 4 models or walking, talking Barbie Dolls. If you sell apparel, offer appropriate sizes. Get nostalgic with Sarah, but don't get maudlin—age is a state of mind, not a lifestyle.

Chapter 6, "Ties that Bind," will show you how to gain Sarah's and Ellen's trust, a trust that will have them e-mailing your URL all over the Internet.

WHAT WE LEARNED IN THIS CHAPTER

o Baby boomer women have a good deal of discretionary income, and they are spending it online.

o Baby boomers and seniors are often lumped together into one group. As a whole, they are vital, attractive, and lively. Sell to them accordingly.

o Gen X and Gen Y women are children of the medium, so to speak. They are as comfortable with the WEB as their parents were with the telephone.

o Gen Xers and Gen Ys want it their way. Give them input into how the end product looks and feels.

o Grandmom, Mom and Daughter shop online for clothes, shoes, jewelry and perfume. They also shop for computers, cars, PDAs, cell phones, and lawn mowers. Really.

6. Ties that Bind

Marketing Tools that Work Online

Q. What do bulletproof vests, fire escapes, windshield wipers, laser printers, and Snugli® infant carriers all have in common?

A. All invented by women.

An April 2003 study done by Pew Internet & American Life Project reported that 61% of Internet users consider the Internet more like a library than anything else. Ten percent consider it a "meeting place." Another ten per cent consider it a "shopping mall."

That means a whopping 81% of Internet users view the Internet as a place to get information, to connect with friends, and to shop. Now, isn't that what *Dickless Marketing* has been telling you all along? But we're going one step further—we're showing you that the majority of that 81% is women—women who shop online.

> **Women purchase 50% of the cars in the U.S.**
> **Half of all business travelers are women.**
> **Women own more than 46% of the homes in this country.**

Scott Adams, in his book, *Dilbert Future,* (New York: Harper Business, 1997) writes: "If you don't believe women spend most of the money, just walk into any Sears store and see what they're selling."

After describing the two things a man would want to buy (both of them tools), Adams goes on to say, "But SOMEONE is buying all that other stuff in there or Sears wouldn't be in business. Someone is buying those fuzzy toilet seat covers. Someone is buying decorative covers for tissue boxes. Someone is buying placemats. Who could it be?"

He considers that a rhetorical question. My question to you, dear reader, is: Have I convinced YOU that it's a rhetorical question?

WOMEN LIKE TOOLS, TOO

Let's step back a moment and think about the Internet as a marketing tool instead of a technology. In Chapter 1 we gave a short tutorial on how the Internet got started and what its true purpose was, according to scientist J.C.R. Licklidder. As a quick reminder: the Internet was designed to share information, but the Intergalactic Network, the founders of the Internet as we know it, headed by Licklidder, had an idealistic vision of getting people of like minds from all over the world to communicate over a network of computer cables. That ulterior motive was to foster a sense of worldwide community.

We have also learned in earlier chapters that women are masters at communication. In fact, even John Gray of *Men are from Mars, Women are From Venus* fame (New York: HarperCollins Books, 1992) notes that women are into communication, writing in his book that "Venusians (women) value love, **communication,** beauty, and relationships." (my emphasis)

As your eyes pass over this page, reading the text and processing the information, women all over the globe are designing, forming, or joining communities that serve a collective, yet individual, purpose. As a sales tool, this gathering of women in communities is a major profit-making opportunity.

In that long ago, ancient 20th century Dick and Jane world, Gloria Steinem said, "We [women] are living the lives many of our mothers only dreamed of." Her words resonate with meaning in the new millennium because women today are forming connections in this world that are making our dreams come true.

Sales and marketing in the Internet age are invigorating a new economy. It is now possible to "window shop" in the comfort of our own home. All because of the capabilities of a computer networking cable—a piece of computer equipment women no more care about than we care about how the street lights come on at night. How this technology works is unimportant. That it is accessible and helps us communicate and collaborate is what makes the difference! We care about the relationship, not the technology.

Women congregating in communities online are building strong relationships with other women all over the world, not just down the street or across town. Their desire to do this gives you, the small business owner, the opportunity to sell in quantity to more women than you will even see in your dirt world store. Why? Because you cannot sell to just one woman. In fact, it's impossible to sell to only two or three women. If you are selling to women, you are selling to a community. Online, members of those communities number in the hundreds of thousands. How many of you see a thousand women at your dirt world store in a day, a week, a month?

If you're developing your Web site to market to women, I assure you that as soon as we're logged on, as soon as we begin reading your sales message, we're also thinking about how your product or service can help not only ourselves, but also every one of our friends and relatives.

RETAILING AMERICAN STYLE

Studies show that American retail marketing has developed through four stages. Following World War II, department stores reigned supreme. People flocked to downtown areas to shop at such notables as Marshall Fields and Woolworths. These were not the department stores of the mid-20th century; they were "all in one" places to shop, a multitude of goods offered under one roof. You could purchase needles and thread, toys, tools, jackets, blouses, children's clothing, even food, at these downtown stores. Their draw was the variety and quality of their goods.

Once the suburbs took hold, the American shopper was reluctant to make that long trek downtown (a 20-30 minute drive to buy a new hat? Not likely!). Stage two marketing involved the indoor shopping mall and the outdoor strip malls that sprang up like daisies in a well-tended meadow. Women with a child or two in tow every time they ventured out the door fueled this new shopping craze. It was nirvana: variety and convenience, dozens of stores to shop in—all in one place, climate controlled for indoor malls, clustered in groups for strip malls—what's not to like about that?

For a time, jaunts to the mall were, in and of themselves, a form of entertainment. Weekends found the malls crammed with families browsing the latest new product colors or design, teenagers cruising for dates, and senior citizens escaping the confines of their quiet homes for some socializing or just a stroll along the concourse to gaze at the storefronts.

While the malls supplied a means to shop for almost anything all in one place, as time went on, the convenience they promised wore thin. Mom wanted to get in and out, but with kids in tow, one clutching her hand and one in a stroller, shopping often ended up taking longer than expected, leaving her stressed and tired by the time she finally got home.

Christmas shopping was especially stressful. The crowds alone made some women crazy. I've known women to stand in line for more than an hour during the holidays to buy one item. I think I was one of them!

When stage three, catalog shopping, entered the picture, buying became a shop-from-home project. Given the advantage of a free phone call using an 800 number, women were drawn to those thick catalogs like kids to the jingle of the ice cream truck during summer vacation. Now they could shop in their robe and slippers, or after arriving home from a long workday, and *have the products delivered to their home, or to the home of the intended recipient!* Catalog shopping was easier than trucking to the mall. As time went on, many malls became teen hangouts, further alienating the folks with real money to spend.

The 21st century finds women still looking for convenience and selection. They want quality goods at reasonable prices. They want companies to offer them a way to shop that doesn't involve loading up the car with all the kids and driving ten miles, only to get sore feet strolling along a concrete floor or up and down an escalator while their three-year-old begs to ride over and over again. Studies from *USA Today* show that Sears and JCPenney are consistently losing mall business, and they're not alone.

The skeletons of at least two local malls in the area of Rochester, New York, pay tribute to the demise of this form of shopping. I hear a new mall is being considered for construction in the area, but I personally don't know anyone, male or female, who believes another mall is necessary.

We're entering stage four in American retailing. In this millennium people are more than happy to do a good deal of their shopping online, many of them are eager to do it online. And that includes buying groceries, cars, electronics, and gifts.

The eager ones are women.

EN-MASS

Can we all agree that marketing, in and of itself, is dependent on mass-communication? That requirement is unchanged. It existed long before Al Gore coined the term "information superhighway" in 1994 to describe the Internet, and will remain true well into this new millennium.

Mass communication in the dirt world involves direct mail, a method that can be cost-effective and generate attention with a wide-audience. These direct mail pieces, designed to get Company X's name and logo in front of us, and to entice us to buy, have a very small response rate. Who among us hasn't cursed under her breath at the number of useless or annoying post cards and one-page flyers stuffed in our snail mailboxes? How many of us discard them without much of a glance? Studies show that only two to three per cent of us respond to them.

This means that a company producing a post card or a sales letter that might reach approximately 20 to 30 people if the initial mailing is at least 1,000 is losing thousands of dollars in time, money, talent and postage.

Direct mail is a true numbers game. In order to receive the most benefit, one should be mailing out well over 1,000 pieces, more in the neighborhood of 10,000 or 100,000 pieces. The average small business cannot afford the time, energy, and talent to do that. I have witnessed SMBs and new start-ups alike send out a select 100 direct mail pieces, then wonder why their subsequent follow-up phone call resulted in a clueless CEO stating that s/he never saw the mailing.

Why were the CEOs clueless? Because their secretaries filed the mailing in the circular file at their feet. In case you are not aware of it, that is one of the things secretaries are hired to do.

If you go beyond the direct mail piece and look to television or radio to do your marketing for you, the odds of a positive result are higher. But radio and TV are inherently expensive. A single 30-second ad during last year's Superbowl ran $2.1 million dollars. A television ad for snack food is not going to get the same attention at ten o'clock in the morning as it will during prime  time, between 7-9 p.m., when more people are watching TV and feeling *snacky*. Negotiating for that time frame costs dearly.

Prime time on the radio translates into morning drive time, 7-8:30 a.m., followed by rush hour time, between 4:30-6:00 p.m. Success on the radio also requires repeating your ad ***during the same time slot*** over and over, for more than three or four weeks, before the listener will actually tune in and hear it. If you're marketing your Web site, how many of those drivers will stop and write down your dub-dub-dub (www.yourcompany.com)? If they don't write it down, it's a sure bet they won't remember it when they get home.

Of course, there are billboards. Billboards were more effective in the Dick and Jane world than they are today. Today we're speeding down that expressway at 70-85mph (I'm not suggesting it, I'm merely reporting it; yes, I know most of the country is stuck in the 55-65mph limit). At those speeds, how many billboards do you read? More importantly, how many do you remember? In my study with women from Colorado to New York City, the answer was, hardly any. We read the billboards, but we seldom remember what they are selling.

I am not advising against traditional marketing tactics. They are still effective—if done correctly—but, in the mobile media marketplace of the Internet, your Web site has the ability to outscore traditional marketing every time. Connecting to people online gets your message in front of your core market more often, for less money. When that core market is women we are talking about numbers in the millions.

SEEK AND YE SHALL FIND

Author Frank Feather (*futureconsumer.com*) says, "Conventional marketing is *four times* as expensive as e-marketing."

Operating on the community principle presented at the opening of this chapter, it's virtually guaranteed that if you get the right message in front of either Sarah or Ellen, she is going to share it with her circle of friends and relatives. You could be selling to a neighborhood of women in a virtual coffee klatch, or to an organization composed of women from all over the country—maybe all over the world! Or you can keep selling to men, leaving messages with secretaries that are trained to tune you out.

> "For Searchers— copy and structure educate and persuade.
> For Search Engines— copy, structure and links accurately describe page content."
> ClickZ author Kevin Lee
> June/2003

I hear many readers asking: "How the heck do you get even one of those thousands and thousands of women to your Web site in the first place?"

The answer is: Optimize your site for the search engines. Notice the plural: Search Engines. There are hundreds of them. I will discuss the top four and show you what you need to do to get a top 10 or 20 ranking—that means showing up on page one or page two of an end-user's search. It requires knowing more than how search engines work. It requires understanding how searchers search.

A common complaint I hear from my clients is that search engines don't work. "Do a search on my company," they say—giving me a specific product description or their chosen keyword phrase—"and see what comes up." Invariably, horror of horrors, their company **does not** come up on that all-important first page of results. In fact, they are quick to point out at least one link that does show up has **nothing to do with their product or company service.**

I am only going to give an overview of search engine optimization. There are better places for you to learn about this invaluable tool, and I have included the two biggest ones in this chapter. However, I will tell you the most important thing you need to know about search engines:

> **The search engines do not care about your Web site. They care about the search.**

As of the writing of this chapter, Yahoo!, one of the giants in the search engine industry (although it isn't a search engine, it's a directory—sort of like a phone book), has just purchased the search engine company, Overture, for a whopping 1.6 billion dollars. If spending billions of dollars to acquire a competitor isn't serious business, I don't know what is.

Consolidation in the search engine industry is happening all over the Internet; expect to see other search engine properties joining the game. Even as this is being written, Microsoft's MSN Search is making noises about purchasing Google, according to Search Engine Optimization expert Danny Sullivan. Google, of course, is considered by some to be the biggest, baddest search engine out there. There is no indication this purchase will ever happen (Google says it is not interested in being acquired), but the fact that MSN is exploring this option speaks volumes about the importance of search engines in marketing online.

Whatever happens, understand that these Internet database companies, and that's what they are—big databases that catalog and store Web pages for inclusion much like a library—are not concerned with your business success. They are in the business of making a profit doing what they do best: returning significant search results to each user's query. The more searchers they attract, the more ads they can sell on their search pages, and the more money they make.

How do you suppose they return such good results to an individual's search? They study how people search, and they hire programmers who use mathematical algorithms, software code (called a *spider*), that travels all over the Internet and reads the TEXT on your Web site in order to include you in their database. If you are not included in their database, your Web site cannot be returned in a search. Since the spiders that crawl the Web need words to identify what you do, if you don't have enough text on your site, the spider goes away unhappy, and your Web site gets left out of the search engine database.

Search engine optimization is not magic. The secrets to optimizing your Web site to rank higher in the search engines are offered at many useful Web sites. You can learn how to optimize your site by yourself at www.searchenginewatch.com with Danny Sullivan, the reigning Guru of this service, or check out Jill Whalen's site, one of my favorites, at www.highrankings.com. I also suggest a visit to www.spiderfood.com for good SEO advice. These are only three of many places to learn more about this necessary online marketing tool.

Danny Sullivan and Jill Whalen will tell you that search engines rely on text; at Spiderfood you will learn that words are food to the search engine spiders. With only pictures to crawl over, the spiders get nothing to munch on and go away hungry. Because we live in a progressively technical world, I expect the programmers who write the algorithms used by search engines will someday find a way to read pictures, but today, the only way they can do that is if you are using alt-text (text that shows up on mouse-overs) to identify your images.

I hear some of you asking, "But how come a Web site called newscorp.com—a communications company, not a cabling company—showed up in the top 10 at Google when I searched on *cable networking?*" You're angry because your company, which does perform cable networking, didn't show up anywhere, not even on page two or three, aren't you?

The short answer is because YOUR company is clearly not optimized for Google. The long answer lies in studying how your site is developed. Remembering that search engines can only read text, not pictures, is your site *optimized* for the phrase you typed in? How many times are you using that phrase on the page? If you are using images, what does your alt-text say?

Secondary information the spiders look for are links to and from sites that you partner with, and value-added content rich in appropriate text, such as *cable networking,* as used in our example above. Value-added content includes articles, tip sheets, advice columns, and anything written to include your key-word phrase as it applies to the Web page or the product on that page. Chances are the sites which did show up, including the communications company, are optimized properly while yours isn't.

> **Search Engine use has jumped from 8 to 15% of all referrals in just the past year. (2003)**

You may occasionally see a Web site that merely *talks* about the search phrase typed in, appearing in the top 10 or 20 search results. When this happens, it generally means the search engine spider could not find enough qualified sites to include. Therefore, it included what was available. Your site would be there if it was optimized properly.

The spiders that crawl the Web looking for good content to add to their database usually review a Web site's source code first. The source code is the HTML your designer, or software package, used to build your Web site. It looks like this taken from a business portal that I use as my homepage:

```
<html>

<head>

<title>CEOExpress: Business portal for executives created by a CEO</title>

<meta HTTP-EQUIV="Expires" CONTENT="Mon, 03 Jan 2000 00:00:01 GMT">

<meta HTTP-EQUIV="Pragma" CONTENT="no-cache">

<meta HTTP-EQUIV="Cache-Control" CONTENT="no-cache">

<meta name="keywords" content="business links, CEO, chief executive officer, senior executives, CEO Links, Business Portal, Business Directory, Small Business Directory, CEO Homepage, CFO Portal, CFO Links, CIO Portal, CIO Links, International Business Portal, C-Level">

<meta name="description" content="Organized business research and news portal for CEOs and executives. Includes email, calender, careers as a customizable hompage and wireless access">
```

Notice the meta tags; *meta* is a computer term meaning "about;" therefore, *meta keywords* are keyword terms in your source code that are "about" your company. In this case, the meta name= "keywords" and the meta name= "description" tell the search engine spiders "about" CEOExpress. They identify the site name and what it does. After reviewing all the meta tags in a Web site's source code, spiders then crawl the remainder of the site checking to see if those specific terms show up in your page content. If they don't, the spiders may decide the site is trying to "spam" its way into the search engine. If this happens, your site will be blacklisted and you will not only be refused entrance into the search engine that caught you, you could easily be refused by dozens of other engines, also. This is because many search engines work together to quantify the content on the Web. They cannot do it all by themselves.

Consequently, good search engine optimization should be done by a professional. If you choose to do it yourself, study how to do it carefully. My advice is to identify three to five search engines you are confident your core market uses and optimize for those. Additionally, there are many industry specific search engines or directories you should consider getting listed in. A qualified search engine optimization company, or a Web designer with SEO experience, can identify industry specific search engines for you. Industry specific search engines and directories are exactly what the term says, specific to a particular industry. These directories might charge a fee, i.e., $20.00 or more for inclusion in their database.

Examples of Industry Specific Search Engines and/or Directories:

http://www.allsearchengines.com/scitech.html
Technology specific searches
http://www.thomasregister.com/
Online resource for finding companies and products manufactured in North America
http://www.freeality.com/women.htm
A search engine for Women's issues

WINNING THE SEO GAME

If you would sell to women online, and I heartily think you should, ☺ you cannot lose if you are optimized for Google, Yahoo!, MSN and AOL. When a woman can't find what she wants at an already saved link in her "favorites" folder, these are the search engines she will most likely use.

http://www.google.com/about.html In 2002, Google was honored as the #1 brand in the world, beating out Coca Cola and McDonald's. Is the Internet powerful, or what? Advice on how to get your site listed in Google is found at this link. Truth is, Google **"spiders"** (sends its software tool out to see what's new on the Web) on a regular basis; therefore, a well-developed, content rich site will get included by default. However, you will not win a high Page Rank merely by getting into the database. Read Google's requirements before you submit.

Google also offers a separate database for listing your company catalog called Froogle. And, the company has its own toolbar for easy use. If that's not enough, Google also has an "I Feel Lucky" button. If you know the name of the company you're looking for but not its URL, type the company name in the search box, click the "I Feel Lucky" link and Google will take you directly to the company Web site without boring you with a list of other possible matches..

http://docs.yahoo.com/info/suggest/ This is the link for advice on getting listed in the Yahoo! directory. Understand that as a directory, Yahoo! does not use spiders. There are specific requirements a Web site has to have to be included in the Yahoo! database. First of all, a real person reviews the site once you've filled out the proper paperwork, and paid your fee. In order to be considered for inclusion, the paperwork must include a category choice. If you choose an improper category (as determined by the Yahoo! editor who reviews your submission), you will NOT get in and you will lose your submission fee. At this time, the cost for inclusion in the Yahoo! directory is $299 per year. Again, payment *will not be refunded* if the Yahoo! editor reviewing your site decides your site does not meet the proper requirements. The good news is, you have the opportunity to open a dialogue with the editor to find out what you did wrong. It's possible to then fix the problem and get listed.

http://search.msn.com MSN has its own team of editors who monitor the most popular searches being performed on the Web, from which it chooses the sites it believes are the most relevant. MSN Search also relies on results from the Looksmart directory. Unlike the MSN editors, the people-powered results from Looksmart are not handpicked to match a query; therefore, MSN uses its own search algorithm to automatically find the sites it believes are the best for particular search phrases. I have found many business professionals prefer MSN search. As this book is being written, MSN, like AOL, is upgrading its search capabilities.

http://aolsearch.aol.com/aol/add.jsp AOL boasts approximately 35 million users. Quoted directly from the link above: "AOL Search is a hierarchical Web directory, organized by subject. All our user-submitted Web content is maintained by the Open Directory Project (http://www.dmoz.org). The Open Directory Project is run by a staff of volunteer editors who choose to evaluate and classify Web sites in one or more categories. The editor exercises the option of choosing to add a site, moving sites between categories and creating new sites." (July 2003) Understand that AOL uses the Google spider to return results on queries that do not match anything in the AOL database. My survey participants, and several women friends, say AOL's newest release, 9.0, is better than ever, making AOL a female-friendly search engine that you should be listed in.

> **July 31, 2003 The *Wall Street Journal* reported that AOL's latest upgrade, 9.0, was hitting the Internet with tools for personalization, antispam, broadband usage, parental controls and more, all designed to put the search engine back in play for a top spot on the Net.**

CAUTION!!!! There are hundreds of search engine optimization companies on the Web that promise to optimize your site and submit it to *the thousands of search engines online today*, but don't you believe it! Without dragging this chapter out for a hundred pages, I can only tell you that you need to speak to a professional—someone who can show you REAL results—in order to have your site optimized successfully. Visit the optimization experts I mentioned earlier, or write to me at the *Dickless Marketing* Web site, and I, or one of my writers, will point you in the right direction. Optimization is more complicated than I have written about it, here. It includes linking to and from other sites, and several other issues best discussed with a professional.

In the end, search engine optimization will give back exactly what you put into it.

PAID SUBMISSION

Search engine marketing (SEM), a cousin to search engine optimization, involves paid submissions and placing keyword-rich ads in boxes or banners on search engine sites. Marketing by placing a small ad on the first or second page of a search engine's results involves understanding Cost Per Click (CPC), and Click Per Thousands (same animal, different color). Paying to have your full banner ad splashed across the top of the search results page is more effective and eye-catchy, but it is also far more expensive. You can read all about the value of top-banners or small side ads at the three sites mentioned earlier.

> Searchers seldom go beyond page 2 of a search result.

Either way, search engine marketing will drive traffic to your site. It will also help raise your rank in not only the search engine you place the ad with, but in other engines. A successful campaign will make you will a popular place to shop and the spiders will see it by recording all the traffic you're attracting.

I urge you to study how to do it right. Visit ClickZ.com and learn a thing or two about SEM from their writers. SEM is a time-intensive task that requires constant reviewing and tweaking.

When you decide to implement this online marketing tool, identify your core market of women and use the advice given in Chapter 5 to draw them in. Remember: your core market is that smaller group of hungry shoppers. For example, within the women's market, are your products better suited to baby boomers or Gen Xers? If it's the baby boomers, are you marketing to stay at home Moms, working Moms, or empty nesters? If it's the Gen Xers, can you offer MSP or real-time chat contact? By beginning at the core level, you will be able to build a stronger, more effective marketing campaign that can, in time, reach out to the larger market available. Think: "sharing." Get one or two of us in, and we'll reel in the rest.

EENEY-MEENY-MINEY-MAIL

A Web Trends booklet (http://www.webtrends.com) I received via snail mail a few months ago discussed the "Law of 5 Rights" for e-mail marketing. These five rights are: "Send the RIGHT people the RIGHT message with the RIGHT offer at the RIGHT time and you'll get the RIGHT response." This was especially pertinent to me since my tagline at Windsor Media Enterprises is "Getting the Right Message to the Right People Via the Right Medium."

After you've optimized your Web site for the search engines, it's time to explore some other marketing options for getting women to buy from you at your Web site.

I interviewed the editor and publisher of one of the first e-zines on the Internet, Abbie Drew of www.demc.com (Direct E-Mail Company). Abbie has been doing this e-mail thing for more than eight years. She is an authority on e-mailing newsletters and e-zines, and her success shows in the over 240,000 subscribers who read her e-zine every week, and in the number of ads she receives income from.

> Show me someone who never gossips, and I'll show you someone who isn't interested in people.
> ~Barbara Walters

I know e-mail marketing is getting a lot of bad press right now, but Abbie isn't giving up on it, and neither should you. As a former teacher who recognized the communication value of the Internet in 1995, Drew suggests marketers hire a legitimate marketing firm to handle their e-mail campaigns—firms that make it their business to keep abreast of the latest issues dealing with the Internet, e-mail marketing, and spam-mail.

Drew's e-zine caters to a niche market, one that is eager to receive her information. "Deliver specific content and your readers will make sure it gets through the ISP filters," she says. Since spam is so prevalent, the members on Drew's mailing list who have AOL as an e-mail client still reliably receive her weekly e-zine because it's recognized as legitimate and because it is designed to pass AOL's filters. Yet, she explained, "My e-mail marketing company also makes sure my content gets through filters." Having that e-mail marketing company as her back up is added protection for her newsletter subscribers.

Because her subscription list is so large, and because she has numerous writers supplying articles, Drew cannot rely solely on maintaining her newsletter list on her own. That e-mail marketing company keeps everything honest, especially when Drew is busy dealing with her writers, her e-mail messages, and other business details that require her constant attention.

"E-mail marketing isn't going away," she says. "People who want the information will always make sure it gets through to them. Be specific, and use legitimate lists or legitimate e-mail marketing firms to help you give your customers what they want."

HI, MOM!

Moms are very much into e-mail, and since many of the women you should be selling to are Moms, or have a Mom, e-mail is still a good way to attract women and gain their loyalty.

E-mail is more than simply sending recipes and/or jokes to job-weary co-workers or your cousin in Kansas. Over the last year, 69% of U.S. e-mail users made an online purchase in permission-based e-mail marketing. Within our gender focus, we can look to AOL as a major player in the use of e-mail for communication and marketing.

Of its 35,000,000 registered users, a study done by Lucid Marketing showed that 58% of AOL e-mail users are females over the age of 45. Most of them, 60%, are married and more than a third of them logon to check e-mail **three or four times a day.**

Are these AOL women Moms checking in on the kids? Maybe. Moms, it turns out, are big Internet users.

> **As of April of 2003, Moms are likely to go online to "Research information (80%), research purchases (57%) and actually buy items (23%)," according to a study by the comparison shopping site, Bizrate.com**

Chuck Davis, President and CEO of Bizrate.com, says, "Moms are one of the most industrious segments of the population, often having to juggle work with home organization. The Web is the perfect tool to help them maximize their family time in the most convenient way, which is why they are hooked."

Today, Moms are as likely to use e-mail to communicate with family and friends, as they are to use the phone. E-mail keeps her in touch with all of her family, 24x7, but especially with kids at college. There are no long distance charges attached to it, and, the Web savvy Moms know they will find their kids online Instant Messaging morning, noon, and night. I confess that rather than get up from my desk to go into the kitchen and call down to my son in the basement, I might IM him from my desk, even though he calls me a dork when I do it.

If your site is female-friendly, Mom will know it, and she'll share that information with her kids at college, with her sister in Duluth and with her best friend in Miami. Bet on it.

CAN I HAVE IT, PLEASE, MOM?

Let's get the spam issue out of the way up front. Various marketing groups are reporting statistics such as, "Fifty per cent of all e-mail is spam." Or "Spam is costing the U.S. business world an estimated eight to nine billion dollars in lost productivity." Plus, "On average, people are getting 200 pieces of spam a day." Yes, spam does give ISPs a headache, and it can clog up your e-mail box worse than mud, but...each of us should take some responsibility for managing our e-mail. If we rely on others, the consequences can be even more trouble.

As of the writing of this book, the government, AOL, Yahoo! and Microsoft, are all working to control spam. No word yet on how they plan to combat this scourge of the Internet, but I'm putting myself on alert; I think if we sit back and let the big tech companies and our friend Uncle Sam decide what gets into our e-mail box, we should then be prepared to receive marketing material from them as an end result. Oh, but they won't call it spam.

> Learn your e-mail program and control the contents of your inbox. "This is spam" is becoming a standard option for letting your ISP know what you consider unacceptable.

I recently attended an online "Webinar" where a spam "professional" was interviewed. To everyone's dismay, he laughed at the proposed CAN-SPAM act, and the "Do Not Spam" registry, both of which are making the news on a daily basis. There are ways around both, he said. He's the professional spammer; I guess he should know. His excuse for engaging in this profession was simple enough. "I don't spam," he said. "I send out broadcast e-mails." His biggest client, so he said, is a large, national financial institution. Naturally, he wouldn't name names.

Truth is, there is no magic wand we can wave to make spam disappear. In the end, I say that divita@windsormediaenterprises.com is the only one who should be allowed to set permissions on what gets into her inbox. Perhaps filtering software is a better answer. I've read reports in *PC Magazine* and other industry publications that some filtering software operates on an opt-in principle, instead of an opt-out one. In other words, you set permissions to accept e-mail from trusted friends, relatives and e-zines or newsletters, and block out all others. This keeps control in the right hands, as far as I'm concerned.

In the end, the spammer in the Webinar is right. Spam is only spam if **you** say it is. For instance, one of my daughters "just happened" to click on an unfamiliar e-mail message one day because the subject line was compelling. To her knowledge she had not authorized this company to send her junk mail (much of what we call spam is merely junk e-mail), but to her delight, the sales pitch was exactly what she was looking for! She called me on the phone the next day to confess that she'd bought something online, through an unsolicited e-mail offer! What AOL and the government would have labeled spam, turned out to be an offer my daughter couldn't resist!

For those of you thinking the majority of spam is "porn", let this be a lesson. Porn is a separate issue and deserves whatever bad things happen to it. But, within the parameters of what can be labeled spam, and what can't, only the individual can answer that hotly contested question.

Now that we've settled the spam issue on our own, I encourage you to consider e-mail marketing and/or developing your own newsletter/e-zine. I offer this advice both from the perspective of a woman who subscribes to a number of newsletters, and because my research shows that because women like to get relevant information on different subjects. E-mail marketing and newsletters are two useful ways to woo her and win her. Visit http://www.demc.com, to learn from Abbie Drew's writers (I admit that I am lucky to be one) how to implement this Internet marketing tool. Meanwhile, here are my suggestions on how to begin.

Before you begin your e-mail campaign or your newsletter, understand these valuable points:

1. Are you giving your potential customers the option to choose your mailing? Permission e-mailing today involves double-opt-in: the user must consent to receive the message, you must send a note confirming, to which the user then replies with a final "yes." Are you prepared to honor this requirement both personally (do you believe it worthwhile) and professionally (do you have software that will support it)?

2. How will you format your message? HTML (pretty pictures along with text) or text based only? Text outranks HTML at this time, but I predict that with the

rapid acceptance of broadband, more users will not only be asking for HTML, but will be wondering about you if you don't at least give them the option to choose it. Users who read e-mail at work may be required by their company to accept only text, but watch that change also.

3. How valid is the e-mail address? Are you able to cull dead addresses from your database regularly? Just because e-mail doesn't carry a stamp from the post office, doesn't mean it's free. The Internet seems infinite but it's already getting clogged with traffic. Every message sent, every Web site uploaded, every piece of information on the Internet costs somebody something. E-mailing to dead e-mail addresses not only loses YOU money, it costs the ISPs in higher broadband connection charges or bigger servers to handle the traffic.

4. Finally, is your message compelling, useful, informative, or necessary? Just like junk mail in snail mailboxes, your e-mail message will get deleted if your reader doesn't find something worthwhile in it.

Once you've answered those questions, you can begin to craft your message, beginning with the subject line. The subject line is arguably the most important part of the e-mail message. It is the text most likely to get caught by spam filtering software, it is the text most likely to convince the reader to open the e-mail or delete it, and it's the text that serves to identify the sender, letting the end-user know this is a safe message to open.

If English wasn't your favorite subject in school, if you thought Charlie's slogan from the fishing site I invented in Chapter 5, ("BEND ME, TWIRL ME, SLICE AND DICE ME: I WILL BAIT THE FISHES NICELY") was a good one, or if you think of cows when someone mentions branding, my suggestion is to hire a copywriter. Hiring a professional writer could mean the difference between a positive ROI and no ROI. And if you don't know what ROI stands for—shame on you!

E-ZINES AND NEWSLETTERS

Jakob Nielsen says e-zines have a "positive emotional" impact because they create a bond between you and the receiver. The differences between a newsletter and an e-zine are few, but let's attempt to identify them here for our use:

An *electronic* magazine, (e-zine,) or a monthly newsletter, sent via e-mail, should be personal and professional.

o   A newsletter comes from a specific site and may only include information from the site owner. Occasionally, the site owner will ask other professionals to contribute to the newsletter, and some newsletters also sell advertising space (very cheap). Newsletters can be sent to as few as 25 recipients or as many as several thousand.

o   An e-zine is a more substantial newsletter. E-zines offer several articles from a group of established professionals, in addition to input from the owner of the e-zine who either writes editorial content or articles herself. Advertising is also cost-effective in e-zines. Chances are, and this is a general statement, e-zines have a larger subscription base. An e-zine usually has several hundred or several thousand subscribers.

The e-zine mentioned earlier, www.demc.com, has a subscription list of over 240,000. If you choose to put an ad in this e-zine, it will get looked at by far more people than an ad put in many other online newsletters. Not everyone will read your ad regardless of where you place it, but an ad in a targeted e-zine has a better chance of being read than an ad placed in a print publication. Most people I know glance at the print ads. Folks have to actually be in the market for a product or service to notice a print ad.

In an online newsletter or e-zine, the subscriber is anticipating the arrival of that information. Because the subscriber trusts the content of the e-zine, she will also trust the ads placed there. Your ad may be the nudge she needs to get that new tool, new dress, new software or gift basket she's been planning to get for so long now.

If you know of a newsletter with a subscription level of 5,000 aimed at members of your core market, I advise you try a series of ads for three or four weeks. It will be more cost-effective than any other method and you have a better chance of reaching at least 5,000 women who want what you're selling than if you were to advertise in an e-zine of 100,000 subscribers who may or may not care what you're selling.

Another way to get attention to your Web site and to your products and services is to offer to write for an online newsletter or e-zine. You may not get paid, but if you have something worth saying, and the newsletter has a good subscription list, you'll get noticed. Free advertising. What's not to like about that?

I hear several readers asking the HTML vs TEXT question. Which one is better? Anne Sherpa of MarketingSherpa.com, who studies various marketing techniques online, sent me (in an e-mail) a report on this very subject. It arrived in my e-mail box just this week (September 2003). According to a study MarketingSherpa conducted with 50,000 readers, "lite HTML" won out over text or full HTML.

What, you are asking, is "lite HTML?" It's a message with HTML and text, where the recipient is offered the ability to click a LINK to get to a Web page that contains the actual content, as opposed to having the content embedded in the e-mail. Lite HTML can also include a company logo [in full color] and a graphic or two, if the sender wishes. This doesn't overwhelm e-mail clients who dislike large files—think Hotmail—and it puts control of the content in the receiver's hands. The study results are located on the MarketingSherpa site at:

http://www.marketingsherpa.com/sample.cfm?contentID=2440

With that in mind, I can honestly say using HTML in your e-mail or e-zine is quickly catching on with a lot of people. It's also an open invitation to get funky. We've already learned the value of color and for the creative among us, here is where you can throw in some animation, add banners and cartoons. End-users who opt-in to receive HTML will expect it.

Remember to break text into headings and sub-headings, keep paragraphs short, and use active voice. Above all—be original. I caution you to make sure you keep to the point of your message: promotion of your products and services. Value-added content should do one of two things, preferably both—it should aid the reader in using your products or services and/or provide related information that will improve the reader's life in some way.

When developing a newsletter or e-zine, having at least one link or e-mail address that asks for a reply builds a stronger connection to your reader. Always request that your readers *forward or share* the e-mail or e-zine. Sometimes even women need a reminder to share things. Sometimes we need to know we have permission to do so. Your e-zine is copyrighted, whether you put the © on it or not, and some women may be reluctant to pass the message along, unless you give them permission. There doesn't seem to be any problem with that issue at this site:

http://www.womens-net.com

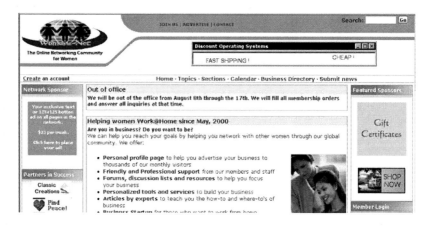

At this community site they encourage and invite input from everyone who stops by. Their monthly newsletter is in HTML and reflects the site design. It includes many of the elements seen on their homepage.

They have a quiz on their homepage and in their newsletter. Women like quizzes. They're fun and interactive and they provide a clear focus on where your reader's interests lie. This is customer relationship marketing at its best. The customer and your relationship with her are the cornerstones of your success. E-zines and newsletters allow you to nurture both of them on a regular basis.

REAL-ATIONSHIP MARKETING

Your Web presence gives you a perfect opportunity to build brand awareness and develop loyalty through *real-ationship* marketing. No, that's not a misspelling. It's a word I invented that truly describes the popular buzz phrase: customer relationship marketing. If you make it your goal to be honest and true with the women who visit your site, the real-ationship you develop with them needs to be as true and honest as the one they hold with each other.

In a society that finds reality TV such a turn-on, giving Web visitors more of the *real* you can only improve your chances of building real-ationships that make sales. One way to accomplish this is to offer visitors downloadable information in the form of an e-document. An e-doc, as it is more commonly called, is a short informational piece normally read on a computer screen. I like to download and print my e-docs, but as a means of conveying information, they are designed for quick reading right online.

Give visitors information they won't get elsewhere—a "valued tips and tricks" list or a "how-to" list that informs or instructs. Offer it in an easily downloadable e-doc or provide a print option. This establishes you as an expert in your field and it provides the visitor with free information she can use at will. The following site is a good example of how to do this successfully. It gives visitors several options on how to treat the content provided.

http://www.marketingprofs.com

Notice in the graphic here how the Marketing Profs site gets the visitor interested in its content by offering a column titled: "Hottest How To's." Next to that is a box asking: "Are You A Marketing Whiz?" followed by a list of testimonials. Visitors to the Marketing Profs site get everything they need in one glance. They can make a fast decision to leave or to stay and explore more.

This site also makes the chore of learning how to market successfully fun and easy with free articles from established professionals. Once you click into an article, there is a header that invites comments, allows printing, and encourages the reader to share the article through e-mail. The site requires registration, which is used to personalize your visit and give you membership status allowing access to the inner pages with even more valuable content. There is no cost attached to registering.

E-docs are now so popular there is a separate location at Amazon.com for them, complete with a "Frequently Asked Questions" section. Amazon describes e-docs as shorter digital documents, usually developed to provide "timely" information on a wide-range of subjects. If you're hoping to build a strong female following by wowing the women who come to your site, write newsy articles and lists; add one small motivational quote each day. It can be the eye-catcher that leads to a downloadable, one page document describing what that quote means to you.

In addition to building interest and establishing brand through e-docs, you can also make some money. As you will learn when you visit the e-doc section of Amazon, e-docs can be big business. Major companies sell their e-docs for upwards of $100 and more. Smaller companies, writers, and marketers usually offer e-docs for a fee of only $5-$10. If you want to sell the e-doc on your site, you will need to be set up for e-commerce capability. This

involves having a merchant account with a bank, or asking visitors to use PayPal. Offering your e-doc on your Web site and on Amazon will net greater profits. You have nothing to lose by exploring this option. You have everything to gain from it.

Generally, e-docs are printed using Adobe Acrobat's portable document format, or PDF, software. The PDF reader is a free download at http://www.adobe.com/main.html. PDF, according to the link, "is a universal file format that preserves the fonts, images, graphics, and layout of any source document, regardless of the application and platform used to create it. Adobe® PDF files are compact and complete, and can be shared, viewed, and printed by anyone with free Adobe Reader® software. To date, more than 500 million copies of the software have been distributed. You can convert any document to Adobe PDF using Adobe Acrobat® software products, enabling business, engineering, and creative professionals to create, distribute, and exchange secure and reliable Adobe PDF documents."

"MOVE OVER, STEPHEN KING"

A June 9th (2003) article in the *Wall Street Journal* titled, "Move Over, Stephen King," spotlighted the growing interest in e-books. Not just in buying them, mind you—but also in writing them! The average citizen who wants to get a book in print is no longer tied to the whims of HarperCollins Publishers or McMillan Publishing, or any of the dozens of other dirt world publishers.

In that tired old century we left behind—the Dick and Jane one, remember it?—getting published was a twisted path to traverse, complete with hidden potholes and dead ends. When I was a young, aspiring writer sending out short stories to the likes of the *New Yorker,* the *Atlantic Monthly,* and *Redbook* magazine, I experienced the same kind of rejection Stephen King experienced early on in his career. King was not an overnight success; "Carrie," King's first published work, was rejected many times over before Simon & Schuster took a chance on it. J.K. Rowlings of *Harry Potter* fame also suffered the disappointment of rejection many times before Scholastic, Inc., gave her a chance to change children's literature forever.

Much like King and Rowling, I persevered, changing my focus from fiction to business, before I achieved publication. Meanwhile, my great American novel lies at the bottom of a box stuck on Chapter 4, somewhere in my office storeroom.

Why? Because getting published using the 20th century way is a long, drawn out, unrewarding task. First, you write the novel, then you send it to either an agent or a publisher. Then you wait. And wait. And wait some more. Until your chosen agent or publisher sends it back with a form rejection saying "thanks but no thanks." Sometimes you get lucky and the agent or publisher expresses interest. This could mean a year or two of conversation and/or editing. In the end, you've lost two years of your life, you may or may not have received a small advance—typically less than $5,000—and the publisher has lost interest or the book gets published but receives little marketing to support sales.

Granted, there are successful writers who hit pay dirt on their first try. And there are successful writers who are making a living using their craft but are recognized only in select circles. For the most part, trying to get a book published using traditional methods leaves one full of confusion, mired in disappointment, and left with the idea of either going to a subsidy publisher or self-publishing.

Subsidy publishing requires a good deal of investment, both in time and money, as the cost of printing is done at the author's expense and any marketing is also at the author's expense. With self-publishing, the cost is even higher; the author must get the book to a printer and bear the cost of formatting and layout, in addition to printing costs, after which he or she will also be responsible for marketing and sales.

DIGITAL DYNAMITE

Enter the 21st century way of getting your book published: print-on-demand publishing.

E-books developed with print-on-demand publishing companies such as 1st Books, the company that produced this book, and iUniverse, or Xlibris, provide a way to publish cost-effectively and within a reasonable time frame. Print-on-demand companies can format your book, store it electronically, and print it in paperback or hardcover *as orders come in*. There is no warehousing, no anxious waiting by the mailbox for that thin envelope containing nothing but a rejection slip, and no pressure to make edits or changes you don't want to make.

- **No paper waste is accumulated.**
- **No trees are felled to develop e-books or POD books.**
- **E-books & POD books are available for purchase 24x7, at the click of a mouse, from the comfort of one's own home.**
- **Supplies are unlimited and no unsold copies are left languishing in your garage.**

Yes, there is a cost. The companies mentioned here charge anywhere from a low of $199 to a high of $2,499, with additional charges for specific marketing plans. Many of the POD companies will obtain your ISBN number for you, and some will copyright your book with the U.S. copyright office for you. The value of POD is that you, the author, are in charge of the production of your work. You determine what the book is going to look like, including the font used, the page layout, the cover, and how it will get marketed. An energetic author with some sales experience can opt for a small marketing package to have notices sent to book reviewers, then perform his or her own marketing, such as selling the book to local bookstores at book signings, and offering the book at trade shows or seminars.

Of course, marketing your e-book on your Web site is a guaranteed way to get it noticed, if you optimize for the search engines and send out e-mail notices. Not only does it establish you as an expert in your field—just as e-docs do—having a book-length document available for sale on your Web site is an impressive accomplishment. Many authors sell a portion of the e-book as an e-doc for under $10, using the content in the e-doc to entice the reader to purchase the entire text, deducting any money already spent.

As of April of 2003, statistics from Amazon.com showed they were carrying 32,000 business volumes in e-book format. Trafford Publishing, another e-book/print-on-demand company, reports that approximately 10% of books today are self-published, and supported by a Web site using this new technology.

E-books are becoming popular with former downsized corporate employees opening their own businesses and looking to the Internet for help. They want and need expert advice and information from others to make a success of their endeavors. These entrepreneurs are eager for advice on how to build a successful business—if you can help, offer them an e-doc.

If e-books aren't your thing, explore the popularity and availability of POD. Both e-docs and e-books are valuable ways to build brand awareness and loyalty. They also help market your Web site, your products, your services, and your own unique form of real-ationship marketing.

R.R. Bowker's database of *Books in Print says* POD books grew from 142,000 in 2001 to around 150,000 in 2002. Forrester research predicts that e-publishing will approach revenue in the $400 million range by 2004.

Before you write your e-doc or e-book and offer it for sale on your Web site, you need to do one more important thing to assure the women who come to buy it that they can trust you. You need to post a privacy statement.

"I KNOW WHAT YOU DID LAST SUMMER"

Joseph Turow, PhD, Robert Lewis Shayon Professor of Communication at the Annenberg School For Communication, University of Pennsylvania, and author of the report "Americans and Online Privacy: The System is Broken" reveals in his 35 page e-doc that "American adults who go online at home misunderstand the very purpose of privacy policies."

According to some statistics in Turow's report:

- o 57% of U.S. adults who use the Internet at home believe incorrectly that when a Web site has a privacy policy, it will not share their personal information with other Web sites or companies.
- o 47% of U.S. adults say Web site privacy policies are easy to understand. However, 66% of those [adults] also believe (incorrectly) that sites with a privacy policy won't share data.
- o 86% of U.S. adults believe that laws that force Web site policies to have a standard format will be effective in helping them protect their information.

The Internet is somewhat like the 1997 movie "I Know What You Did Last Summer," (Directed by Jim Gillespie), where a group of teens is terrorized by a stranger who has knowledge about them that they would rather keep hidden. Venturing on to the superhighway of the Internet without bothering to read the road signs is a sure guarantee that someone, somewhere is going to collect information about you that you might not want to share.

Most of the time the information gathered is aggregate facts—your location (gleaned from the IP address attached to your computer, which is part of your physical location), your surfing habits (how long you spent on the homepage, how many links you clicked on, whether or not you actually put an item in a shopping cart and what that item was), and what you did while on the Web site; i.e., Did you download an e-doc? How many pages did you visit? Did you fill out a form? Did you share your e-mail address? All of this is done through the use of Internet cookies.

Everyone who understands Internet cookies raise your hand.

I see a lot of hands, but, if this exercise were being conducted in a real classroom or a seminar, I would bet (just a little—maybe $10—I'm cheap) that few of you would be able to define what an Internet cookie really is. In my survey, I asked every woman if she knew what an Internet cookie is and less than half of them offered up an explanation. Of those, only a few gave a correct answer.

Here is what an Internet cookie is not:
- o Edible
- o Flavored
- o Packaged in boxes or bags
- o Viewable by the naked eye
- o Intended to steal personal information about you

Here is what an Internet cookie is:
- o A software tool that collects data
- o A good way to measure Web site effectiveness

- Used by marketing professionals to track visitor actions on a Web site
- Technology likely to leave crumbs scattered around

The issue with privacy and cookies lies in the last bullet: likely to leave crumbs scattered around. Moms really don't like crumbs all over the house. Women in general have been fighting the crumb-war for centuries. We have a reputation for wanting a clean house and some of us are fanatical about it. Even those of us who don't give our homes the white glove test on a regular basis rebel against crumbs on the kitchen floor or the carpet.

Therefore, imagine how we feel about leaving little bits of information in the form of data (crumbs) all over the Internet for some unscrupulous marketing firm to share with companies that pay them for this information. Mostly, we don't like it. Some of us dislike it so much, we go into our Tools menu, click the Internet Options link, and tell our system NOT to accept cookies. Many women are savvy enough to click the security tab in options and disable the *third party cookies* option. This allows us to view any site requiring cookies, but it prevents that blinking banner ad at the top of the page from sending any information back to its owner.

We may not like Internet cookies, but we do value our **privacy**.

You do have a privacy statement reassuring us that you can be trusted, don't you? It's that link at the bottom of every page that clearly says: PRIVACY or PRIVACY STATEMENT. Clicking the link downloads the privacy statement in all its glory, informing us how you are using our personally identifiable information—if, indeed you are—whether or not you use cookies and what for and how your Web site protects the information we share with you in that e-mail we send requesting product information, or that form we fill out requesting company details.

In cases where a site has products which may interest children, your privacy statement needs to include a paragraph detailing how you handle information children may share with you. This is a requirement of the Children's Online Privacy Protection Act (COPPA).

For more information visit:

http://www.ftc.gov/bcp/conline/pubs/buspubs/coppa.htm

Turow, in the study I mentioned earlier in this chapter, discusses much of this. His overall conclusion is that few people understand privacy statements. I agree. Most privacy statements are too complicated. They contain too much text in all caps, which is inherently difficult to read, especially on a computer screen, and in their attempt to reassure the reader that his or her privacy will be protected, privacy statements often include language such as this, taken from an anonymous site:

"On the Site, we place links to other Web sites operated by other parties. Some of these other Web sites contain our brand names and trademarks and other intellectual property that we own; others do not. When you click on these links and visit these other Web sites, regardless of whether or not they contain our brand names, trademarks, and other intellectual property, you need to be aware that we do not control these other Web sites or these other Web sites' business practices, and that this privacy policy does not apply to these other Web sites. Consequently, the operators of these other Web sites may collect different kinds of information about you, and may use and disclose that information in different ways than we would if it were collected on the Site. We encourage you to review their privacy policies and remind you that we will not be responsible for their actions."

If that gives you the warm fuzzies, you must be a lawyer. Personally, I, and the women I spoke with, would prefer simple language. We understand that your lawyer wants to cover all the bases, and that's a good idea, but write it in normal English, not legalese.

Note how the same site addresses the COPPA requirement in clear English:

"Please note that nowhere on the Site do we knowingly collect personal information from children under the age of 18, as we require that all users represent to us that they are at least 18 years old."

We can't fault any site for trusting that registrants admit to being 18, even if they are not. Whether or not someone is of age is not an issue you can do much about. That's why a privacy statement, stating exactly what you do with the information people share with you, is so important—for your visitor's protection, and your own.

From a visitor's viewpoint, your privacy statement should assure her that her visit is safe, that any information shared is not going to be sold to third party vendors, and that you respect her willingness to buy or spend time at your site. Unfortunately, the language used in most privacy statements gives readers a headache. This in no way excuses you from having a privacy statement. Instead, it outlines why a privacy statement is crucial to building trust, and I hope it shows that a carefully worded privacy statement is as good as a handshake.

To read a privacy statement that doesn't resort to legalese or convoluted "might dos" visit: http://www.aarp.org/ .

BETTER BUSINESS ALL AROUND

In my survey I also asked women if they knew of, or understood, the BBB: Better Business Bureau; Verisign: an online site working to make the Internet a safer place; and TRUSTe, a site that promises to protect consumer privacy. Most knew the BBB, few knew or had even heard of Verisign or TRUSTe.

Displaying the Better Business Bureau seal http://www.bbb.org on your site is a plus. Prominently displaying the Verisign symbol showing that any information collected is properly encrypted also rates high points in assuring visitors you can be trusted. http://www.verisign.com

These companies are the most notable ones involved in privacy issues. For more information, visit http://www.w3.org/P3P, the World Wide Web Consortium's *Platform for Privacy Preferences* which, according to their site, "is emerging as an industry standard providing a simple, automated way for users to gain more control over the use of personal information on Web sites they visit."

In addition, there is another digital certificate site which operates to protect consumers from fraud, identity theft, and other privacy issues. Site http://www.thawte.com operates on the "open source" principle, as stated on their Web site: "Thawte focuses all its energy and resources on creating a world where *every single person* can communicate and trade securely, profitably and privately across technologies and beyond borders, a world in which code is freely and securely distributed as part of the open source movement."

The open source movement is not a part of our marketing venue, but as an explanation, it's fueled by programmers who believe computer code should be free and accessible for public use. The war between the open source community and the likes of Microsoft, with its proprietary software solutions, is not important here. Understanding what open source is, is important. Because it supports a growing faction of believers in helping keep the Internet safe and free to all.

My reason for asking survey respondents the BBB, Verisign, TRUSTe and Thawte question was to see how aware they were of the privacy and security options online. By and far, they recognized the BBB. To my surprise, a few also knew Verisign and had heard of TRUSTe.

In other words, learn how to write an effective privacy statement. Join your local Better Business Bureau. Explore TRUSTe and Verisign membership. Look at what Thawte has to offer. The more safe and secure you make us feel, the more likely we will be to buy your products and services.

Try it yourself. We'll like it!

TO ERR IS HUMAN

To error is human, to really foul things up requires a computer; so the saying goes. In the dirt world, if you need help purchasing something, you often go off and find a customer service rep, or a clerk, or a sales manager, and s/he will assist you. Online many small businesses think they cannot afford the kind of software that offers visitors real-time chat screens to solve their problems. Often, the only customer service offered is a "Contact Us" link that lets visitors send an e-mail to— someone in authority, we hope.

An example of the effectiveness of understanding your market can be seen in this report from NetCreations, an e-mail marketing firm which reported a 60% increase in click-through rates during the fourth quarter of 2002. Kris Oser, writing at ClickZ.com, writes that the factors contributing to that 60% show a direct result of the company's knowledge of *how users react to information online.* The company used a clear, informative registration form; provided easy navigation; offered opt in functionality; and supplied an explanation of what the information is for and how it would be used. Finally, the company sent an e-mail confirming visitor sign up.

That confirmation e-mail is so important! I urge you, however, to make sure you include a link back to your site in that e-mail. Any e-mail we send that ends up in cyberspace, or lost in the webmaster's e-mail box, is a clear indication to us that you do not care about us. An empty silence as a reply to an e-mail sent with questions, or as a response to an order confirmation, truly speaks volumes. Within that silence the word "Good-bye" comes through loud and clear.

Sadly, this is a problem with many brand name sites. I caution the reader to think carefully about this aspect of your Web presence. Instant chat screens are what we really want, but if you can't afford the technology to implement a 24x7 chat, at least program your e-mail system to auto-reply to every e-mail you receive and include an option for the receive to send you a reply. It's imperative after that first auto-responder to follow up with a reply from a real person—someone who can be a contact for us, in case we have more questions.

> If you're not five minutes early, you're ten minutes late. ~Anonymous

Women are adamant about this. As mentioned in Chapter 5, "Sarah-Ellen Xceptions," having an 800 number which operates 24x7 is one excellent way to attend to a Web business that reaches national customers. Implementing that chat screen is another. If these options aren't in your budget just yet, use e-mail effectively by programming your auto-responder and sending a real-ationship note that involves a reply from a real person, *in less than 24 hours.*

Giving customers immediate attention builds trust—e-mail us to remind us what we ordered and then tell us when it will be shipped.

THE FINAL F WORD: FREE! TO LOYAL CUSTOMERS

Free anything works—for women and quite a few men, too. Free subscriptions to newsletters, free accessories, free information. Free can be offered as a printable coupon to be used in a dirt world store, or it can be an incentive to buy more than once.

At Barnes and Noble, for instance, for a small registration fee, shoppers receive a card resembling a charge card. When used with purchases, it records how many items the shoppers is purchasing; after a certain amount, the shopper is rewarded with free merchandise. This is a loyalty program and it works. Hallmark uses the same principle with its Hallmark Gift Card. In Hallmark's case, it's the sum total of the purchase that accumulates points, giving the shopper free merchandise when she reaches a certain point level. A bonus to the Hallmark model is a direct mail notice sent quarterly to inform us how many points we have accumulated, complete with suggestions on how to spend those points on more Hallmark merchandise!

Loyalty programs are replacing coupons online because it's much easier to track visits and sales with software, than to expect shoppers to download and print coupons for redemption. If you prefer to offer coupons online, use the numbering method: assign a number to the coupon, ask the shopper for her coupon number at check-out, and make sure your shopping cart program can handle the calculations. In the Rochester, New York, area at this time, one local grocery chain will not accept coupons printed off of the Internet. I have no way of knowing where this will lead, but it shows reluctance on the part of the dirt world to participate in the whole online coupon thing. Be aware of what's happening where you are. Reward us with quality, service, and price, and we will reward you with sales.

Beyond the coupon offerings and loyalty programs, one area that gets the highest marks is free shipping. In my survey, I asked women, "What would get you to buy online if you are not buying online today?" The number one answer was free shipping.

This is not as prohibitive as it sounds. It doesn't mean you need to lose money on shipping costs. It means an opportunity to do some serious math. For instance, if you consider how much shipping is costing you, then work in how much you can recover by increasing the cost of certain products just enough to cover shipping, you will attract twice as many customers.

Amazon.com is the poster child for the success of using this marketing tactic. According to an article in the Rochester, New York, *Democrat and Chronicle,* January 2003, free shipping is becoming an online standard. "Amazon, other retailers bank on free shipping," the headline reads. While not a new concept, as a way to lure customers and get them to click that buy button, the experts at Amazon.com have perfected it.

Bill Curry, spokesman for Amazon, is quoted in the article, saying, "When customers love something, it's our job to figure out how to do it." As a retail store selling a variety of goods, and partnering with other department store sites, Amazon is an attractive place for women to shop. Old hands at catalog shopping, women know and understand the value of free shipping, perhaps better than men. When a woman can get free shipping on orders of only $25, it's a good bet she will spend a few extra minutes adding to her shopping cart to get up to that amount, rather than settle for that one item at $15.99.

You can't go wrong following Amazon's lead. In June of 2003, the top e-commerce site for both men and women was Amazon.com.

Following that, the second place for both genders was Barnes and Noble. In third place it's CDNow for both, then Buy.com for men, but eToys.com for women. Each of these sites offers free shipping, with some restrictions.

What's not to like about that?

WHAT WE LEARNED IN THIS CHAPTER
- o Getting women to like and trust you builds brand awareness online and offline.
- o Women are loyal to sites that offer loyalty programs.
- o E-mail marketing is in flux right now. Stay tuned to see how it develops.
- o E-books and e-docs are excellent ways to establish expert status and build loyalty.
- o Free shipping is better than a two-for-one sale.
- o "We will not sell or barter your personal information. Period." Short, simple, and private.

7. Meeting at the Well

Working with Communities, Non-profits and Partnerships

Women are the real Architects of Society
~Harriet Beecher Stowe

In 1985, Stewart Brand and Larry Brilliant founded the Whole Earth 'Lectronic Link. The WELL, as it came to be known, was the first online community, gathering attention and open dialogue from people in all countries throughout the globe. The concept was unheard of in its day. Discussion groups expanded and grew exponentially until The WELL became a literal "watering hole" online; a place for great thinkers to gather and—well, think out loud. I can hear the furious clicking of their keyboards even now!

It isn't hard to imagine the hundreds of WELL users hunched over their keyboards, fingers flying over the letters that would form the words they were thinking. Hundreds, no, thousands, of great minds surfed to The WELL to engage in conversations in those early days. Conversations that were blunt, uninhibited, and intelligent. Everyone visiting The WELL had something to say and no one was afraid to voice his or her opinion, openly and without reservation.

The WELL was unexplored territory; its worldwide appeal came from the open atmosphere—no walls, no rules, no barriers to voicing opinions, radical or not. It was a virtual community, yet the core *meeting room* became so enthusiastic that some groups stepped away to gather in forums separately, as if shuffling off to a room down the hall or across the way.

In its original format, The WELL was designed to offer people a place to meet online without *anonymity*. Anyone with a keyboard and a

modem was welcomed to The WELL, where the credo was "You Own Your Own Words." Bios were encouraged to keep folks honest, and over time, the concept of an online community-meeting place took firm hold.

Today, The WELL is owned by online subscription-based e-zine, Salon. Its cluster of electronic meeting forums stands as a testament to the power of community in the electronic age.

This chapter of *Dickless Marketing* is about community and how it plays an important role in marketing to women. I will introduce you to a few online communities that cater to a female clientele but also welcome men as friends and partners. Learning how important community is to women will give you some insight into how to use it to your advantage.

Within the community mantra, this chapter will touch on the roles of philanthropy and non-profits and how supporting charities is a vital part of marketing to women. I will talk about the role of partnerships, both personal—new entrepreneurial businesses that have been started by husband and wife teams—as well as business partnerships where senior management is comprised of both women and men.

NEW AND OLD TOGETHER

> **Make new friends, but keep the old;**
> **Those are silver, these are gold.**
> **New-made friendships, like new wine,**
> **Age will mellow and refine.**
> **Friendships that have stood the test—**
> **Time and change—are surely best;**
> **Brow may wrinkle, hair grow gray,**
> **Friendship never knows decay.**
> **For 'mid old friends, tried and true,**
> **Once more we our youth renew.**
> **But old friends, alas, may die,**
> **New friends must their place supply.**

> **Cherish friendship in your breast—**
> **New is good, but old is best;**
> **Make new friends, but keep the old;**
> **Those are silver, these are gold.**
> **Joseph Parry**

This poem is a perfect description of how to increase business and sales. Studies show that existing clients are the lifeblood of any business. Yes, a business needs to be adding new clients on a fairly regular basis, but the real test of success is in how long existing clients stay with you.

Clients and customers that stay with you are your best salespeople. They provide better advertising than any TV commercial, radio ad, or e-mail marketing campaign. Referral business—an introduction to a possible new client from a satisfied existing client—yields far better results than cold calling or prospecting on your own, no matter how great a salesperson you are.

Existing clients are like old friends. Friendship, which I have been touting throughout *Dickless Marketing*, is the cornerstone of women's communities. Like minds meeting in various places to discuss—oh, everything under the sun. That's really what communities are all about. Women started overtaking men online when we realized we could get together with our friends and family quickly and easily, without having to use the phone. Or we could find new companions online, unlimited by the physical boundaries of our lives. It wasn't because we were eager to shop online, although that myth continues to float about cyberspace.

It's time to get nostalgic once more.

In the ancient days of the '60s and '70s, the baby boomers introduced the term "hippies" to the American dialect. This was a generation of Americans that hit the road to relocate, sometimes thousands of miles, away from home. They gathered in communes in Haight Ashbury, listened to strange psychedelic music, and smoked funny cigarettes. The hippies made the news in their day for their wild escapades, free love, and outlandish clothing, much the same way the Gen Xers and Gen Ys make the news today for their Internet exploits and their tattoos and body piercings. The ironic thing is that some of them are wearing bell-bottom jeans and crazy colored T-shirts, straight out of the '60s.

Some of the Hippie communes eventually morphed into suburban communities made up of people related not by fashion, music, and drugs, but by goals, achievements, religious beliefs, and a desire to make America a better place for their children.

The world the *hippies-turned-suburbanites* built was founded on the prosperity of the post Vietnam era, full of white-collar workers who looked at credit almost as a normal means of support. Cars, houses, clothes, toys, even food, were bought on credit; and sometimes a new credit card was used to pay off or supplement the old one. The baby boomers were the first generation to feel "entitled" to their "stuff." And they amassed a lot of it! From televisions to workout equipment; from gourmet foods to freezers full of steaks and ice cream; from lava lamps (leftover from their college years) to bread makers; they were good consumers. When the PC became a household appliance, they accepted it as a necessity as quickly as they accepted the "necessity" of color television.

The computer begat the Internet, of course. And, by the time the boomer's kids came of age in the waning years of the 20th century, they were sold on the high tech toys that IBM, Microsoft, HP, Apple Computers, and all the other tech giants were marketing to them. They lug their laptops and PCs to college as if carrying along an extra set of Nikes or a pair of sunglasses. Today colleges all offer broadband Internet connections and free e-mail addresses. (They have to or they wouldn't have any students.) Today's college kids are still at home, though—at least in spirit. Their screen names are highlighted in Mom's and Dad's IM box.

This was the beginning of digital "reaching out to touch someone." It was AOL that lured women online to reach family and friends through e-mail, then Instant Messaging. AOL with its massive advertising campaigns showed even the novice computer user how easy it was to logon and stay in touch. E-mail and instant message have, in some ways, brought back the challenge and the pleasure of letter writing. Both of them require using words to express feelings and share thoughts in what can be a sincerely private way.

E-mail and/or Instant Messaging means using words that can be edited before hitting the send button. It gives the writer control. The timing is never off. Unlike an intrusive phone call, e-mail notes can be read and replied to at the recipient's leisure. Strangely enough, notes written on a computer have become both more personal and more private than any phone conversation or any snail-mail letter.

When women discovered how simple and easy this new form of communication was, we began looking for other ways to use this new tool. It wasn't long before we realized we could form communities with other women online. We could gather together online and talk to each other freely. We could discuss what was in our hearts and minds with other women; morning, noon, and midnight. This ability to connect, to communicate, to confess, is the real reason there are more women than men online today.

> **Yes, now we know that e-mail is not private, and that e-mail messages can be used as evidence in court trials, but that is not part of marketing to women online.**

I recognize the danger of that kind of communication, but there are ISPs, law enforcement officials and politicians policing the legal issues of misrepresenting oneself online. For our purposes, we will err on the side of trust. Most women, not all, are who they say they are. For that matter, when you communicate with them, they expect you to be who you say you are.

SIZING UP THE SALE

Am I naïve for admitting that shopping is not the primary reason women go online, considering the focus of this book is how to sell to women online? I don't think so. It's precisely because women view the Internet as a vehicle of communication that I believe women are your core market, no matter what you sell.

We use e-mail and Instant Messaging to keep the lines open with family and friends. Our e-mail exchanges are emotional and focused; sometimes on family issues, sometimes on careers and health; other times on psychology—and even where to buy the best laptop!

We care. In that caring is a need to find answers to problems affecting friends and family members. We log on to the Internet looking for those answers every day of the week, morning, noon and night, over and over again, in a never-ending cycle.

If you give it some thought, your site may be the one we visit to learn how to help our daughter decorate her basement apartment, or to find the latest treatment for our new grandson's colic. If we're looking for advice on how to treat a sibling's pain in his or her esophagus, a

> Being a woman means caring and sharing. Share with us and we'll share with you.

link on your site to a medical dictionary will be just the thing, regardless of what you're selling. It goes back to the value-added content I talked about in Chapter 5.

The communities we form and populate have pages and pages of value-added content. Some of it we write ourselves. Some of it we get from—you, if you've bothered to check out our community and have good insight or advice to offer. Using value-added content to inspire us with uplifting quotes or daily affirmations will get us to your Web site, guaranteed.

> If you think you're too small to have an impact, try going to bed with a mosquito." Anita Roddick, entrepreneur/ founder of The Body Shop

It's those warm fuzzies, again. It's that handshake welcoming us into your living room. Give us a reason to trust you. Write articles or buy ads on our community homepage, put notices in our community newsletters. Display strong business ethics coupled with genuine integrity. Help us be better than we are. You don't have to be Wal-Mart, or Target, or JCPenny. All you have to do is show up and show you care. We want to make friends with you, if only you will give us the chance!

Remember, in *Dickless Marketing* friendship= S-A-L-E-S.

Anyone who still believes the myth that women log on to the Internet because it's a gigantic mall sending out strong subliminal messages, read this sentence carefully:

Building community comes before spending money.

Now let's see why women's communities online are so powerful.

DR. MOM

Bob McDowall, a contributing writer at www.it-director.com noted distinct behavior patterns in women's online communities, in an article dated January 2002.

At the core of his article, "Women and the Web-are they a different community?" he reinforces what I've been showing you throughout DM. As a general rule, women don't go online to play games, look up stock quotes, or buy tools (although we may do all of those things). Instead, women logon to the Internet to meet other women in an online forum or community in order to interact and discuss family, career, politics, and support issues. By support I am not talking about alimony or child care, although that is probably a topic in every woman's community online. I'm talking about emotional support. That virtual pat on the back, which can mean, "Good job!" Or "There,

there, I understand." Or "This has worked for me. Maybe it will work for you, too."

One area that women have controlled since the beginning of time is the health and beauty industry. Recent information from research firms emarketer.com and Cyberatlas.com show that the health and beauty industry, H&B, is tallying up numbers too big to fit in this paragraph! Numbers aren't necessary if you're willing to admit that we live in an age where the use of health aids such as  nutritional supplements, power drinks, vitamins, and more, are no longer optional personal items, they are now considered necessities. A view into the skin care industry reveals another new development—men are rapidly adopting the daily routine of moisturizer, toner, and even make-up. These are clear indications that the H&B industry will generate billions of dollars in profits during the next decade.

When thinking of the health and beauty industry, which gender comes to mind first?

I submit that it's the one the quarterback waves to on camera at the end of the ballgame, when he says—with a big, toothy smile, "Hi, Mom!" It's Mom because she is the one who generally buys the most beauty aids, the most band-aids, the most hair treatments, moisturizer, make-up, nail polish, laundry detergent, dish detergent, soap, glass cleaner, mouthwash, and on and on.

This is not because Mom is cleaner than Dad, or because she is more concerned with cleanliness and skin care, but because women *purchase the majority of all household goods*. I dare say that with the new popularity of men's skin care products, we will see women increase their spending on these products as they buy for themselves and for the men in their lives. After all, they already make sure that their men do not run out of deodorant and shampoo!

In a market heading towards $2 billion during 2002, reports showed that "this group [H&B buyers] represents a select group of mature online shoppers who purchase much more than the basic books, music, or gifts online." Their purchases run to healthcare and pharmaceuticals, beauty products, gourmet items, and pet supplies.

A March 2003 report from Forrester Research predicts that "the Web will become the foundation for a new healthcare industry infrastructure that supports complex, multiparty transactions among consumers, providers, insurers, and medical suppliers." The report showed that 32% of online shoppers buy healthcare products online. How many of them are women? I leave the figuring up to you. But it behooves the smart marketer to figure out a way to tap into this community.

Futurist Frank Feather, *(futureconsumer.com),* says there are five discount H&B shopping sites online to watch:

1. WebMD.com

2. CVS.com

3. Drugstore.com (powered by Amazon.com)

4. Quixtar.com (online shopping portal)

5. Walgreens.com

Of these five sites, Quixtar may not be as familiar to some readers as the others. Launched in late 1999, this online retail portal gained premier status as a shopping site in the short space of three months. By the end of 2001 Quixtar was ranked #1 in the Health and Beauty online space, commanding 20% of the market (*Business 2.0,* December 2001). Today it shows promise of overtaking the other four sites listed here, fueled by Independent Business Owners (IBOs). These IBOS are entrepreneurs from all walks of life who have a stake in making Quixtar a worldwide success as an online shopping channel. Since the launch of the 22,000 pages Web site, Quixtar's IBOs have generated $3.1 billion in sales and generated over $200 million for Partner Stores such as OfficeMax, Disney, Catalog City, and more.

Quixtar boasts a personal product line of over 450 products, including all natural cleaning products, vitamins, energy drinks, snack bars, and skin care. A certain measure of Quixtar's success comes from its partner companies, but the greater success is in the IBO partnerships composed of husband/wife teams. In the next five to ten years, we will see more husband/wife teams in all areas of business, pushing the focus of marketing away from male-dominated ads to ads that attract women because it may be the woman signing the check. We will talk more about husband/wife teams later on in this chapter.

Television, an old hand at reaching the right market, is actively marketing to women. For example, Yoplait® yogurt is having success with its commercials featuring several young women commenting on the lusciousness of the yogurt. In the most recent commercial there are several young women enjoying their Yoplait in a beach setting, each one commenting on how "good" the yogurt is.

A recent Pantene® commercial shows popular female celebrity Kelly Rippa, of *All My Children* and *Regis and Kelly* fame, speaking directly into the camera, as if talking to the viewer, showing off her beautiful hair, compliments, she says, of Pantene.

Carmakers are also aware of the power of marketing to women. An August 2003 Nissan *Quest* commercial on TV clicks rapidly through a variety of women in one second displays, with a voice-over announcing, "Moms have changed. Why shouldn't the minivan?" Their Web site notes that the new minivan was an effort to "produce a family hauler with style."

The Web site goes on to mention why they are approaching the sale of this new vehicle as they do, "We feel this new work is a more natural fit when talking to confident, fun-loving and intelligent women across the country. We built the Quest for them and want to make sure our messages connect with them emotionally," according to Kim McCullough, senior marketing manager.

Nissan gets it. Pantene and Yoplait get it. They get it so well, they are spending millions to advertise on television. Can you afford to compete with that? If you're online, you don't have to. As a small business with a Web site, you can put your marketing dollars into advertising on women's communities, and reach double the people those TV ads reach.

TV is expensive and forces you to choose a time frame: prime time, afternoon soap operas, or the 5:00 News, each with its own price level and market share. Cable commercials may be more cost-effective, but they can't match the value of advertising online. Online you reach your core market at *their convenience*. Using the community approach, you can outsell your competition for pennies on the dollar.

> **An online advertising campaign by Kraft Foods focused on reaching Moms from 25-54 to sell Oscar Mayer Lunchables®. Research by Kraft showed that women with children are heavy Internet users.**

Think of women's online communities as digital meetings at a virtual well; we may be there to get water, but it's a sure bet we're going to come away with a new tip on how to bake homemade bread, or how to keep our children and husbands healthy, or how to develop an online business. If you're supplying that information, you have our attention—sell us something.

Community is so strong; the American Sociological Association (ASA) spent three years studying interactivity on the Internet and how online communities worked. Their findings, reported in October of 2002, reveal that folks with a high-speed Internet connection are more likely to be active in their community, both on and offline. The study reported that the Internet can actually expand and strengthen relationships on a local level with neighbors and family, especially extending to friends and relatives who have moved out of the region.

The ASA report showed that:

- o Folks with high-speed Internet access recognize, talk and visit with more of their neighbors, than those without.
- o Having access to a local computer network (think cable or DSL) introduces new methods of communication, ultimately improving

              communication between friends, relatives, and neighbors.

- o This interconnection beyond the computer showed that wired residents are more likely to know neighbors living elsewhere in their suburb, not just those who are next door or across the street.
- o Neighborhood e-mail lists increase in-person socializing (barbecues, holiday parties) as well as fostering political action and involvement within the immediate community.

THE WELL REVISITED

The WELL was just the beginning. Women dominate online communities today because we like to talk to each other, even virtually. I have listed a few of my favorites here. Visit them, join them, advertise on them, and take the time to explore them to learn about the women who belong to them. I'm confident you'll find your core market in one or more of them.

COMMUNITIES DEVOTED TO CARING:

www.womans-net.com : A gathering place for professionals of all sorts, work at home Moms, stay at home Moms, and anyone interested in selling to them. "It's not only WHAT you know that makes you successful, it's WHO you know."

www.womensforum.com: "Whether you're a busy mom, career-blazer, or superwoman trying to do it all, you're in the right place. Our motto is come as you are and throw perfection out the window! So join the fun, find a community that suits you, and make womensforum.com your own."

www.ivillage.com: This site has it all: groups, quizzes, magazine links, sales, advice. Find out what's on our minds by perusing iVillage, and use that information to sell us your stuff!

www.bhg.com (Better Homes and Gardens): Food, garden, house, home, holidays, crafts, health, family, store…want more? It's there.

www.suite101.com A unique publishing community online with a focus on "global community." Women play a big part on this site but it's open to all. Visit it and find your niche.

www.umbc.edu/cwit/ (Center for Women & Information Technology): According to ABC.com news, this is the "Best Resource for Women in Technology on the Web."

www.digital-women.com/ "An International online community for women in business, business women, and all women around the world." Going international? This is a great place to start.

www.oxygen.com/ "Oxygen Media, a 24-hour cable television network, puts a fresh spin on television for women." This site is associated with Oprah Winfrey.

In addition to these community sites, there are dozens of others that can be found by merely searching on "women's communities" in your favorite search engine.

The Internet has also become a safe haven for women of faith, be that of Christian faith, Jewish faith, Muslim faith, or any of the many other spiritual sects that gather to engage in fellowship with each other. These communities often focus on health, family values, and a hankering to return to the days of old, but *they are doing it online.* There are thousands of women, women with husbands and children, mothers and fathers, sisters and brothers, who visit these communities on a daily basis and who might be in the market for your products or services, if only you would approach them in their own environment.

PUTTING IT ALL TOGETHER

You need look no further than eBay for an example of a successful, powerful online marketing community. This interactive auction site started out small but it has grown to be a giant among giants, easily giving Amazon.com, Yahoo! and Google a run for their money as top Internet property. No longer serving as an online garage sale or weekend shopping portal, eBay is a runaway success today. A visit to its portal opens avenues to purchase from the likes of IBM, Microsoft, Dell, Apple, Sony, Levis, and many other logo-touting giants.

Notice how this description of eBay, taken directly from its "About Us" page, describes the community aspect: "The World's Online Marketplace^{TM} for the sale of goods and services by a diverse community of individuals and businesses. Today, the eBay community includes tens of millions of registered members from around the world. People spend more time on eBay than any other online site, making it the most popular shopping destination on the Internet."

As such, it has attracted many an entrepreneur. In June of 2003, as I was watching the evening news, a story on partnerships in this so called "new economy" world we live in caught my eye. The reporter was interviewing small business owners who were setting up shop on eBay. In three out of four cases, a woman, in partnership with her husband, owned the business.

"It's my business," one woman gushed, then, with a twist of her head, added, "HE works for me," indicating the man standing next to her whom she identified as her husband.

In the same story, this comment from Meg Whitman, CEO of eBay, says it all, "Community is growing at a phenomenal rate. It's no longer a flea market." We should all heed her words. She's a Fortune 500 female who knows whereof she speaks.

When she joined eBay in 1998, Meg brought a keen sense of what works online and what doesn't. She came from managing the preschool toy department at Hasbro, Inc., followed by a stint as President of FTD. Meg was instrumental in launching FTD's online presence, making it easy to see that her strength and intelligence, along with a dab of woman's intuition, worked to her advantage.

Meg and women like her recognize the value of nurturing and caring. We find ways to help it empower us, not defeat us. In Meg's case, I believe being a leader in the preschool department of a toy company, then following that with a position of authority in a flower business, speaks significantly to nurturing and caring.

Fortune magazine ranked Meg Whitman the third most powerful woman in business, in 2002. The CEO of eBay, a top Internet success, a Fortune 500 female. What's not to like about that?

OUR OTHER HALF

> **From *Businessweek* online (January 2003)**
>
> ***1 in 3 Wives Now Out Earns her Husband***
>
> **"All talked about how crucial their husbands were to success," says Barbara Stanny (author of *Six Figure Women*, Harper Publishers, 2002).**

The community aspect of our lives is growing exponentially with the tightening of our budgets. The day of the coffee klatch where neighborhood women spent mornings gathered in suburban living rooms sipping coffee while the children played at their feet is all but over. Today, women are gathering in groups online to network and advance their careers or to talk about breast cancer or to congratulate friends on the birth of their new grandchild.

There is a resounding roar coming from these communities. It's the Janes of the world starting new businesses in record numbers. These are home-based businesses, and they include husbands, or significant others. With estimates from the U.S. Census during the late 1990s revealing that couples owned or managed approximately 2 million businesses and the IRS showing an increase in businesses formed by male/female partners up from 433,000 in 1986, to 750,000 in 1997, Jane has something to roar about, indeed.

Technology is the great equalizer, as I have mentioned in *Dickless Marketing* before. Many of the home-based partnerships we see today are getting their start online. Women and their partners are choosing the Internet as their "location", their carefully selected piece of real estate that will give customers convenient access to their businesses. Their 'spot' online, designed and devised for success.

It makes sense. In the dirt world, where can a new small business go to set up shop? To an indoor mall with half a dozen empty storefronts? To a strip mall where traffic is dictated by the weather? These options are money-grabbers—physical space is very costly, both in rent and maintenance, and they are inherently risky, always banking on the "location" to draw in customers. Furthermore, what if the "location" is good, but the store layout is bad? What if the "location" is good, but a fire burns down the building next door making the whole area an eyesore?

Online your Web site is your location. You pay for hosting, yes, but it's far cheaper than rent on office space. Traffic is dictated by how well you attract your core market, an easy job if you follow the rules and guidelines outlined here. But the best part of being online is that it's cost effective and it gives business owners the ability to manage everything from the comfort of their own home.

I'm not saying having an offline presence isn't necessary in some cases. Many businesses need somewhere to stock inventory. Or their services require a physical location for meeting clients. I'm saying you need to get out of that outmoded Dick and Jane mentality that rules the dirt world. Get on board with *Dickless Marketing* and pull women to your online presence and make some sales!

The new millennium is promoting multi-channel consumers, folks who shop while watching TV, while they are on the phone, and certainly, while they're online. Twenty-three million Americans are now shopping both online and off. If there is hesitancy to buy online, some of them will research products online, then buy offline, much like Ellen from Chapter 5. Estimates of spending range somewhere around $500 a pop when they buy offline after researching online. It's business suicide not to have a Web site to sell to these eager shoppers.

Sometimes, being on the Web gives you an advantage that having a physical store can't match.

Case in point: I interviewed Suzanne Clarridge, CEO of www.mybrandsinc.com, a Web site that offers shoppers out-of-stock items no longer available at their local grocery chain. From the moment she thought of the idea back in 2000, Clarridge knew that MyBrandsInc. had to be a Web-based business. Coming from a background in packaged goods at Hefty, best known for its plastic sandwich and garbage bags, she had firsthand product knowledge of sales and marketing in the grocery industry. Her experiences at Hefty sparked the idea of giving consumers grocery products they really liked but could no longer purchase locally.

Clarridge endured the trials of the dot-bomb explosion during the selling of her idea to investors, but she never gave up. MyBrands now has a warehouse, two telemarketers, and two small offices, one for Suzanne and one for her partner.

Today MyBrandsInc. handles orders and fulfillment for 14 manufacturers, including Nestle, Hefty, and Maple Grove Farms of Vermont. Whenever someone calls one of her manufacturers wondering where her favorite food item has disappeared to, the manufacturer refers the caller to the MyBrandsInc. Web site or to the company's 800 number.

"The site attracts a primarily female clientele," Clarridge says. She guestimates the percentages at "57% female, 43% male." The women are mostly over 35 and they never flinch at cost. Obviously purchasing a hard-to-find product isn't done one box or one bottle at a time; MyBrandsInc. sells by the case. The company has a unique concept that is a perfect Internet model, marketed through partnerships with manufacturers. What's not to like about that?

What struck me about Suzanne Clarridge, besides her insight into building a future in a niche market that serves as a great Web-based business, was her willingness to admit that, at the time of our interview, her Web site was "in need of work."

The Web site she had at the time of our interview had been "thrown up" just to get her online with the added database support she needed. Now, "we have to go back and do a redesign for functionality and usability," she admits. She understands that a better Web site can help build business. Manufacturers will be more likely to want to do business with her if her Web site is a clear representation of her business.

"It needs to provide "personal attention and ease of use to the consumer, but should also attract new manufacturers and convince them to sign on," Clarridge told me. She admits that hyperlinks from each manufacturer's site to her own can make or break her success. In this instance, Clarridge could function with only an 800 number, but she would lose out on a lot of attention—the kind of attention a Web site gives to a truly niche market.

In parting, Suzanne confided that she could never have made the progress on her business without the help of her husband, and several senior level males in the food industry who helped her get funding while she was building her business plan. Suzanne found a few good men who weren't tied to that Dick and Jane world of marketing. They recognized a good thing when they saw it, and they encouraged the strong woman who presented it to them to move forward with her dreams.

SPEAKING OF CEOS

After interviewing Suzanne Clarridge, I went back to my mouse-to-mouse survey to check on one specific question. I had asked women: "If you could speak to the CEO of your favorite store, what would you tell him or her?" and I wondered how the answers would relate to *Dickless Marketing* and reaching Dick through Jane, which is what Suzanne does, and does so well.

The answer to that question was repeated by many of the survey participants. That answer was: "Get a Web site!" Suzanne recognized the inherent value of building a company that would be Web-based, which seems to be more than many dirt world CEOs are recognizing.

Some of the women in the survey complained that shopping at their favorite store was not convenient to their daily schedule; it wasn't open late enough or on Sunday. To the CEOs of those stores, I say, "Get a Web site!" A Web site, of course, is open 24x7, 365 days a year.

If a woman can't shop at her favorite store when it's convenient for her, where do you think she is shopping? At your competitor's Web site, that's where.

WE ARE FAMILY

Developing leads and sales through a well-designed, well-thought-out Web site, is easier, faster and cheaper than renting office space and supporting all the other physical requirements of being in business. Women know this, and their willingness to partner with significant others or willing dirt world professionals to build an online business is testament to its effectiveness. The Pointer Sisters put it succinctly in their best-selling record, "We are family," when they sang, "I got all my sisters with me."

Owning a home-based business is growing more popular in the techno-world of e-commerce. Generally, these are businesses composed of a woman on her own, a husband-wife team, or a woman in partnership with a significant other not necessarily her husband.

With this form of business model, and telecommuting becoming easier and easier to manage, it's time to accept that in today's business climate the signature on those company checks just might be a woman's.

> **Little Known Women Entrepreneurs:**
> Ruth Handler
> Martha Coston
> Kate Gleason
> Bridget "Biddy" Mason
> Hattie Carnegie
> Martha Matilda Harper

Traditional business models, back in the days before the Internet became the name of the game, show that women had an influential role in family-owned businesses, whether she was the wife of the CEO, or the mother. The six women listed in the box above were unique in their day. They bucked a system that continually tried to box them in, ultimately bridging the way for women of the 21st century to make the move from the kitchen to the boardroom, sometimes without getting out of our chairs!

Their biographies at http://www.onlinewbc.gov/morestories.html show remarkable courage and persistence, traits women today are just as proud of. The difference today is that women are not only eager to build something solid and unique, we actively do so with our "significant others," men or women who support our dreams and goals.

This is new millennium entrepreneurship where the partnerships can be as diverse as those with groups of several women, those with one woman and a husband or a male business professional, or those consisting of a group of creative individuals, both male and female, brought together by a strong, determined woman leader. Many of the partnerships today began on a truly emotional level, building into a collaboration that serves each partner according to his or her ability. Early studies show that within these partnerships the women continue to perform the same duties they did before the partnership began, and the men, or significant others, fulfill a role that compliments their skills and strengths.

Cooperation and determination is the name of the game; a game women entrepreneurs know well. That's what Mary Anne Shew, owner of Shew Technologies Inc. which designs Web sites for the SMB market in Rochester, New York, had to say about building her technology business, www.shewtech.com.

"After 25 years in corporate America, I realized I was a round peg trying to fit into a square hole. I wanted to help small and medium-sized businesses get on the Web as soon as possible," she told me. Working with a female coach who encouraged her to take "the leap," Shew's business is thriving today, and she continues to give back to the community by belonging to several women's networking groups. And she admits that she knows more about the Internet than she ever thought she could.

Especially impressive is the fact that she credits much of her success to her husband, Dennis. "I couldn't have done it without him," she stated. "He's always there to help me no matter what the problem is." Clearly, this is a case of life- partners unified in moving business forward as equals.

What's not to like about that?

I AM WOMAN, HEAR ME ROAR

Family-owned businesses constitute more than a third of the Fortune 500 and generate 80% of all new job creation and 50% of this nation's gross domestic product. It's easy to see the marketing potential here. Following the tragedy of the Twin Towers in New York City, many people in the U.S. began withdrawing to the warmth and security of their homes, happily nesting in their homes, using technology (VCRs, DVDs, television) to build home-entertainment centers—cocooning, as it were. This social change added another level to the new multi-purpose home and to the women who are at the center of all its activities.

> **"I am woman, hear me roar;**
> **my home is now my store,**
> **my office and so much more!"**

This could be the new battle cry for women of the new millennium. In the home-based business arena, women are taking charge. Welcome to the real age of the Jetsons, where Jane is telecommuting, managing her business through video-conferencing, while her husband and partner, George, is managing the inventory and telecommuters using Instant Messaging and CRM software.

Women want the advantages of earning a living while being there for the kids when they get home from school. These are women tired of the corporate glass ceiling still holding them back—forward-thinking women who view technology as their ticket to financial success, where they can have it all, and on *their terms*!

When I read reports such as the one out of Michigan State University's Department of Marketing and Supply Chain Management (2003), citing "Online Grocery Shopping Showing Fortified Strength," I know that women are one step closer to having it "our way", both in our personal lives and in our professional lives. We already shop online, we're opening new businesses in record numbers, and we value convenience and quality above price. Isn't buying our groceries online just another method of making our lives simpler and easier?

The study from Michigan State states, "Customers of these grocery services are learning to appreciate and value the great convenience, time-savings, improved service and potentially fresher foods." The study doesn't cite gender statistics, but if the majority of those customers aren't women, I'll eat my hat! Honestly, I have been waiting—and waiting—and waiting, for the online grocery industry to finally get it right.

I know I'm not alone in this desire to click a few boxes and have my groceries shipped to my home. The study by Michigan State has me salivating in my computer chair; it openly says that online grocers "can opt to ship products like meat and vegetables directly from distribution centers, resulting in home deliveries of goods that are fresher than those found in a store!"

Imagine my delight when I also came across this article from the *New York Times*, as I was writing this chapter: "Whipping Up Supper, Mouse in Hand." Written by author Michelle Slatalla on September 4, 2003, the article is a firsthand report of how great it is to buy your groceries online (www.freshdirect.com). Slatalla admits, "I was shocked. Like a lot of people, I have pretty much written off online groceries. But that night, as I fought my husband for the last slice of pizza, I couldn't ignore the facts."

The fact is that this is another successful niche market. It serves the Northeast (Long Island, Chicago, Boston, and Westchester) and it's a convenience for busy families and professionals who don't have time to shop at their local store in person every week. Slatalla says customers are buying "an average of 60 items, with an average order size of $143."

At the Quixtar shopping portal we spoke about earlier, purchasing groceries online is as easy as point and click. They are offering staples such as cereal, dry soup, microwaveable meals, frozen pizza and more. Since women instinctively want to replenish their pantry or kitchen cupboards in one fell swoop, women who shop at Quixtar go on to also order those health and beauty supplies which are the biggest online market today. While there, today's woman can click into a partner store, such as OfficeMax, to order her home-based business supplies. By shopping online, she has saved hours of time, and she gets it all delivered to her door. OfficeMax even guarantees overnight delivery!

What's not to like about that? And, how helpful is that going to be to the home-based business owner? The ability to conduct business at home, through the Internet, just got easier. Making dinner just got easier. Ordering office supplies just got easier. Looking at the bigger picture, how much influence is this online grocery and business supply model going to have on online shopping as a whole?

> **One of every 11 women in the U.S. is a business owner. Women-owned businesses showed an annual revenue increase of 32% in 2002.**

Stop and think about the advantages to YOUR business—beyond the convenience of home delivery of your own food and H&B supplies. Think of your business and how running out of printer ink or paper is such a hassle. With just a few clicks of your mouse, you can get all of the sundry items offered at a grocery store, and add your business supplies at the same sitting. It's convenience for convenience sake. Start thinking about how to parlay this into attracting more women to your Web site.

For example, can you offer a link to an online grocery site in your area? Better yet, can you *partner* with the site to share customers? Can you help promote their services, and get a free banner ad on their site? Can you offer their customers free advice on consumer spending or how to protect their identity?

Why not post articles on what's new in the online grocery business and who has this service available now? Talk up the value of shopping online for business supplies, and then show women how easy it is to buy your products, too. Give women who visit you a taste of what's to come, and remind them they heard it from you first.

Offer a forum, a discussion group, or feedback form to find out how the women who visit your site feel about the food industry moving online. Build a rapport by letting them voice their opinion! Remember to monitor and update this value-added information for relevance to your location or region. Be creative—make these new ideas work for you. Getting interactive with us is a win-win situation.

And, if you can do it in our native language, the door to success will only open wider.

CUANDO EL INGLÉS NO ES LA LENGUA MATERNA

"Only one in 20 people worldwide have English as their mother tongue and we are at the point where English is no longer the dominant language of the Internet," according to Global Reach Express http://www.global-reach.biz .

The total Internet world population is purported to be around 648 million. Non-English speaking members make up more than half of that number. In the U.S., I urge you to begin courting Hispanics in community groups.

MediaMetrix, a Chicago-based research firm that routinely reports on Web activity, says: "some 12.5 million people in the U.S. of Hispanic extraction are regular Internet users." That number alone is reason enough to put some of your marketing focus on Hispanics, but when you stop to also realize that this group is America's largest minority group, the big picture begins to come into clearer focus.

Sears understands marketing focus. A July 2003 report in *Business 2.0* focused on the Miami-based host of the Spanish-language TV show, En Casa de Lucy—Lucy Pereda, touted as the Hispanic Martha Stewart. The study at *Business 2.0* calls Hispanics the "most prosperous and fastest-growing minority demographic."

This explains why K-mart is also tapping into this market, joining forces with an as yet unnamed Mexican soap opera star. It also explains why Office Depot has developed a Spanish language site.

The Hispanic market is ripe with prospects. Look at the numbers shown for *The National Association of Hispanic Publications*, found online at http://www.nahponline.org. This non-profit site boasts that it represents "more than 200 Hispanic Publications serving more than 55 markets in 28 states and Puerto Rico with a combined circulation of over 12 million." I like those numbers. Don't you?

One caveat: translation tools online are fallible. Don't insult prospective customers by marketing to them in language from an online translation tool. If the error in word choice doesn't send them clicking away, the awful accent will! For example, General Motors **Nova** is a classic example of the pitfalls that can be encountered if you aren't careful how you approach markets in a language other than your own. It is hard to imagine a worse name than Nova for a car you want to offer to a Spanish speaking public: in Spanish *no va* means *doesn't go!*

> **Look to Superstar J-Lo and her influence on the Hispanic market, and also to Latin singing star Gloria Estefan, who led the way to pop music's recognition of Latino style, for ways to approach women in this market.**

COLOR BLIND

We have already established that the Web is a technological tool with no emotional attachment to you, to your Web site, or to your customers. It bears noting here that the Web is also indifferent to gender and it is also colorblind. I advise you not to be Web-like—develop an emotional attachment to your Web site, and certainly to your customers. Court the hidden female customer, and I am going on record saying that in your goal to get her attention, you should also not be colorblind. Ignoring the growing numbers of African Americans going online is bad business.

If you do not approach the color issue, if you ignore minorities and women because you don't see them in the marketplace, you are already missing out on a good many opportunities.

A February 2003 report from Nielson/Netratings showed that African American numbers online are soaring upwards of 10 million. While they still account for less than Caucasians and Hispanics, this community is a dynamic one and worthy of your attention. In the U.S., broadband Internet access is a driving force for sales online. My research shows that African American households are eager to log on using high-speed access at a greater rate than others; their adoption of broadband jumped 55% in one year.

Forbes magazine notes that this group is earning MBAs in greater numbers than ever before. Better education is also leading to a rise in entrepreneurship. When we look at the numbers, we see that African American women are an untapped group.

> **11% of black women hold executive and managerial jobs today—more than the 9% of black men in those positions. (*BusinessWeek Online* July 2003)**

The fact that black females are succeeding in a white world is a product of "steely determination, unwavering excellence and sista-girl support," according to a *Businessweek.com* article citing optimism as an ingredient in the black woman's march to success. "Ask black women," the report says, "and they'll tell you tomorrow will be a better day."

Keenan Davis, CEO of Unorthodoks Marketing, a Web design firm for the online African-American community, writes in his August 2003 newsletter, "Blacks Online & The Web sites that Serve Them," that, "The online African-American community is more interested in career advancement, professional development, education, family & relationships, entertainment, health care, news and travel information than the general population."

I submit that women of all races and nationalities are among that group. Davis does not break this market down into specific sub-groups or relate it to other minority populations, nor does he need to. It's enough to know that his description applies to a diversity of women, including African Americans, Hispanics, Caucasians, Asians, Native Americans, and many, many more, I am sure. Women in general offer a kaleidoscope of opportunity to Web site businesses that care to take note.

The common denominator for women as well as minority groups is community. Community is what brought us online in the first place. No matter what our age, color or nationality, women are online for a reason—seeking companionship, answers to health issues or family concerns, career advice, political commentary, and, of course, great places to shop.

WOMEN AND PHILANTHROPY

Can you stand to hear it one more time? Women care.

We care about our kids, our husbands, our moms and dads. We care about the dog and the cat, the bird and even the fish. Our caring is often shown in our eagerness to feed the masses (who reminds the kids to feed those fish, now really?). How did food get to be such a comfort tool, anyway? I submit that women, the keepers of the kitchen, made it the answer to depression (chocolate, anyone?), the answer to little Jeffrey's tumble from his bike (here, have a popsicle, it'll take your mind off of that scraped knee), and the ultimate reward for a job well done (cheesecake, chocolate cake, an expensive dinner at a posh restaurant).

Megatrends for Women talks about this need we have to feed the world. "Women have an instinctive desire to feed," according to Alice Waters, owner of Berkeley's Chez Panisse restaurant in San Francisco. "Women are more concerned with whether people like their food than with making a statement." Consequently, women are always looking for good things to offer to their families, whether it's groceries, toys, or health and beauty items.

It all comes back to caring. In our role as caretaker, we feed everyone in an effort to generate smiles and happiness. This need to take care of the world has U.S. women focusing our energy outward, looking for ways to affect social change for the better.

> **In 1997, women represented more than half of all foundation's CEOs, doubling their percentage since 1982.**
> **~Women's Philanthropy Institute 2002**

The Women's Philanthropy Institute says we make up 1.3 million of the top wealth in the U.S. Our combined net worth is almost $1.8 trillion. Factoring in women's longer lifespan, the Institute says that leaves us in charge of as much as $41 trillion over the next 50 years.

That caring gene—if we can call it that—the one that dictates the drying of children's tears and the holding of elderly parents confined to a hospital bed—plays a prime role in how we share that wealth. In *Marketing to Women,* Martha Barletta writes, "Somewhere along the way, women were handed the 'guardian of civilization' cloak. It's generally agreed that when it comes to the altruistic stuff, women are in charge of everything: the earth, the arts, and the unfortunate; morality, spirituality,  culture, and civilization—you name it, women are on the committee."

The Business and Professional Women's Association reports that "women business owners are philanthropically active: seven in 10 volunteer at least once per month; 31% contribute $5,000 or more to charity annually; 15% give $10,000 or more. Women are also more likely to serve in volunteer leadership positions than men."

While research online shows that women are focusing much of their charitable spending on their own gender, especially on young women and girls, we are also participating in local community efforts to support our favorite causes. That cause may be Humane Society improvements because we're animal lovers, or better food for the soup kitchens, or actively supporting the United Way; regardless of what the cause is, you will find women on the planning committee, or serving in supporting roles making phone calls and writing letters.

Showing community spirit by supporting charity and non-profits is a good way to get women engaged in your business. We like to do business with companies that are environmentally aware, companies that get involved in recycling, senior issues, children's issues, animal rights, the list could stretch for pages. A good place to begin learning how you can help is to start at The Hunger Site http://www.thehungersite.com/. This site is a favorite of many women I know, but I was introduced to it by one of my brothers-in-law. Environmental and community issues are areas that everyone cares about. You should too.

The point is, whether you support world hunger or your local soup kitchen, women in particular need to know that you care. We like sites that show involvement in charities, fundraisers, and non-profits.

Over one-half of U.S. non-profits will increase their fundraising efforts in 2003, and 43% will spend more on technology.

As a caveat, be aware that the Web is a good way for legitimate charities and non-profit organizations to reach out and get attention, but, increasingly, unscrupulous scam artists are using the Web to pad their personal bank accounts. Women want to help you raise funds, but if you fail to exercise due diligence and we get caught in a net of chicanery because you lured us into a scam we will all lose, but you will lose most of all, because we will never trust you again.

When searching for a cause online, or when approached by a charitable organization asking for funds, do yourself a favor—don't be fooled by fancy Web graphics and animation or by a site that harbors on the maudlin. True charity and non-profit organizations are upfront in their appeals. Check with http://www.give.org to see if the site is listed, and then look for a copy of the IRS form 990 at http://www.guidestar.org or http://www.nccs.urban.org/990.

True charitable organizations and non-profits are up front in their appeals. They have legitimate *terms and conditions;* read them. Then check out their privacy statement—look for the "opt-out" clause—before agreeing to anything.

WHAT WE LEARNED IN THIS CHAPTER

- o Women share thoughts, feelings, and ideas in numerous *community* settings online.
- o Hispanics and African-Americans are part of the growing success of diversity online.
- o Women are caregivers; we care about charity and non-profits and if you care about them, too, you'll win our favor.
- o Women have been entrepreneurs for more years than you have been in business.
- o Today's female entrepreneur is working her business hand in hand with a partner, most often a husband or a significant other.
- o Send chocolate. Or cheesecake: divita@windsorenterprises.com

8. Risky Business

Ignore Jane's Buying Power at Your Own Risk!

By means of electricity, the world of matter has become a great nerve, vibrating thousands of miles in a breathless point of time ... The round globe is a vast ... brain, instinct with intelligence!" ~ Nathaniel Hawthorne 1851

- Consumables Market Takes Larger Share of E-commerce (CyberAtlas, January 2000)
- Internet Advertisers Target Women (CyberAtlas, January 2000)
- Online Holiday Shopping Rings Up $13.8 Billion (Newsbytes News Network, January 2002)
- Victoria's Secret Leads Apparel Web sites in visits, NetRatings Reports (Internet Retailer, June 2003)
- Online Retail Keeps Getting Better (Internet Retailer, June 2003)
- Shoppers Look for Deals Online, but Usability Determines Where They Buy (Internet Retailer, June 2003)
- Online Catalogers are Most Profitable E-Merchants (Shop.org, May 2003)
- 80% of Paid Search is Controlled by Hundreds of Thousands of Small, Niche and Regional Businesses (MarketingSherpa, August 2003)

I've heard it said that risk is the price you pay for opportunity. In a world caught in the hype of a new emerging technology, connected from one side of the globe to the other, and teeming with women, I hope you have figured out that continuing to ignore

Jane's buying power and her willingness to shop online is truly risky business.

By the time you read this book, there will be new stats and new reports, but in September of 2003, I can tell you that with the Christmas season approaching, Jane is already on the lookout for online bargains.

I know this because latest reports from the aggregate shopping site, BizRate.com, showed that women dominated sales online during the second, third and fourth quarters of 2002. They issued that report in July of 2003.

It's easy to see why women are dominating sales online. Women control most of the spending in the home and influence 90% of what they don't control, both at home and at the office. From the stay-at-home Mom to the middle manager to the VP of Finance, women command marketing dollars that they could be spending at your Web site, if only you would market to them correctly!

The woman pictured here is probably ordering online. She just happens to be on the phone utilizing her favorite Web site's 800 number.

When you factor in the realization that opening business for yourself is inherently risky, recognizing the sales opportunities in marketing to women is just good business sense. You may have the greatest idea, the greatest product, and the greatest service in the world, but if you fail to get it in front of the right people, *at the right time,* especially women, your success will be a vain struggle.

No matter what products or services you're selling, without a notable presence online you are already behind your competition. If you are represented well online but you aren't focusing some of your marketing dollars on the largest consumer demographic in the world, you are risking a chance to make thousands of dollars more than you would be making otherwise.

For a very short recap on who makes up the largest, most willing demographic spending online: she's female, she's friendly, and she likes free stuff. Make friends with Jane—remember how we spell friend in *Dickless Marketing:* S-A-L-E-S.

In this chapter, I dig deeper into the statistics above to reveal their inherent truths about online sales, and to support the reasons you should be spending more time, thought, and cash on marketing to women.

CONSUMABLES MARKET TAKES LARGER SHARE OF E-COMMERCE (CYBERATLAS, JAN 2000)

We live in a consumer society; consumption drives our entire economic process. What are consumables and who buys them? Consumables are those products human beings use up on a daily basis and need to buy every day, in order to consume them again.

Consumables include things like health and beauty aides, an industry already identified in *Dickless Marketing* as an online bonanza, but it also includes health*care* and medical products, groceries, household goods, gourmet food, and pet supplies. Within this list, I can identify dozens of items that I, along with millions of other women, shop for on a weekly basis—items such as cosmetics, toiletries, paper towels, aspirin, Tylenol, ibuprofen, cold remedies, dog food, cat food, Guinea pig food, personal hygiene articles, and so much more.

Jane and her sisters are the undisputable leaders in purchasing consumables. Anyone who cares to dispute that fact can talk to my mother, any one of my sisters, the dozens of women who filled out my survey, his or her own mother, etc., etc., etc., as King Mongkut of Siam was fond of uttering in the popular musical, *The King and I* (Rodgers and Hammerstein, 1951). King Mongkut was a powerful man with numerous wives, but it was the English governess who held him spellbound and influenced both his personal and political decisions.

No doubt, if she were advising the King today, the governess would advise him to invest in consumables. In the still emergent sales world of the Internet, online retailing of consumables is the aisle with the most traffic.

You don't have to sell a huge variety of consumables to attract women to your site and get them to buy from you. You don't even have to advertise consumables to get us to buy from you. Brainstorm ways to talk about consumables. Do you have a pet at home? Talk about your pet. Talk about buying pet food online. Give us a reason to commiserate with you. We're more likely to buy your products, if we see that you're someone just like us.

For example, if you are a service-oriented company, offer relevant information on the growing acceptance of shopping online for consumables, and segue it into a description of how you, or your wife/mother/sister or significant other, find shopping online for these items so much easier. Then, smoothly bring the reader back to your service. Reel her in with language that lets her know you understand her. If you both shop online, you have a connection already.

> Spending on consumables claims 56% of online shoppers' sales dollars.

Studies show that consumers who shop online for consumables also spend more of their cash online for goods such as office supplies, home and garden tools, sporting goods, jewelry, and clothing. We will talk about which gender spends more money on clothes later on. (As if you don't already know!)

At the very least, consider offering a link to information on how to make judgments on the consumables we may be purchasing online. Or sell your products to us using consumables as a lead in. Mary Lou Quinlan, in her book *Just Ask a Woman* (New Jersey: John Wily & Sons Inc., 2003] says, "For many women, the Internet has evolved into a surrogate friend to be called on for reinforcement or validation."

Make friends with us. You won't regret it.

INTERNET ADVERTISERS TARGET WOMEN (CYBERATLAS, JAN. 2000)

In terms of Internet time, looking at statistics from 2000 may seem counterproductive. If the Internet is "real-time," shouldn't the information on it be "real-time" also?

The statistics cited in this book were gathered from the most reliable sources on and off the Internet, sources which spend a great deal of time and money studying what Web surfers do as they surf the Internet. However, the time required to complete marketing studies can range from a few weeks to a few months. Therefore, a study done in 1999 and reported on in 2000 may seem to be reporting "old news" when, in reality, it is the most recent news available.

By following advertising news over the last two years we can see a shift in Internet marketing away from men towards women. *PC Magazine,* in their August 2003 issue, showed a "Tallying Up Online Sales" chart that listed clothing, including shoes, as the leading product being bought online. Clothing sales took 50% of U.S. spending dollars. Computer hardware and software, books, concert or theater tickets [including movies], CDs or DVDs, consumer electronics, flowers, home-delivered groceries, stamps, and pet food were the rest of the items in the chart.

Consider which gender spends the most money on clothes; it's women, that's a no brainer. Yes, I know young men are more clothes-conscious today, but women's closets are still bigger, still jammed with more "stuff" and, in the end, women are the ones buying skirts, shirts, and suits for all of the other family members, including sons and husbands.

A March 5, 2002 press release out of Burbank, California, "Cyber Dialogue Research Commissioned by Disney Online Reveals How America's New Cyber-Family Looks to the Web for Information, Entertainment, and Influence on Purchasing Decisions," shows that women, moms in particular, (haven't I been telling you moms love being online?) are using the Web for research, shopping, and communication.

The press release goes on to say, "During the past six months, 86% (of women) say they made an online purchase while 85% said they clicked on an online ad." Ken Goldstein, executive vice president of Disney Online, is quoted in the release saying, "The Internet is fast becoming the most powerful, cost-effective medium for reaching today's cyber family and particularly the moms who influence the overwhelming majority of all family purchases." Clearly, the social *and financial* power of women is being recognized at last.

Further supporting the move to reach women online, the American Homeowners Association in October of 2002 formed an alliance with the popular woman's portal, iVillage. This alliance guaranteed AHA a "minimum of 8 million monthly impressions."

Who wouldn't like 8 million monthly impressions on their Web site? Get over to iVillage and discover how you might be able to form a partnership with them. http://www.ivillage.com/partners

> **"The trend in American demographics has more single female heads of household and working couples," says Greg Bibas, vice president of business development for the American Homeowners Association. (October 2002 Reed Business Association)**

These figures show not only why you should be marketing to women, but also why you should be advertising on women-specific sites such as the ones suggested in Chapter 7. In addition to those sites, Media Metrix and AdRelevance show these sites (in no particular order) as high traffic Internet property that attracts women visitors:

o Onhealth.com	o Valupage.com
o Freeshop.com	o Kbkids.com
o ToysRUs.com	o Etoys.com
o Coolsavings.com	o Egreetings.com

ONLINE HOLIDAY SHOPPING RINGS UP $13.8 BILLION (NEWSBYTES NEWS NETWORK, JAN. 2002)

During the last few decades I have seen Christmas go from a mid-winter holiday starting after Thanksgiving, to a long winter holiday beginning at Halloween and stretching through the first few weeks of January. It's a season full of inspirational music, family get-togethers, good food, camaraderie, and, of course, shopping.

Despite the state of the economy at any given time, it's a good bet that women all over America will open their wallets for some serious shopping during the months of November and December. In our family, we anticipate the after Christmas sales, always saving a little mad money for the January markdowns.

According to a Nov. 2002 report found at http://www.conference-board.org/index.cfm, a Web site that "creates and disseminates knowledge about management and the marketplace to help businesses strengthen their performance and better serve society," last year [2002] Americans were expected to spend anywhere from $200-500 on Christmas gifts. Online purchases were expected to be highest in books, clothing, shoes, toys, games, and music CDs.

Christmas gift spending throughout the U.S.:*	
New England=	$552
Middle Atlantic=	$496
E.N. Central=	$532
W.N. Central=	$505
South Atlantic=	$489
E.S. Central=	$393
W.S. Central=	$476
Mountain=	$423
Pacific=	$468

*figures represent average planned household expenditures: ConferenceBoard.org

The boomers and seniors were well represented in those figures. The 55-64 year olds were expected to spend the most, (it was determined they had the most cash to spend), followed closely by families with incomes at or over $50,000/year.

Shopping just increases, across the board, during the holidays, despite economic predictions or layoffs. More importantly, people are mousing it instead of malling it. The thought of fighting those crowds, of hanging out in the checkout line for eons and eons, is just too much these days. Women are no longer willing to circle the mall parking lot endlessly searching for a parking place when they can go online and get *all of their shopping done* in the comfort of their own home!

> **Jupiter Media Metrix, January 2002: "Shopping online was up 50% from 2000, with 51.3 million unique visitors per week (Nov-Dec 2002) doing their shopping online."**

We're learning that online spending is following offline spending when it comes to seasonal shopping. Summer in America seems to encourage folks to purchase movie tickets online, check the weather, research Real Estate, and buy consumables. More importantly, the research indicates that apparel sales were up more than 50% in 2003, suggesting a shift from malling it to mousing it.

With online retail shopping numbers continually going up, and with the numbers of women online keeping pace, a logical conclusion is that women will continue to do what they like to do best, shop—only they will be mousing it instead of malling it. As more women become more comfortable with this convenient way to purchase our goods and services, don't you want your Web site to be one of the places we shop?

It won't be, unless you've underlined and studied what *Dickless Marketing* has been telling you.

VICTORIA'S SECRET LEADS APPAREL WEB SITES IN VISITS, NETRATINGS REPORTS (INTERNET RETAILER, JUNE 2003)

The lingerie and other apparel items offered through the Victoria's Secret catalog, also mirrored on its Web site, attract shoppers of both genders. Because of this site's attraction to both genders, it achieved a top unique visitor listing for apparel during the week ending June 1, 2003. During that week, Victoria's Secret logged 460,000 unique visitors.

That's the fun statistic. The great statistic, the one that shows not only do sex and underwear sell well, but jeans and T-shirts do, too comes from OldNavy.com, a site we talked about in Chapter 5. This site placed a strong second, just behind Victoria's Secret, with 454,000 unique visitors.

Following OldNavy.com, Gap.com attracted 400,000 visitors, LLBean.com, scored 256,000, and YourAvon.com, lured in 248,000. The AdRelevance Report (from Nielsen/NetRatings) went on to say that YourAvon.com held visitors for the longest amount of time—30 minutes, 29 seconds.

So, why did the report lead off with Victoria's Secret in the title? Because Victoria's Secret is an attention grabber! Some people think *Dickless Marketing* is an attention grabber. They're right. Attention is a good thing. Get us to your site using creativity, but when you get us there don't try to sell us a bill of goods. Victoria's Secret and *Dickless Marketing* don't dick around with our products and services. We turn your head with our wit and winks, and then we deliver the goods, as promised.

How is this relevant to you, and to getting Jane to shop at your site? There is no doubt about it; retail spending online is going up, up, up. Forrester research predicts that retail spending will go up 26% this year, to $96 billion. In order to manage that increase, smart sites are introducing customer relationship software, or improving what they already have in place.

In addition, since the Internet makes shopping so accessible and so varied, you need to know which sites are making the most impact, and how long people are spending on them. Victoria's Secret, Old Navy, The Gap, LLBean, and Avon are competing heavily in the women's market. You would be smart to study them and learn how they continue to be successful at it.

The sites are female-friendly by virtue of their dirt world design, but they have replicated that on the Web into a user-friendly site that reflects the growing desire by women to "have it their way." No doubt visitors to Victoria's Secret, male and female alike, get to the site by typing in "Victoria's Secret" or the full URL into their browser. The same is probably true for Old Navy, etc. Women know them and shop at them online and offline. It isn't because they have "brand." These dirt world companies have taken the time to develop a dialogue with women. They speak our language. If you've been paying attention in *Dickless Marketing,* you should have the fundamentals of woman-speak down pretty well by now.

The attention to detail demonstrated in the sites listed above shows the value of learning how to communicate with your core market *in a virtual neighborhood.* No doubt the companies above used focus groups and surveys, but I am sure they also continue to test new approaches and to interact with customers to determine how to maintain or increase the online edge in their market.

Watch them carefully. Their success can easily spill over into your Web site. If you visit each of their sites today, you will see that they engage the shopper, they get personal, and they make the shopping experience easy. Is this true of your site? If it isn't, don't despair. Identify the areas in which you need improvement, and work on them one at a time. The note below can be a first step in improving sales on your Web site.

78% of e-tailers offer in-store returns of online purchases. (Shop.org May/2003)

Remember that your prime goal is to get found. If women don't already know you, or have you listed in their "favorites" folder, studies show they will do a search in a search engine first. Get optimized. Following search engine searches, women often go to an aggregate site—something like CatalogCity.com—and search for specific items, knowing they will be offered in more than one store for comparison shopping. If you want to be included in Catalog City's database, or whatever directory online serves your industry, look for a partner link or open the "About Us" page. Information on how to get included at that site may be in there. Another place these aggregate sites place information is on their "Contact Us" page. At CatalogCity, there is a "Become a Merchant" link on the homepage, in the upper right corner.

We shop at Victoria's Secret, Old Navy, the Gap and Avon, because they are familiar to us. We would be happy to get familiar with you. But we would like to be introduced first, thank you just the same.

ONLINE RETAIL KEEPS GETTING BETTER (INTERNET RETAILER, JUNE 2003)

A June 2003 article in *Businessweek online* reported that "Every year millions more people around the world use the Internet to interact in more ways than ever before, incorporating it into all corners of their lives."

Internet Retailer supports that view with this note: "Online sales continue their acceleration, up 40% for the week ending July 27."

August 2003 reports were showing a strong audience for back to school shopping. Once again, we see Old Navy represented, with 614,000 unique visitors August 3rd through the 9th. Aggregate shopping site Buy.com sponsored a "Back to School Superstore" which generated 1.2 million unique visitors. A senior analyst at Nielsen/NetRatings was quoted saying, "Even as overall retail sales tick up, consumers continue to be value-driven and look for deals and discounts online."

Spending online dominated the entire shopping year for 2002. Jane and her friends showed an overall spending rate of 55% compared to 45% for Dick and his friends. Who should you be getting your marketing message in front of, again?

B2B SPENDING IN HIGH HEELS

Let's not forget women entrepreneurs. Within the bigger e-commerce arena, B2B is a viable, strong market, and women are a large part of it. The number of companies owned by women jumped 11% to 10.7 million (twice the rate of all companies, according to the Center for Women's Business Research), making one in eleven U.S. women a business owner.

> **24% of women in business said technology assisted them in improving their marketing efforts, compared to 17% of men entrepreneurs.**

Women-owned businesses are financially sound, they have proven themselves credit-worthy, and they are eager to get established and grow their business buying the same products and services their male colleagues buy. Women business owners are also more likely to have an Internet presence than men. Women-owned businesses have a more diverse employee structure, and they like buying online. When seeking out the technology to run their business, women are more likely than men to use the Internet.

Women-owned businesses, many of them entrepreneurships and online retailers, employ more than 18 million workers. Those workers need desks, computers, monitors, desk phones, headsets, cell phones, PDAs, briefcases, pens, pencils, paper, office supplies, and all the other materials needed to operate a business.

Even Web-based businesses need supplies—a virtual office doesn't run itself, no matter what people tell you. Virtual office space requires Web hosting, a Webmaster, encryption tools, a privacy statement, a merchant account at a bank, software, hardware, phones and/or e-mail capability with chat or IM; they need copy writers, newsletter managers, sales people, and telemarketers to satisfy their women customers.

> Mother Teresa was an active, successful fund-raiser. She knew the power of money and its ability to effect social change.

SHOPPERS LOOK FOR DEALS ONLINE, BUT USABILITY DETERMINES WHERE THEY BUY (INTERNET RETAILER, JUNE 2003)

When women shop we want value, convenience, and respect. Yes, we buy a lot of clothes and shoes, and we shop routinely for toys, but don't revert back to those old Dick and Jane days of thinking those are the only things we purchase.

Looking at a March 2002 report from *E-commerce Times*, identifying itself as "The E-Business and Technology Supersite" (www.e-commercetimes.com), readers might come away with the idea that being big spenders on clothes means we don't buy big-ticket items. Yes, as this quote says, "Clothes will become more popular among Web shoppers as women— who spend more on apparel than men— conduct more of their shopping online," women like to buy clothes. But note this quote: "online purchases of kitchen products, small appliances and large appliances, all of which are popular with women and older consumers," is expected "to show strong growth over the next five years."

My mouse-to-mouse survey said the same thing. A majority of the women who took the survey said they were quite capable of buying big-ticket items: cars, refrigerators, lawn mowers, computers, etc., without the man in their lives standing there giving them advice. I will admit that they also said they would often take a man—husband, brother, uncle, whathaveyou—with them when making bit-ticket purchases. This was only because many sales professionals still live in that Dick and Jane world.

American Road and Travel provides a list of demographic highlights in a "Female Buyer Study" on its Web site, http://roadandtravel.com showing that:

- o Women spend $300 billion annually on used car sales, maintenance, repairs and service.
- o Female buyers are the fastest growing segment of new and used car buyers today.
- o More than 53% of all women use the Internet to research product information and resources online compared to only one-third of female buyers reading a print automotive magazine.

I remind the reader that women buy for more than just themselves. In many instances they are buying *for someone else*. Consequently, you will find women online looking at lawnmowers, PCs, shoes, baby clothes, business suits, gift baskets, pharmaceuticals, consumables, and even cars.

The key to getting us to click the "buy" button and not abandon our shopping cart on your Web site is in the ease and functionality of the shopping experience. I touched on this topic in Chapter 4, "You Don't Know Dick," where I discussed Web design, but it bears repeating here.

Web design is the equivalent of store layout. When women shop at a dirt world store, we like aisles that are easy to get through with a cart. We like merchandise displayed to its best advantage, making it easy for us to determine at a glance if its something we're interesting in. We like the price to be prominently posted, on the item or on a shelf. We like choices and variety. And we like plenty of cashiers for a quick and easy checkout.

Studies show that not only will visitors to your site abandon their shopping cart if they have a poor user experience they will also stop purchasing from your physical store, if you have one. Remember that Web design is more than pretty graphics, colors, and fonts. Your Web site needs to have eye appeal, it needs to give women a clearly defined purpose—written in words we don't have to look up in the dictionary—nothing fancy or erudite (Erudite? If we have to look up, get rid of it!), easy navigation that moves forward and back in three clicks or less, and a shopping cart we can fill with items, then go back to shop some more, *without losing what we have already placed in the cart!*

A good Web site wants to attract women. To do so, it should have an 800 number with a real live person at the end, ready to answer questions on merchandise size or color shipping, returns, and where to sign up for your newsletter.

> **So long as the merchant provides a good online experience, 29% of online consumers are inclined toward merchant loyalty as well as being relative high spenders. Jupiter Research Inc. (*Retail Consumer Survey June 2003*)**

A good Web site provides value-added information women can use in other areas of their lives. It can be links to consumer reports on products and services, interesting details on your company and how you make the products you make, or an anecdote on how you got started doing what you do, and how your visitor can do the same thing.

It's not about making you look good. It's about information design. Information design refers to all of the elements of building a good Web site including the site's usability and functionality. Web site's look and feel is your introduction to us. We're looking for qualities such as personalization, free shipping, and loyalty programs. When all is said and done, women will not stay on a site that is poorly designed, even if it's selling brand name items the visitor usually buys.

It's because women shop online for the convenience that you need to be aware of these requirements. Just the other day I was discussing my online shopping experience buying groceries with a woman friend and she admitted that she shopped online for—of all things—her husband's underwear!

"It's so much easier to go online and buy it in quantity, than run around to all of the malls trying to find one that carries the brand he likes," she said.

She went on to say she bought her underwear online also, and she most often shopped at Lands' End, because if there was ever a problem she could return the item to her local Land's End store.

What's not to like about that?

ONLINE CATALOGERS ARE MOST PROFITABLE E-MERCHANT (SHOP.ORG, MAY 2003)

Shop.org is the online retailing division of the National Retail Federation (http://www.nrf.com) "the world's largest retail trade association with membership that comprises all retail formats and channels of distribution including department, specialty, discount, catalog, Internet, independent stores as well as the industry's key trading partners of retail goods and services."

The NRF says catalogers are the most profitable e-merchants to date. This information comes from a survey of more than 130 retailers, conducted by Forrester Research. The survey showed that online retailers without stores or mail-order catalogs, referred to as "pure-play" merchants, continued to lose money throughout the fiscal year 2002. Yet, retail sales overall went up 48% from the year before, an increase attributed to sales at online catalog sites.

Catalog shopping has always been convenient and easy. It usually comes with an 800 number and offers clear-cut sale items, often by brand name merchants. It sounds a lot like shopping online! This is another form of multi-channel sales. For the catalog retailers who are moving their catalog products online, it's a sure win-win situation.

First of all, online catalog shopping means less trees being cut down to make the paper used in the print catalog—appealing to a woman's sense of caring about the environment. Second, online catalog shopping utilizes the Internet to promote products, saving the merchant on postage and keeping customers' snail mailboxes freer for that all-important note from Ed McMahon. Online catalog shopping also allows the order to be acknowledged by an e-mail response—*as soon as the shopper clicks the buy button.* This sense of security is something both shoppers and merchants feel good about.

A visit to CatalogCity shows why catalog shopping is popular, and why it's aimed at the female market. Just glance over the product pictures; definitely aimed at the woman in the family. We have a *Fall Preview*, with a man and woman in a playful pose. One space over is a *Get Fit* graphic of a woman in workout gear. The next eye-catcher is *The Outlet*, showing a Sale tag. Following that, the graphic depicting a figure of a woman (headless, but clearly female) toting a large bag, the kind women take shopping with them, shows the header *Specialty Stores.*

Glancing at the left-hand navigation, the top 15 links are arranged in a list obviously geared towards women:

o Auto	o Food & Drink
o Baby	o Furniture
o Beauty	o Gifts & Occasions
o Books	o Garden
o Clothing	o Health & Wellness
o Collectibles	o Hobbies & Crafts
o Electronics	o Home Improvement
	o Jewelry & Watches

Catalogs are a great way to sell your products. But the reason catalog shopping is such a big success online is because it's another way to make shopping easy for women. We get variety, brand items on sale, personal contact, and unique and unusual items—items that are often not offered in a merchant's print catalog (see Lehmans.com call-out below).

> **http://www.lehmans.com:** **"Your source for old-fashioned, hard-to-find items such as** pickle kegs, grain mills, wooden barrels, hand water pumps, wood cookstoves, heating stoves, canning supplies, **and much, much more. In all, we have over 3000 items online...more items than in our** print catalog!"

It's in the information design. Whether you're selling products or services, whether you have two items to sell, or 200, if you make it easy and friendly for us to buy from you, we will do so. If you can't put together a catalog of your own, partner with others who have similar or complementary products. Those readers who are complaining because they are service oriented and don't sell products, begin putting your expertise into e-docs and e-books. Sell them on your site and at partner sites.

'Nuff said.

80% OF PAID SEARCH IS CONTROLLED BY HUNDREDS OF THOUSANDS OF SMALL, NICHE AND REGIONAL BUSINESSES (MARKETINGSHERPA, AUG. 2003)

The best, as they say, is always left for last. Here is my final reason to fit marketing to women in your plans for the future—which starts today, by the way. In Chapter 4, "You Don't Know Dick," I talked about search engine marketing. This is online advertising at the search engine level. The banner ads and box ads flowing down the right side or across the top of each search page returned in a visitor's search have these ads. This is paid search. Get in front of women using paid search. It works.

This book is not intended for companies with over 500 employees, although they are welcome to read it. I know many of them should read it. But *Dickless Marketing*'s goal is to get more sales for the small-and-medium-sized businesses. It's your opportunity to take your online success to greater heights by marketing to the biggest group of shoppers the world over.

> **Multi-channel retailers reported that the Web influences 15% of their offline sales.**

Not only are women the biggest group of shoppers the world over, we are, statistically, the greatest portion of those thousands of small, niche and regional businesses controlling paid search today.

According to Connie Glaser, author of *When Money Isn't Enough, How Women are Finding the Soul of Success* (DIANE Publishing Company, September 1998), "Women-owned businesses have attracted the attention of American corporations, many of which seek them out as vendors under supplier diversity programs." Remember Chapter 3, where we talked about women qualifying for minority funding? Remember Chapter 7, when we talked about communities and how women gather in them to share business advice, career choices, and shopping tips, all online?

The power of the new millennium woman as entrepreneur is tremendous. We've been talking about her throughout *Dickless Marketing*. She's young and eager to change the world. She's middle-aged and snappy, ready to leave her dead-end job and start her own consulting firm. She's over 50 and qualifies for induction into the AARP (American Association for Retired People) but she isn't ready to retire, she wants to open a florist's shop, or go back to school to get her teaching certificate.

Today's entrepreneurial woman is embracing the Web. To the cynics out there, I remind you, "A cynic knows the price of everything but the value of nothing." Marketing to women is a value proposition. If you know how to approach us, if you learn to speak our language, you will get our sales and, as a bonus, our loyalty—for life.

The *Wall Street Journal* knows it. Writer Jeffrey Zaslow knows it. In his June '03 article, "Staying in Touch: One More Thing That Women Are Better at Than Men," Zaslow says, "Men tend to build friendships until about age 30, but there's often a steady fall-off after that."

Sell to a man today—he will likely buy elsewhere tomorrow.

Further in the article, Zaslow quotes Karen Roberto, director of the Center for Gerontology at Virginia Polytechnic Institute and State University, saying, "If women are friends at 40, there's a strong likelihood they'll be life-long friends."

Life-long friends support each other.

How do we spell friend in *Dickless Marketing?* (try SALES)

Our loyalty, and the loyalty we inspire in friends and colleagues, is real. It's so real that when portfolio manager Helen Young Hayes left the investment firm Janus Capital Group, a number of investors "abandoned" the mutual funds group. Hayes was well known and respected, and she commanded the respect of many well-heeled shareholders. It may be that unanswered questions led the investors, including some with corporate retirement plans, to move elsewhere, but whatever the reason, Ms. Hayes caused a big ripple in the investment firm's business when she packed up her desk and went home.

It's a trust factor. It's a service issue. It's a community focus. Research says that women will buy from you if you offer quality goods at reasonable prices; excellent—not merely *good*—service; if you guarantee privacy and security; and if you show community spirit and support. These are the things we care about, online and off. The thing is, most of us are going online to shop today, so your nice dirt world store is not our first place to look for the things we want to buy.

Market to us as if you actually care.

> **WHAT WE LEARNED IN THIS CHAPTER**
> o E-commerce is expected to increase substantially over the next five years.
> o Consumables, products more women use and buy than men use and buy, command the #2 spot in retail sales dollars online.
> o Women buy more than stockings and toys online. We buy electronics, appliances, cars, and lots and lots of clothes.
> o Women business owners look online for products and services from technology to bookkeeping.
> o Women like catalog shopping because it's easy and convenient. Use information design to mimic catalog shopping, or partner with another company.
> o Our loyalty is not for sale. It comes with the territory when you make friends with us.

9.   Can You Handle It?

Bad, Baad Web sites! Are YOU Guilty of these Mistakes?

Let us be thankful for fools. But for them the rest of us could not succeed. ~ Mark Twain

In this Chapter, I examine several Web sites for information design, including functionality, navigation, content, and whether or not the site is female-friendly. I selected these sites by doing a Google search on selected keyword phrases appropriate to women's issues, then clicking on several of the top 20 sites each phrase returned. After going through these sites, going as far as attempting to "buy" from them to see how easy or hard the purchase process was, I made my choice to focus on the following sites. The best part, of course, is always saved for last. So don't miss the final review at the end of this chapter. It includes a review of a site that's a winner in all categories of being female-friendly. Make sure you check it out to see why.

The scoring was done on each section of the sites, using the *Dickless Marketing* Dick-e-meter 5-point scale:

5 = Excellent.

4 = Good job, but needs improvement in certain areas.

3 = Too egotistical; the Web is not about YOU, it's about THEM.

2 = Okay, you're on the Web, but — who cares?

1 = Works better as a 404 page ("404 page not found" is an error indicating the page searched for does not exist on that server).

Section scores were added together to provide an overall score at the end of the review.

Dick-e-meter elements scored are:

  a) Information design: Visual appeal using color font and white space. Also, functionality and indication of company purpose and what it sells.

  b) Navigation: Are links easily recognized and clickable? Do they compel the visitor to act?

  c) Real Estate: How effective is the layout of the homepage? Is the content easy to read? Does it speak to the visitor? Are there clear indications on how to view and buy products?

  d) Company Information: Do I know at a glance what this company does? Does the URL match the content on the page? Is the content useful information? Is there a call to action?

  e) Contact Information: Is there an 800 number and/or an e-mail address to connect me to an actual person? Does the site show consideration for me, for my time, and for my wallet?

Since *Dickless Marketing* is aimed at the small to mid-sized business market, readers may wonder why I am beginning this section with a review of a luxury site.

First of all, I believe in dreams and I hope all of my readers are dreaming of the day their business becomes so successful it affords them the opportunity to shop at or compete with a luxury site such as Gucci's.

Second, many people look to the Fortune 500 companies as standards on which to model their own business. Certainly new business owners can look to the leadership of IBM, Microsoft, Coca Cola,

McDonald's, and Starbucks, as well as many others, as models of business success.

Third, one of the areas showing outstanding success on the Web is women's designer jewelry, handbags, and accessories. This convinced me that a review of a known designer's site would help readers learn something about how women shop online, and what needs to happen before they will buy from you online.

Fourth, as I was researching for sites to review, I came across an article in the *Wall Street Journal* noting that luxury retailers were reluctant to go online. According to the article, luxury items did not transfer well to the Web because shoppers need to actually "touch and feel" them before they will buy. Right away I wondered, don't those of us with less than million dollar incomes need the luxury of touching and feeling our merchandise, too?

Of course, we do. Therefore, the only conclusion I could come to was that companies that sell luxury items don't understand the Web. A site that allows the shopper a sense of touch and feel is vital to any site hoping to attract and sell to women.

WWW.GUCCI.COM

Since Gucci was mentioned in the *Wall Street Journal* article, I surfed on over to its site and began my review. The Gucci.com site is a good example of a company serving a wealthy female clientele successfully offline, but not even coming close online. Here's why.

a) DESIGN: On download, my pop-up stopper killed a pop-up, which turns out to be the true entrance to the site. (I closed the pop-up killer and re-entered the site to see what I'd missed—it was the doorway into the site.) After enabling the pop-up, I waited patiently, staring at a totally black screen, until I was finally rewarded with another totally black screen shot showing the word "Gucci" in white text.

In the prime real estate section of the site were the words: "Step inside our new online store" in tiny white text. A note beneath that sentence informed me, "At present, purchases available in the continental United States only." Below that sentence, was an even smaller link inviting me to "enter." I entered.

The entire site is done in Macromedia Flash, which opens and closes the frame, sliding from left to right, to display product depending on the link clicked. On the next page that opened up, I was entranced by a picture of an attractive, smiling woman holding a baby. The model was dressed for a brisk fall walk, but the baby was naked. Of course I know that Gucci is a designer of men's and women's clothes, but the smiling woman and her cute baby did little to tell me so.

I immediately looked for the "buy" button. The only indication that the site offered product for sale were the words "fall winter" in tiny white lettering on the left hand navigation bar. Below it were the words, "Shopping bag," which I took to indicate the presence of a shopping cart. Clicking it took me to another shadowy page that indicated I had no items in my shopping cart. I went back to the "homepage" where a new model appeared, also holding a naked baby. The new model was blond and not nearly as attractive as the original woman on the first page I had viewed. Is this the reward for progressing through the Gucci site?

Realizing that the entire site is a Macromedia Flash presentation, including the navigation links, left me wondering what the designers were thinking when they designed it. Using Flash throughout leaves the site out of the search engines' purview. I guess Gucci is so famous the company doesn't care about being found in the search engines.

Out of curiosity, I did a Google search to see where the site placed. I used the company name as my first search term. It brought up the Gucci URL right away. Clicking on that took me to that horrible black page where the word enter is supposed to be, but—this time, offered only a broken link. Three other searches using terms I thought women would use to find Gucci were unsuccessful in returning a URL that even pointed to the site. I searched on "NY Designers," "Designer Leather Jackets, NY" and "Women's Designer Clothes, NY." The Gucci URL was nowhere to be found. The site is invisible to the search engines, and by default, to anyone who doesn't know the URL. Gucci may like it that way, but the company is failing to get in front of the women it wants to reach by limiting access to only those who know the URL already, or who learn it through a visit to a dirt world Gucci store.

I clicked through a few more pages on the site; both on the men's and the women's fashion side, but I found the overall design of white text (or gray, it was hard to tell) on a fully black background ominous and depressing. Page after page of models in badly done make-up did not inspire me to buy. A friend commented that the site and the models reminded her of badly dressed mannequins. Leaving aside questions about the actual clothing or handbag/shoe designs, I can personally say the site made everything surreal, leaving me anxious to move on to the next site. But there was still more Gucci to see.

The Gucci site may be a designer's dream video, but after that first friendly screen of the woman and the baby, the design spiraled into a nightmare of dark images and poorly presented product. To add insult to injury, after many, many page views showing ghastly runway models, I was blocked from purchasing by not having my very own personal shopper. More on that in the Real Estate section. **Dick-e-meter rating: 2**

b) NAVIGATION: Site navigation is sparse. Links are limited to tiny white text on the left, which repeats throughout the site. Since the site is done completely in Flash, one is forced to endure the opening and closing of each window as the movie slips a gray shadow from left to right each time one wants to access a new page. Even with my broadband Internet connection, this repeated opening and closing of screen shots took more time than I would have been willing to spend, had I not been reviewing the site.

In an effort to keep track of the navigation options, and to try to get a clearer picture of some of the designs, I took advantage of an option to print the page. I was rewarded with a totally black piece of paper. No text, no product, nothing but a big black box and a few white boxes where the text and product should be.

This site has no "Home" button. The opening and closing of each new window takes the shopper back to that navigation bar, so technically, you never leave "home." **Dick-e-meter rating: 2.5**

c) REAL ESTATE: What real estate? Real estate consists of the totally black background and a few graphic images of male and female models on a runway. The only invitation to buy comes from a "buy product online" link. Clicking it took me to a statement saying the site only offers handbags for sale online. To buy one, I was asked to contact a "personal shopper" via e-mail. The personal shopper, I was told, would then contact me when my item was available. **Dick-e-meter rating: 1**

d) COMPANY INFORMATION: The "About Gucci" link led to a nice history of the company. I found this section of the site interesting. It contains short paragraphs describing the company's progress from the 1920s to the present, accompanied by graphics from each decade—a nice touch. **Dick-e-meter rating: 2**

e) CONTACT INFORMATION: Clicking the "Store Locations" link opens a flat map of the world. The visitor needs to mouse over the map to see which section lights up a possible link to a Gucci store location. Clicking on a country causes the rest of the map to disappear, focusing then on the country chosen. Separate text links appear, then, showing where one can shop at a Gucci store in that country.

The "Client Service" link offers clients in Europe an e-mail address. Clients in the U.S. are advised to contact their closest Gucci store. **Dick-e-meter rating: 1**

So much for luxury. Gucci may not care that their site is unattractive, unappealing, and female UN-friendly, but they should. No matter how big and important your business is, your clients should still come first.

Dick-e-meter rating overall: 7.5. This site is not female-friendly.

When some of the readers of this book get to be multi-millionaires by getting women to flock to their sites and spend lots of money on their products and services, I hope they will still treat us with kindness and consideration.

WWW.ATOUCHOFHOMECRAFTS.COM

Many of the women in my family are wild about crafting, and I know from spending weekends with my sister that as a hobby or a business, crafting is popular with women. So I feel a special connection to what is supposed to be happening at this site. Although the site may attract its fair share of men, "A Touch of Home Crafts" sounds very female to me.

a) DESIGN: I really like what Cheryl, the site owner, is trying to accomplish. The wallpaper background and fancy scripted font convey a homey, kitchen-like environment. Unfortunately, it also detracts from the purpose of the site—to sell Cheryl's products.

The words on either side of the center paragraph—the site introduction—are links to other pages, but only a seasoned Web shopper would know that. The text introducing Cheryl and her site is itself an issue. The gray text on the printed background disappears. And, while being quite chatty, it's too full of "me, me, me." I need Cheryl to tell me more about her craft experience, and how her products are going to look great in my kitchen or my family room. Shoppers still want to know, "What's in it for me?"

If Cheryl extended her first sentence to include more gift ideas, "Whether you're looking for a birthday gift, a baby gift, an anniversary gift, or a housewarming gift, you'll find lots of great stuff here!" I would be more willing to click those side links to discover more of what she has to offer. Instead, she talks about country wood signs with "witty sayings" and "clichés", then moves on to a sentence promising to introduce more of her "favorite creations." What if her favorite creations are not MY favorite creations? Then she loses me right there on the homepage.

Since she has no way of knowing the answer to that question, and doesn't even ask it anywhere on the site, I advise her to give her visitors a voice by supplying a feedback form.

The two opposing links located on the bottom left and on the bottom right of the page are more compelling than her other links because they are more eye-catching, but "Nurse Angels" and "Teacher Gifts" do not a call to action make. It would help if Cheryl added the word "buy" to them. On monitor settings of 800x600—and many of Cheryl's core market customers are using this setting—these compelling links are **below the fold**. I fear folks who fail to scroll down are missing them. **Dick-e-meter rating: 4**

b) NAVIGATION: I consider myself a savvy Web surfer. But when I get to a site that does not have clearly defined links across the top of the page, or along the right-hand or left-hand border, I get frustrated trying to figure out how to move around the site. In Cheryl's case, it took me a few seconds to realize her fancy-fonted words were links. Since I found the text on the homepage difficult to read, I did not spend much time on it, and did not see her statement at the end explaining that the words are links. I wonder how many other visitors fail to read all the way through that text?

Cheryl's effort to be original and creative is losing customers for her. By focusing on what she does as a crafter, instead of what the customer might want to buy, Cheryl is underselling her own products. **Words as links, with no accompanying text, can be more confusing than helpful.** Her other problem is that she makes getting back "Home" difficult since the only pages with a HOME button are the ordering pages. **Dick-e-meter rating: 3**

c) REAL ESTATE: I have mentioned before that your homepage is prime real estate on the Web. In Cheryl's case, she has set up shop in a popular strip mall that has the potential to bring in hundreds, if not thousands, of visitors, but she's put out a sign that few, if any, visitors can read as they stroll casually by.

In addition to the gray text competing with the striped wallpaper background, the page does not offer an "About Us" link, a "Contact Us" link, a "Shopping cart" link, or any value-added content to back up Cheryl's claim to credibility—that she's been in the business for over eleven years. The site is designed for Cheryl's tastes, not for the shopper's experience.

I did click farther into the site and viewed some of her products, which left me wanting more; not more Cheryl, more descriptions and better graphics. Cheryl is a talented woman. She has many adorable products for sale, but the display of her dolls and other crafts do not do them justice. If she would only place the dolls on a child's bed, or show a child playing with one, the shopper would feel more personally connected to them.

In addition, a description next to each product, with a call to action: "On sale this week only," or "Specially priced for Thanksgiving," would help improve sales. **Dick-e-meter rating: 3**

d) COMPANY INFORMATION: Other than the sentence or two on the homepage, I learned nothing about Cheryl. I do not know how trustworthy she is. I do not know how she got started in crafting, nor how she chooses what style of dolls she makes, nor how she chooses the sayings on her plaques. She has many links to other crafting sites, which is helping her ranking in Google, anyway, as you will see from my comment below. The numbers showing on the counters of some of the sites to and from which she is linked show that they get few visitors. This is not a good announcement to make on your site. A conspicuous site counter is a bad thing. If you have one, get rid of it now!

I was happy to see that the description of Cheryl's site as described in my browser window was full of great keyword phrases, not the usual "Homepage" or "Products Page" that some sites use. Using those keywords I did a Google search and Cheryl's site showed up in the top 5. Good work. No doubt, much credit can be given to those shared links I talked about above. A visit to them will show you that Cheryl's site is several steps above many of them, proving that you are often judged by the company you keep. As one of the best sites in the bunch, A Touch of Home Crafts gets priority listing. But, as we've seen so far, this site still needs work.

Shopping on A Touch of Home Crafts was not difficult, but I never received indication that my credit card information would be safely encrypted and the lack of a privacy statement left the shopping experience on shaky ground. Cheryl needs to address these important issues with her merchant account bank, or whoever handles her shopping cart. It's apparent that buying Cheryl's products takes one to a completely different site.

Having a shopping cart handled by an e-commerce company is not a bad thing. Many small businesses out-source their sales process. However, before I click that "add to shopping cart" button, I need to see a privacy statement and have Cheryl's assurance that my personal and credit information is safe with her. Saving it for that last moment when Cheryl wants me to click "submit" might be too long. **Dick-e-meter rating: 2.5**

e) CONTACT INFORMATION: Once into the site to view the dolls and crafts, the shopper will find several links at the bottom of each page offering access to "e-mail," "products," and "home." Cheryl also has a link to e-mail her right on the homepage but this address is from MSN, not from A Touch of Home Crafts. On her "ordering information" page Cheryl has a postal address.

Visitors with questions may call Cheryl at a number she provides, using their own quarter. Cheryl has no 800 number. Cheryl needs an 800 number. Eight hundred numbers are not expensive and having one is a good way to build a personal relationship with your customers. **Dick-e-meter rating: 4**

Cheryl has the makings of a good site here. With some adjustments, a softer background, some personal information, including her picture and a paragraph or two about how she got into the business of crafting, a privacy statement, and a BBB link, I think she could increase her sales substantially.

Dick-e-meter overall Grade: 16.5. Fairly female-friendly.

WWW.ELREYCHOCOLATE.COM

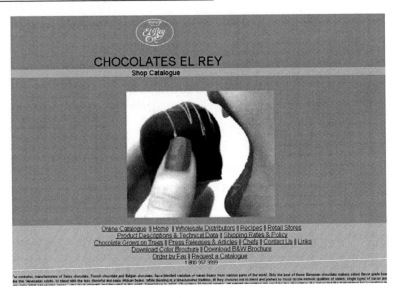

No one likes chocolate more than I do. Not your sister, not your cousin, not your boyfriend, not your neighbor three doors down, not your grandmother in Florida, not the little kid you pass at the grocery store every Wednesday. NO one likes chocolate more than I like chocolate. Which is why this site disappoints me. It makes a lot of promises it never fulfills!

a) DESIGN: The homepage fills the screen with a deep turquoise background. Sixteen text links are set below the prime real estate graphic image. These links are in faded turquoise. The center graphic of a woman ready to take a bite out of a piece of chocolate commands the visitor's attention. It certainly got my taste buds tingling. Chocolate aficionados might imagine, for a split second, that they have entered nirvana.

But it's only a dream. As it goes on, it slowly becomes a nightmare.

In the banner space beneath the site title there is a link to a catalog, showing the visitor right away that the site has product for sale.

Beneath the attention-getting center graphic of a woman taking a bite out of what looks like a truffle to me, those 16 links are crowded together like a run-on sentence. Furthermore, finding them requires shoppers to scroll down even on a monitor set at 1024x768. On monitors set at 800x600, the text gets bigger, causing even more scrolling.

Meanwhile, below the links is a long paragraph attempting to describe Chocolates El Rey company background. Information contained in this paragraph—and there is a lot of good stuff there—is essentially invisible to the reader. The type is so small it gave me eyestrain. It stretches from left to right in one big jumble and even on a monitor setting of 800x600 it may be too small for seniors or some baby boomers to follow.

Few visitors will actually take the time to squint at that text and learn how the chocolates at Chocolates El Rey get made. **Dick-e-meter rating: 2**

b) NAVIGATION: The navigation fares little better than the homepage design. The links set in that crowded group at the bottom of the homepage carry through on every page, but they don't get any easier to read! The links work but the pages that open from them do not flatter this site. Nor does anything on those pages compel visitors to buy.

The densely written paragraph talking about the company and describing how the chocolate is made is carried through to every page also—to what end, I cannot imagine.

Clicking on the links to review the rest of the site gave me no joy. The "Recipes" link offers recipes, but there were empty boxes where the pictures of the product should be. The "Product Descriptions" page was informative, but is presented in a long table requiring extensive scrolling. In addition, the only pictures were of cocoa beans. (A repeat visit several days later displayed the proper pictures until I clicked links that took me to the recipe ingredients and details. Then, once again, I could not view the picture of the end product.)

An attempt to find something that would redeem the site led me to click on the "Download Color Brochure." I received a PDF showing chocolate being poured from a vat. So far, so good. Imagine my disappointment when pages 2-6 were blank.

Not only is Chocolates El Rey losing women shoppers by not displaying its chocolates well, it's making life difficult for us by putting potholes in our way as we stroll through the site. Male shoppers probably click out with the same rapidity they use on their TV remotes when they're searching for a weekend ballgame. **Dick-e-meter rating: 1**

c) REAL ESTATE: Short and sweet—this site is wasting real estate by not presenting text and graphics in an attractive way to get visitor's taste buds tingling. First of all, the site navigation needs an immediate redesign. Put it across the top of the page for immediate, easy viewing, or list it vertically on a left-hand navigation bar, which most Web users are used to. Having a catalog and announcing it up front is good use of the prime real estate section, but there is no real call to action—anywhere on the site!

In fact, entering the catalog section of the site opens up a whole set of new problems. I clicked a few links, but the product I was shown did not seem aimed at home-shoppers. It suited retail restaurants or bakeries better. I did come across a spice called "Mole Rub with El Rey Cacao." Without some explanation of what it was and how to use it, I certainly didn't make any attempt to buy it.

Another failure to use real estate efficiently was glaringly apparent on the "Press Releases and Articles" page. This page has some good content, content that could get this site noticed both by search engines and by searchers, but it's presented in gray print on a turquoise background giving the text shadows that make it difficult to read. In addition, the press release requires scrolling for more than two page lengths. It should be broken up into smaller paragraphs with sub-headings to keep the reader's interest. **Dick-e-meter rating: 2**

d) COMPANY INFORMATION: As noted in the design section, the company information is contained in that densely written, tiny printed paragraph at the bottom of each page. I read it because I was reviewing the site. It was an interesting story. The owners of Chocolates El Rey should consider putting it in an "About Us" page or more prominently on the homepage in 11-point type that everyone can read.

My next goal was to try to buy some chocolate. As one moves through the process, it becomes even more apparent that this site is geared toward retail merchants, yet a bit more searching finally turned up some individual items for sale which I attempted to purchase.

Unfortunately, as I moved through the purchasing process, I became more and more uncomfortable. Nothing on the site gives any assurance that my credit card is protected by encryption. The only privacy notice I could find was on the "Terms and Conditions" page. At the very bottom of that page, I found one sentence reading: "Transaction information provided by you is not shared with third parties." Not good enough. **Dick-e-meter rating: 1**

e) CONTACT INFORMATION: The "Contact Us" page shows information for Venezuela, North America, Japan, England and France. A company doing this much international business should be able to afford a decent Web site. Since I am located in the U.S. I checked out the contact information for North America. My options were to write to Randall Turner, President, in Texas, or call him at what appears to be an 800 number. If I prefer to e-mail him, the address is a hotmail box.

Two other contact names were offered, both with e-mail contact information using a Chocolates El Rey e-mail address. I find it strange and suspicious that the "President" of the U.S. division does not have an El Rey e-mail address. **Dick-e-meter rating: 2**

Chocolate El Rey has missed out on a great opportunity to attract a swarm of women shoppers, and a passel of men shoppers. With a Web site so poorly designed, developed, and produced, it's a good bet that Godiva has nothing to worry about.

Dick-e-meter rating overall: 8. Not female-friendly.

WWW.JOBHUNTERSBIBLE.COM

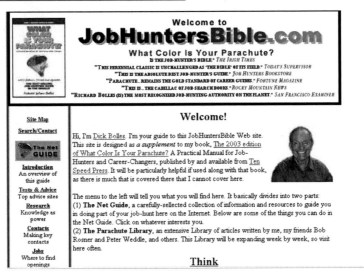

Richard Nelson Bolles, author of the best-selling book, *What Color is Your Parachute?*, doesn't seem a likely candidate for the Bad, Baad Sites chapter of *Dickless Marketing,* does he? He isn't a candidate for this chapter; his Web site is.

There are several reasons I chose his Web site for inclusion in this chapter. I will cover them in the actual review, but for the record, the following evaluation focuses **solely** on the Web site. My review is not intended to reflect any positive or negative comments of Bolles' book, his writing, his personality, or anything else about him.

Because there are more women online than men, and because more women are choosing to become entrepreneurs, I believe attracting more women to his Web site would be to Bolles' advantage.

a) DESIGN: Bolles is on the right track. He has a homepage that conveys its intent as soon as it downloads. I especially like his smiling face beaming out from the top right. It's a genuine smile, not a studio produced headshot taken to make him look younger or smarter or whatever it is those studio headshots are supposed to do for people.

I found the black border around his book and its testimonials off-putting. My guess is he built this (or the designer he hired built it) to make a point—and it succeeds, but how much better would it be if the book itself were the focus, with the testimonials in more readable text below? The real world continues to show that trying to read text in all caps—as Bolles' testimonials are written—is difficult on the eyes. Generally it sends reader's eyes scurrying for something simpler to focus on.

Below the box promoting his book, Bolles welcomes his visitor. Since he's already done that in the book promo, I fail to see why he needs to do it again. From that point on we are treated to a great deal of content. There are several link headers in a centered table explaining what we will find on the inner pages, but their arrangement prevents the reader from easily settling on one topic.

Perhaps Bolles doesn't know that readers don't automatically read a printed page—online or off—they scan in a Z pattern. Reader's eyes start at the top left of the page, move to the right, then skim through the body of the page in a diagonal to the bottom left, finally ending at the bottom right. The bottom right is where the important information should be—think: 1-800-Call Me Now! On this site, we can't move our eyes in that Z pattern—the content forces our gaze to jump around like a Mexican jumping bean.

The very last link at the bottom of the page encourages us to "Learn How to Navigate this Site." When the site owner has to teach visitors how to get around his site, it's a good indication that the site is too complicated. Still, if Bolles had put that link at the top, my life would have been easier. **Dick-e-meter rating: 4**

b) NAVIGATION: Since I found the content on the main part of the homepage too much work to get through, I moved my gaze to the navigation bar on the left. I was happy to see that there were appropriate links to other parts of the site there. The best link is the "Site Map" which is located above the "Home" link. A site map is an excellent tool to help visitors navigate your site. It also serves search engine spiders by sending them to a page that allows them to search the entire site quickly and easily. Unfortunately, the navigation links here have nothing to do with the content in the prime real estate section of the page. They merely offer more information for the reader to assimilate. This is information overload taken to the extreme. Bolles could easily incorporate several of the topics into one, give it a relevant heading and a drop down menu for options, or even a link-tree to give the reader a heads up on what's available and what she will get when she clicks on it.

The navigation links do tempt the visitor to act. They offer career or resume how-tos, solutions, advice, and even spotlight career counselors. The final section of the navigation bar contains three links, one labeled "For more Information," which leads to "Books," "CD-ROMs," and "E-Mail a Counselor." I expected to be able to buy books on the books page, and CD-Rooms on the CD-ROMs page, but it's just not so. The pages offer no product, just more content. (We will get to "E-mail a counselor" in a moment.)

Midway down the navigation bar is a provocative link titled, "Working Wounded." I clicked it out of curiosity and found myself on what—at last!—appeared to be an interactive page. There is a question from a "visitor" which is answered by Bob Rosner, a career consultant, whose connection to Bolles is—a mystery. The site doesn't give one and I did not try to find one elsewhere. The page offers two other "question/answer" links, but they have that musty, attic feel about them—as if they've been around for more than a few weeks.

While this is a content-rich site, it does not sell itself well. Time spent on it is not useful because there is so much to take in. Visitors can easily get confused about what to click on next when information is offered like this; in large sections scattered across the screen and throughout the site. **Dick-e-meter rating: 3**

c) **REAL ESTATE:** Bolles makes poor use of the real estate throughout the site. He maintains the centered table throughout, making it hard on the reader to settle on one topic to click into. A simpler, focused format, NOT CENTERED, would help visitors quickly peruse the possible content, and choose an area to explore.

Once again, that option at the bottom of the left-hand navigation bar (showing a "books" link, a "CD-Rom" link, and an "E-mail a Counselor" link) leads only to more content, not to a shopping cart. My attempts to purchase Bolles' book took me back to the homepage, where I clicked on the book icon and was finally rewarded with entrance to Bolles' publishing company, Ten Speed Press. The book was offered for sale there, nowhere on the Jobhuntersbible site.

Back to the "E-mail a Career Counselor"—this page offers advice from Jim, Carol and Dave, professionals Bolles' describes as having "over 75 years of career counseling between them." As an introduction, it leaves one blinking in wonder. This does not qualify as a handshake. I still don't know who these people are or what their qualifications are. Why would I bother to e-mail them my career questions? On Bolles' say so? Not me.

At one point, I thought I'd ventured into a cartoon site. On the "Tests and Advice" page, there is a "Fairy Godmother's Report," which talks about Career Tests, Personality Quizzes and Salary Surveys. Somehow, I don't feel that career issues, personality quizzes and salary surveys are issues that lend themselves to fixes with a magic wand. The page title works, but the fairy godmother thing is frivolous, and if Bolles insists on keeping it, I ask him to please choose a better image. The one displayed looks more like a cartoon from the 1960's sitcom *Bewitched.* I found nothing fairy godmotherish about that.

Bolles has compiled a great deal of insight and content on jobs and careers; he even includes advice on how to use the Internet, but it's all a puzzling jumble of links and text. It needs better organization and clearer navigation. **Dick-e-meter rating: 2.5**

d) COMPANY INFORMATION: While the Jobhuntersbible.com site is heavy in content, the only company information is the page with a bio of Bolles, and it isn't easy to get to. I finally found it by clicking on the site map where I found an "About Richard Nelson Bolles" link. **Dick-e-meter rating: 3**

e) CONTACT INFORMATION: Contact information is limited to the "Search and Contact" page that allows the visitor to e-mail Bolles or the Webmaster through a link that opens the viewer's e-mail client.

Actually, this can be a good thing. By not having your e-mail address displayed on your Web site, you limit the amount of spam directed your way. Providing a way to contact you is what's important.

Bolles also offers an 800 number, located on the Ten Speed Press site. This is the only actual "sales" area. Purchasing at Ten Speed Press can be done through fax, e-mail, or secure online ordering. So they say. I saw no indication of security. After filling out the form, and waiting for the fulfillment page to download, I was treated to a sentence assuring me that my credit card is secure because it is processed offline. That one sentence promise, stating that personal information, along with credit card information, is safe with him, doesn't do it for me.

I would like a lock, please. Or the **https** indication in the URL where the extra **S** indicates encryption. Or a connection to the BBB. Just something more substantial to protect both my privacy and my credit card information.

Ten Speed Press does have a simple privacy statement, which covers all the bases. Why doesn't Bolles put one just like it on the Jobhuntersbible.com site? Even if he isn't selling anything on the site, he is asking visitors to interact with him through e-mail. He needs a privacy statement. **Dick-e-meter rating: 2**

I wish Bolles had taken as much time developing and producing his Web site as he did writing his book. His site wants to be professional and friendly at the same time. It does not pass the female-friendly test, however. I give him points for offering good content. If only he would improve his site so more of us could benefit from his expertise.

One last note—kudos to his search engine optimization. He is #1 in Google on the search term "job hunting" and #3 on the term "job hunter." Once again, that proves that even an average site can get ranked up at the top of the search engines, if it's optimized properly, and its competitors are not.

Dick-e-meter rating overall Grade: 14.5 Sort of female-friendly.

HTTP://MEMBERS.AOL.COM/COACHMJW/PP22.HTM

To: Coach Michael Wells

From: Dickless Marketing

Re: Your Web site.

Mr. Wells, your site showed up on the third page of a Google search and after looking it over, I couldn't help myself. I knew I had to put it in my Bad, Baad Sites chapter. You have made a valiant attempt at presenting some good stuff to interested folks, but there is a better way.

I hope you will take a second look at what you've produced and go back to make it more female-friendly—after all, girls play basketball, too!

To my readers: This appears to be a homemade page. Coach Wells is to be commended for taking the time and effort to develop something with so much content and such "interesting" animation. Understand that my review is not meant to discredit or insult the coach's attempt to put useful basketball content on the Web. It's to show how he might improve what he started by putting effort into attracting the women's market, thereby improving his sales.

a) DESIGN: I can hear basketball enthusiasts all over the country sneering at me, now. Coach Wells' site shows a counter at the bottom saying he's received over 998,000 visitors in six years. I would venture a guess that many of those visitors like his site. After all, it has a lot of dancing basketballs, a couple of small video icons of people playing basketball, and a whole lot of linked information about the game of basketball. I also venture to say that many of the visitors to Coach Wells' site are his own students, sent to the site with some encouragement from the Coach himself.

What's not to like about that?

Well, for starters, the site is pretty much contained on one page and scrolls all the way to Toledo, or Miami, or city of your choice. The point is, there is too, too much for the reader to assimilate, leaving much of Coach Wells' hard work unappreciated. As with other sites I've talked about, scrolling is only one online sin that users hate. Text that stretches all the way across the page making it difficult for readers to read is the other. The addition of dozens of bouncing basketballs invading the page while the reader is trying to concentrate on the content is just too much.

As for the counter at the bottom—counters are passé. Their only purpose is to broadcast popularity, yet the numbers most often reveal that the site is not as popular as the owner would like it to be. The counter for this site is showing six figures, at present, but over a six-year period, that translates to a little over 166,000 per year. If we factor in the number of repeat visitors—I checked the site out at least 10 times in three days, so using my visits we can guesstimate that the actual unique visitor count is less than 17,000 per year.

Admirable. But it still begs the question…so what? We have already established that some of Coach Wells' traffic may be students required to visit the site. If not, I am quite confident many visitors are there to get a good laugh at the dancing basketballs. A male member of my family made a rude remark I will not include here when I showed him the site, but his comment supports my thinking that the site needs help.

To the Coach, I would ask, do you monitor what your site visitors do and how many of them click to buy some software, but never complete their purchase? Those are the numbers that are truly important. Not the ones on a site counter. **Dick-e-meter rating: 2**

b) NAVIGATION: Because this site is contained on one scrolling page, hosting provided by Coach Wells' ISP (AOL), there is no true navigation. There are over 150 links on the site, not including the boxes thrown here and there offering what the good Coach must think are "calls to action" as they open sales pages for his training software. Navigational links set in a table three columns across are really doors to entirely different Web sites. Clicking on any of them takes the visitor to other basketball sites or sports information sites. Click one and you have left Coach Wells' bouncing basketballs and can only return to them by hitting your back button.

Bad move, Coach. Never willingly send the visitor to someone else's site. Links on a Web site should open a new window, which keeps the visitor on the original site. Once the new window is closed, the original site is there beneath, patiently waiting for the visitor to continue her stroll—or scroll, as the case may be— through the site. **Dick-e-meter rating: 1.5**

c) REAL ESTATE: Wasted space. What else is there to say? The site reads like a bad term paper. The bouncing basketballs interrupt everything; the links throughout the site are not arranged for easy reading and assimilation. Moving through the site is like trying to play basketball in a field of overgrown weeds with hoops attached at uneven levels on elm trees. It can be done, but it won't be much fun.

This site wants to be an "Everything You Ever Wanted to Know About the Game of Basketball" directory, but it's designed and organized like a crowded bulletin board that few can or will even attempt to read. Worse than that, I only saw one link referencing girls playing basketball. It was a link to a site called "Girls Can Jump." This was a site that spent another long scrolling page discussing cruciate ligament repair. Apparently girl basketball players suffer from this more than boys.

Where, Coach Wells, is the information on girls' basketball styles, moves, and plays?

I hope the Coach will redesign his site, reorganize all of the marvelous contact information, and reformat his text, so the site can get the attention it deserves. This will make not only the Coach look good, but will also improve the impression of Admiral Farragut Academy, Coach Wells' school. And I hope he will include some relevant content for girls, next time around.

Dick-e-meter rating: 2—with a qualification because I think a lot of people do care. That's why it's important to understand the Web and how people cruise Web sites. No doubt basketball players and their parents will find this site useful, if only Coach Wells will make it easy for them.

d) COMPANY INFORMATION: Coach Wells gives visitors to his site a resume on himself in a boxed link at the very bottom of the page.

Next to his resume link there is a notation that this is an award-winning site. Since visitors are not appraised of WHAT honor this site has been awarded, I will guess the award is for creative use of animation, sometime back in the previous century. **Dick-e-meter rating: 2**

e) CONTACT INFORMATION: Several links throughout the page allow the visitor to e-mail Coach Wells. On the pages where he attempts to market his software, showing diagrams of basketball plays, and a very large "Buy" button in red, there is no contact information. My attempt to move through the buying process was unrewarded one day [I received a server error several times], but worked the next day. A separate page opened with a form to fill out, but…no assurance that my credit card was protected. Nowhere on the site did I see a privacy statement or an 800 number. **Dick-e-meter rating: 2**

This is a good place to get valuable information in a niche market—playing basketball—but it is too cluttered, too complicated and not user-friendly. If you're making money selling your software, Coach Wells, I predict that if you redesign and reorganize your site to be female-friendly, you will reach more women (and men), and you may just double your software sales.

Dick-e-meter rating overall Grade: 8.5 Not female-friendly.

WWW.KATESPADE.COM

Gucci eat your heart out! Kate Spade knows design; she knows handbags; she knows shoes and accessories; she knows women, AND she knows the Internet!

What's not to like about that?

Since I started this chapter with a designer that earned a rating of 7.5, I thought I would end it with one that, as you will see, deserves the excellent rating she gets.

Lest anyone accuse me of favoritism by presenting a site I adore, selling products that take my breath away, let me make one thing perfectly clear: I learned of this site on *the day before* writing this chapter. As I was putting my site list together, my sister asked if I'd been to Kate Spade's site—my sister, like myself—is a shoe hound. She had discovered Kate Spade because Kate is big in shoes.

a) DESIGN: This is a complex site that appears simple and covers everything a female-friendly site should. One might expect it to accomplish that task because it's a female-owned company, yet, if you've been following *Dickless Marketing* so far, you know being a woman is no guarantee your site will be female-friendly. Many female-owned companies fail to attract women to their Web sites because they are taking their cues and advice from decades of male-dominated marketing—all offline!

Kate Spade is not one of them. The homepage of the site is testament to her thoughtfulness in designing and producing a Web site that women will feel comfortable shopping at. I expect she hired a Web designer to put this site together, but it's clear to me that Kate had a hand in how the site was going to look to the end-user. I also have to believe that she worked with the designer to make sure visitors to her site would feel welcome, that visitors would enjoy their click-throughs, and that it would be easy for them to buy.

Kate Spade's site revolves around product and visual appeal. Her homepage displays several handbags (at the writing of this review, anyway) with one handbag featured in a larger graphic box in the prime real estate section. There is plenty of white space on the page, which serves to enhance the appearance of Kate's designer handbags while also keeping the shopper's eye on the products.

The site uses color sparingly, displaying a green logo on the top left, immediately followed by "the collection" and two links, one to an "About Kate Spade" page—good reading, by the way—the other a link to shops that carry her products throughout the U.S.

Eye-tracking studies insist that the human eye is attracted to text on a page before pictures, and as a writer, I like to remind people of that now and then. However, eyes cannot help but notice graphics when they are relevant to the written content, and at the same time command a greater portion of a page than the text. Kate Spade's site uses graphics to enhance text. It is impossible not to notice the designer handbags, shoes, or other products as they are displayed. But the content describing each product also shows the shopper how to purchase them—what's not to like about that?

This is an upscale shopping site. The products are for the well to do, but they also appeal to mid-range women shoppers out to treat themselves to something extraordinary. Prices are displayed without embarrassment, allowing the visitor to the site to make an upfront choice on whether to go further into the site, or to crawl away to one of those discount stores talked about in earlier chapters.

A nice touch to the Kate Spade homepage is the advice written above the products: "Click images below," which tells the visitor right away that she will get more information on that product by clicking the image. Unfortunately there is no alt-text describing the images, so the search engine spiders are missing out on enjoying what the visitor can see. And Kate is losing traffic that could be coming her way. **Dick-e-meter rating: 5**

b) NAVIGATION: Shoppers at Katespade.com are guided through the site by easily noted links and product pictures. While the site does not have a true "Home" button, clicking on the text which is set along the logo-line will always get the shopper back to the homepage. As more and more people become used to surfing the Web, a company logo will serve both as a branding tool but also as a way to direct people "Home." For small businesses just getting started online, I still recommend an actual "home" link.

At the bottom of each page of this site there is a "customer service" link that opens a page showing the site's privacy statement, a page that serves as an FAQ page, and an 800 number for quick and easy contact.

I have two issues with the navigation on this site. One is that the links are presented in such small type. I would ask Kate to rethink the font size in view of the fact that many of her clientele may be baby boomers just learning to use the Web and they dislike having to squint to read text.

The second issue is that I see no call to action. Perhaps it is assumed that if we have come to the site, we are probably interested in buying. Her homepage does note that the products showing right now—as of the writing of this book—are the "fall collection," but no where does she encourage or urge the visitor to shop; "Buy Aunt Helen her Christmas gift early," or "Treat yourself to a new wallet, a new handbag, new shoes," whatever. It may be that designers expect visitors to shop, but I would caution readers that sales copy, subtly crafted, is never a bad thing. **Dick-e-meter rating: 4**

c) REAL ESTATE: I like what the Kate Spade site has done with its real estate. This is definitely not a content site, it's a shopping site, and there are plenty of products to look at, with proper descriptions. Products are purchased through a link to Nieman Marcus, but with links to the NM site throughout, buying is a quick and easy task.

In monitor settings of 1024x768 no scrolling is necessary to reach the bottom of the page where that all so important Nieman Marcus link is located. Monitor settings at 800x600 cause a small bit of scrolling. In that case, the text is larger, so the issue of squinting has been taken care of. [I have a 17-inch monitor set at 1024x768]

A nice touch at this site are thumbnail pictures of the products in different colors which, when clicked on, display the product in that color in full view. On the full-view page, the shopper can click a "previous" button to return to the previous page, or a "next" button to get to the next page.

I am not pleased that Kate keeps all of her text in lower case. It is unique, giving her site a "signature" other sites don't have and since she is a talented, creative and successful young woman, I will grant her this preference. However, I do not suggest my readers follow her lead. Use proper punctuation, please. **Dick-e-meter rating: 5**

d) COMPANY INFORMATION: Here's where I think this site shines. It may be my predilection for story-telling, but if you click on the "About Kate Spade" link offered at the top of every page, you will be treated to an inspiring look into how this young woman became a top designer of women's handbags and shoes. Not only that, this link also offers an "about jack" link, which opens a new window to a site called www.jackspade.com. Jack Spade sells men's bags, luggage, computer cases, and more.

Here is true new millennium marketing online—a woman's site and a man's site that complement each other. The Jack Spade site sports a publication with columns by writer Rory Evans, from which I borrowed this snippet:

THE QUEST
Rory Evans
NEW YORK CITY 09.11.00
Dear Paul,
You know how little kids with back-road lemonade stands, when they finally see a car coming, will stand up and hold up their posterboard sign, and then inch toward the middle of the road, hollering louder, desperately brandishing the sign, all but throwing themselves in front of the car to make a twenty-five-cent sale.

Many a woman who clicks into the Jack Spade site to see what it's all about, and surfs through it thinking of the man in her life (boyfriend, husband, son, father, whomever), will click on the "happenings" link and get a real treat when she finds Rory's column on little kids selling lemonade. She doesn't have to be someone's mother. She doesn't have to be a baby boomer. She only has to be human. The story is timeless—it touched my heart, it will touch other women's hearts, also. I bet it touches a few good men, also.

Content on the Kate Spade site goes well beyond the ordinary in welcoming visitors into her world. She does more than shake our hands—she gives us lemonade and cookies. **Dick-e-meter rating: 5**

e) CONTACT INFORMATION: Contact information is on every page through the "customer service" link. Kate provides an 800 number and a way to e-mail her. She offers a link to a mailing list for product updates, and she offers a site map to let eager shoppers find the right link at once, rather than waste time clicking randomly through the site. **Dick-e-meter rating: 5**

While shopping online at the Katespade.com site requires a click-through to Nieman Marcus, Kate makes that an easy and fast task. Because she has developed the site with the end-user in mind, offering easy navigation, eye appeal, and a way to contact her without waiting for a reply e-mail, she deserves her **overall Dick-e-meter rating of 24, Totally Female-Friendly!**

Visit the Dick-e-meter rating at www.dicklessmarketing.com and view some more Female-friendly sites.

WHAT WE LEARNED IN THIS CHAPTER

- www.gucci.com which serves a largely female clientele, is NOT female-friendly.
- www.atouchofhomecrafts.com has a lot of potential, but misses the point in a number of easily fixed areas.
- www.chocolateselrey.com is selling delicious sweets, but purchasing them is not an easy task.
- www.jobhuntersbible.com has some great content but it needs to focus on better organization and an easier way to buy.
- http://members.aol.com/coachmjw/pp22.htm Coach Michael Wells knows a lot about basketball, but he needs a new design and better organization on his Web site.
- www.katespade.com is the Jewel in the Crown. She has great products, she shows them off well, and she makes it easy for shoppers to buy.

Yes, the truth hurts but on the Web improving your business presence doesn't involve moving mountains. It merely requires changing some computer code.

10. Was Will Eine Frau Eigentlich?

Don't ask Freud What Women Want, Read On...

When a train goes through a tunnel and it gets dark,
you don't throw away the ticket and jump off. You sit
still and trust the engineer. ~ Corrie Ten Boom,
author and Holocaust survivor

Throughout the writing of *Dickless Marketing* I had this vision of Freud in my mind. I could see him standing tall in his office, his back to a woman patient leaning forward on his couch, hands clasped between her knees, head down in despair; someone with whom he was just finishing a therapy session. In my vision, I imagined him throwing his hands up in the air, shaking his head in exasperation, posing that tired old question he is so famous for "Was will eine Frau eigentlich?" translated by Google as, "Which wants a woman actually?"

Chapter 10 is going to tell you "Which wants a woman, actually." Or, to put it in more understandable terms, "What do women want, anyway?"

THE KEYS TO THE KINGDOM

The truth is, women want it all. This should not be news to anyone. A pink-haired Cyndi Lauper sang, "Girls just wanna have fun," in the 1980s, while at the same time, pop-icon Madonna was singing about a "Material Girl" in a "material world."

Lauper, Madonna, and other pop icons did contribute to the role of women breaking free from the myth we talked about in Chapter 1, but I believe it was all the way back in 1957 that the seed of today's love

> 64% of all women ages 18-34 want to become business owners.

affair between a woman and her computer really began. That was when Katherine Hepburn and Spencer Tracy starred in a movie called "Desk Set" (Directed by Walter Lang). While the movie did not endear the computer to women, or men, it opened the door to the idea of women succeeding in business, and it gave viewers a glimpse into the future of what computing was. The computer in the movie takes up an entire wall. I encourage readers to rent the movie and watch just for the enjoyment of watching that monstrosity perform.

Katherine played "Bunny Watson," a TV-network research whiz, to Spencer's "Richard Sumner," a time-efficiency expert. Sumner wanted to replace Bunny and her all-female crew with a computer he claimed could outthink human beings—especially women researchers. Bunny was not impressed. In the movie, she and Sumner parry wits and engage in heated arguments over the value of the human brain over a simple—simple?—machine, but, in the end, Bunny wins when the computer crashes (hardware issues—some things never change).

To me, that movie was a positive portrayal of an attractive, ambitious woman with a brain, smitten by a man battling against her intelligence. His attempt to introduce logic and linear thinking to her comes in the form of his computer. His failure to change her is testament to the female will. When we're right, we're right, and we know it. And I'm right about women being the dominant gender online, spending their money on everything from flowers to bathroom fixtures, from toys to tea and coffee, from coaching to cabling.

In "Desk Set," Sumner finally succumbs to Bunny's feminine wiles— which are nothing more than a woman using her brain and intuition to master a situation. It would seem that even back in the ancient days of the 20th century, when Jane was relegated to second place behind Dick, women and men thought differently, approached life and business differently, but still fell in love and learned to work together.

Yes, Lauper and Madonna were right—women (girls) do want to have fun (rent "Desk Set" and watch the Christmas party scene!) and we are material beings. Bunny's ambition in "Desk Set" wasn't part of a feminist goal to have enough money to buy perfume—her ambition and her need to defeat Sumner's computer embodied a desire to get her an executive chair at the network. But, oh the fun she had doing it! (Check out the link below the picture here for more shots of old, old computers.)

http://www.chstm.man.ac.uk/nahc/#what

The waning years of Bunny's century brought the computer from the size of a moving van to the size of a breadbox. During its strange shrinking phase, women were busy evolving into beings that could compete with men at work, in school, in sports, and in politics. It was our destiny to enter the 21st century on the cutting edge of technology and business. Unlike the men in our lives, we haven't merely learned how to use the technology. Instead, we're holding it in curious hands and deciding on how we can own it, experience it, give it life.

Judy Hoyt Pettigrew calls this a "reawakening." In *Women Mean Business, The Secret of Selling to Women* (New York: Creative Consortium Books, 2000), she says, "Today we have a more powerful medium for communicating our experiences—the internet. I believe this single tool, more than any other, has been responsible for the reawakening of connectedness in women. It has truly given her the keys to the kingdom."

The kingdom Pettigrew is talking about is bigger today than Lauper or Madonna imagined in the '80s.

It's a realm of bits and bytes spidering through a broadband Internet connection from woman-to-woman, mother-to-daughter; from sister-to-sister, family-to-family, and nation-to-nation. Every year it grows larger. Each new technical development giving women faster, easier access to each other's thoughts, words, and experiences is influencing world society in ways we will not understand for years to come.

For now, it serves to admit that yes, whether we are 15 or 50, 10 or 100, women are holding the digital world in our hands and we like it just fine!

VIEWS, VALUES, AND BEHAVIORS

According to David Wolfe of Sales Overlays, Inc., a marketing services firm specializing in marketing for the Fortune 500, "The aging of society is driving historic changes in leading views, values and behaviors in the marketplace." Chapter 5 of *Dickless Marketing* talked about the youth of America growing up—about the differences between the baby boomers and the twentysomethings.

This is also what Wolfe is talking about—marketing to women, but especially women over 40.

Companies that refuse to acknowledge the maturing of America will soon feel it in that most vulnerable place—their quarterly financial statement. It's because any discussion of people over 40 must, by definition, include more women than men since there are more women than men in the over 40 group. Remember what I said in the Preface—it's not Dick holding the digital world in the palm of his hand, it's Jane.

I've shown how the increase of TV ads targeting women is taking hold in the dirt world. Yet, while TV, radio, and print will continue to drive sales for the Fortune 500, small to mid-sized businesses are hard-pressed to compete in that arena. Instead, I say look to the

> In the 1300s, ale brewing was a female-dominated enterprise. By 1600, women were forced out due to lack of capital and a growing misogyny.

cost-effectiveness and reach of the Internet to drive your online sales message.

Look to Jane for your online success. Jane is holding those keys to the kingdom. I say, look to the wives, mothers, sisters, businesswomen, entrepreneurs, and partners who need your products and services. Believe that women have the power to research, influence and buy whatever it is you're selling. And believe that we are doing so in greater numbers every day.

MY SURVEY SAYS...

When I decided to write a book on marketing to women online, I knew getting real feedback from real people would be more valuable than statistics reported by experts all over the Internet. I wanted readers to know what the *average woman* actually says about how she shops online, and how her shopping habits have changed over the last few years, moving from mallspace to cyberspace.

To help my readers understand women and their online shopping habits, I conducted a mouse-to-mouse survey, using permission-based e-mail to contact survey participants. I also used word-of-mouth, asking friends and relatives to e-mail or otherwise share the survey with their friends and relatives. You've already seen some of the results of the survey quoted in the previous chapters of this book. Now we will get into the overall results.

In my survey I specifically questioned women about what was important and what wasn't when shopping online. Dubbed "the longest survey on the planet" by one woman, it generated enough interest to substantiate all of the statistics presented in this book. It showed that as a whole, women are shopping online for the convenience, the savings in time and money and because they are tired of running to the mall.

Women who participated in the survey came from as close as my own neighborhood, to as far away as across town, across the state, and across the nation. Their only incentive was to help me, another woman, compile statistics that, while not "formally gathered," would reflect the thoughts and feelings of the women who shop at small and mid-sized companies online.

Here are some of the things women reported through my survey:

o **An 800 number** is vital to online success. Alternatively, women will accept an online chat program. It's an issue of getting our questions answered while we're adding items to our shopping cart. In the dirt world we would approach a sales clerk. Online, we want you to accommodate us and post an 800 number. Yes, we still accept e-mail options, but if the issue is one of a certain color or size, and there is no way to contact a real person, that e-mail option is not going to do it.

1-800-NOW

o **GOOD CUSTOMER SERVICE** is more than important, **it's essential!** This goes beyond that 800 number. Good customer service means clearly posted shipping information: i.e., how long it takes to ship, how much it costs, complete with options to ship overnight if we're willing to pay the extra cost. It includes how easy it is to return products and whether or not we will receive an e-mail confirmation of our order, along with tracking information.

More than half of my respondents said customer service is more important than price. One woman wrote, "Make sure employees know and understand store policies." On your Web site, this means citing store policies openly, not making promises you can't keep, and having a feedback form where visitors can post comments or complaints.

o **AN AUTOMATED, QUICK, EASY BUYING PROCESS—** click, click, click. Women want your shopping cart program to do all the work. It should allow them to add items to their shopping cart, go back to shop for more, and not lose the contents already in the cart. It should figure the sales tax, if there is any, and post shipping costs up front, not at the end of the shopping experience.

o When shipping costs are posted at the end of the shopping experience, the number sometimes causes sticker shock. The shopper often isn't prepared for that shipping cost. If it's higher than she expected, she will abandon her shopping cart and click her way into a competitor's site.  Ninety percent of my respondents preferred free shipping. Free shipping also received a 90% "want to have" rating at eBrain Market Research, announced in an August issue of *Entrepreneur Magazine*.

o **WOMEN WANT CHOICES**—give us color size, design, and style options. One woman wrote, "Keep sizes and brands in stock. I wish more stores carried tall sizes." Another woman remarked, "Have ads with women of all colors, shapes and sizes." Still another said, "Plus size women are fashionable, too!" At the Gucci site I felt that the women shown looked ghoulish not only because their make-up was stark, but because they were breadstick thin. Even thin women have trouble identifying with that kind of promotional appearance. Don't treat us as if we're all one size, or one shape.

Service companies should take this advice, also. If we're looking for coaching, technical services, Human Resources outsourcing, networking services, and you have stock photos of models from a catalog on your site, how can we be sure you will take good care of us? The pictures on your site represent your impression of your perfect customers. If you don't recognize our diversity enough to display it as an introduction, we won't do business with you. As one woman wrote, "Read your online feedback!"

o **NO MORE COUPONS OR FEE-BASED SHOPPING CLUBS.** Women from my survey said forget the coupons, "Give us quality goods at a reasonable price." Other marketing studies done online show that loyalty programs work, but these are in place of coupons or fee-based clubs. One woman in my survey commented, "Treat the people who frequent your site extra special." We want to be rewarded for shopping at your site, for being loyal, but trying to lure us there with sales and coupons, or by charging a fee intended to *allow* us to shop at your site, doesn't work. There is no privilege in shopping at a fee-based chain. Be different. Thank us with free merchandise.

o **QUALITY GOODS AND SERVICES.** An overwhelming majority of my survey respondents said quality was more important to them than price. According to one young woman, "Quality is what keeps me coming back." Another woman put it this way, "Cut cost without sacrificing quality." The Internet affords any small business an excellent way to do this. You can cut your overhead cost immediately just by building a good Web presence and downsizing your office space. You may need warehouse space to store your products, but make your Web site your showroom and you will definitely save money.

For a service-centered company, develop your Web site to show customers how to manage on their own by putting control of your service in the customer's hands—be available, but give the customer/client the tools she needs to handle issues and problems up front, calling you only when absolutely necessary. We've seen in earlier chapters that women are very much into learning new skills today. Your willingness to show them how to do something new will win their favor every time.

o **WOMAN BUYS REFRIGERATOR ON HER OWN!** Nice headline, don't you think? It could happen. Not only were a majority of the women who took my survey comfortable shopping online, they were also comfortable buying big ticket items without help. That means cars, refrigerators, financial planning, even houses. They like to discuss it with husbands, boyfriends, or significant others, but they are fine with making the purchase on their own.

One woman did say she was not comfortable shopping online. However, she stated that she **researches online,** and then **buys** offline. The refrigerator headline could easily apply to this woman, and others like her. I have already shown how online research drives offline sales. Seventy-seven percent of U.S. Internet users gathered information about products to buy, and 60% of them went on to make offline purchases in 2002 (AOL, Roper ASW March 2003). Get your products in front of us. We want to know about them upfront—often before we step foot in your dirt world store.

o **BRAND YOURSELF**. Women are particular about what they buy, and from whom they buy it. My survey showed that brand name was important enough to stir interest; Target and Wal-Mart got high marks, with JCPenny only a few points behind. The surprising store winner, however, was Home Depot! What, I ask you, does Home Depot have that Wal-Mart and Target do not have? Women shoppers, according to the women who filled out my survey.

Branding is all about selling to us using the advice in *Dickless Marketing.* You can be the next Home Depot or Target, if you get enough women to shop at your Web site.

While buying by brand got high marks, the numbers of women who like to shop at the Dollar Store were also quite high. This is a clear indication that women like to shop at stores they know and trust: Target, Wal-Mart, JCPenny, but our desire to find just the right present, gift, or personal item, also leads us to frequent smaller, less well-known stores, like the Dollar Store, looking for bargains.

If you would compete with the name brand stores here, including the Dollar Store, study what they're doing right, and try to be like them. I hear that imitation is the finest form of flattery. Voltaire says, "originality is nothing but judicious imitation." Since it's a woman's prerogative to change her mind, she might switch from that brand name store she's used to shopping at and go shopping at your Web site—if you make the shopping experience easy for her.

TOP 12 REASONS WOMEN SHOP ONLINE:
1. The buying process is easy.
2. Site offers free shipping.
3. There is an 800 number posted.
4. The site is a trusted brand name.
5. The shopper saves money buying online.
6. Trust is established on the homepage.
7. The return policy is posted openly.
8. The merchant describes his/her product and provides convincing pictures.
9. The site is referred by a friend.
10. She is too tired or too busy to go to the mall.
11. Customer service is posted on all the pages.
12. We like it.

SIX WAYS TO GET MORE WOMEN TO BUY AT YOUR WEB SITE:
1. Have an 800 number.
2. Offer free shipping and handling.
3. Include information on return policy.
4. Show a consumer guarantee. (BBB or other trusted seal)
5. Offer bargain prices for quality goods.
6. Show a privacy statement.

FIND OUT WHERE IT HURTS

Professional sales people know they've made their sale when they have identified the client's area of greatest pain and they know their product or service can alleviate that pain.

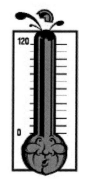

Women have pain. Our pain is knowing someone in the family is having a birthday this month and we need to purchase the perfect gift for him or her. Back to school shopping gives us lots of pain! Thanksgiving and Christmas shopping give us pain I am certain many of you can soothe. Then there's the pain we suffer when we suddenly remember that next month is our parents' anniversary, or our best friend's housewarming party, or time to shop for our first kid going off to college. We have pain at work also; so many of us are starting new businesses without knowing how to network our computers, or how to do our bookkeeping, we need you to help us out, please!

Every day more women go online to see what's new. Every day more women buy from online merchants. Every day we aren't buying from you, we are BUYING FROM A COMPETITOR OF YOURS! My last words of advice are these: Don't WOW us with how great YOU are. WOW us with product information, zoom-in images, a list of in-stock items or items on back order, personalization, product reviews from other clients or customers, wish lists, and a search function right there on your homepage.

Every time you WOW us, we'll either buy something, or send your URL to a friend, who will buy something. What's not to like about that?

According to Margaret Thatcher, former Prime Minister of the UK, "If you want anything said, ask a man. If you want anything done, ask a woman." Someone asked me what I'd like to do more than anything else in the world, and I said I would like to write a book on marketing to women online. A male friend suggested a title, and I ran with it.

I hope *Dickless Marketing* has alleviated your pain by giving you information on how to build a functional, female-friendly Web site. One that will make you shine. One that will have women all over the Web talking about you.

Before signing off, I would like to share some of the answers to two particular questions on my survey—those that asked women to name a 20th century woman and man she admires, and then tell me why.

Here are the most interesting replies:

NAME A 20TH CENTURY MAN YOU ADMIRE AND TELL ME WHY YOU ADMIRE HIM.

Bill Gates: Great business sense and donates to a lot of charities.

My father: He is a loving person who is very family-oriented. He provides for his family, he is a marathon runner and I admire his dedication.

Dave Thomas (founder of Wendy's): Not only for building a successful franchise, but also for his work with adoptive children. And he did it all while still seeming to be just a regular guy.

My father: He grew from a humble background, in a country with a fairly rigid caste system and he moved up and did not complain or talk about what happened—yet, he grew to be a quiet, yet determined person.

My father: He is very smart, patient, and driven.

Bob Hope: For his dedication to our Armed forces.

Harry Truman: Because he was decent and honest, a straight shooter. And because he was an underdog who won.

Martin Luther King: For his ability to think big, his efforts to eliminate racism and for his fight for equality.

My husband: Smart, handsome, willing to take risks, rolls with the punches, very caring and devoted to his family.

NAME A 20ᵀᴴ CENTURY WOMEN YOU ADMIRE AND TELL ME WHY YOU ADMIRE HER.

Susan B. Anthony: Supported women's rights with courage and conviction.

Oprah Winfrey: For all that she has been able to accomplish in the man's world of media/entertainment.

Queen Elizabeth: When I was a little kid she was a teenager much in the public eye. I've seen what she has gone through in her life, not by her choice but because of whose child she was. She has never wavered from what she sees as her higher duty, regardless to the cost to her as a person and as a woman.

My mother: She has never let anything keep her from her dreams or ambitions.

Audrey Hepburn: For using her celebrity status to help those in need.

Eleanor Roosevelt: Because she tried to bring about changes in American society for both men and women.

Cher: She has come a long way in her career.

Katherine Hepburn: She was her own woman, didn't take stuff from anyone, talented, worked hard, achieved greatness in her profession.

Juanita Bynum-Weeks: She is a great inspiration to women of color because she has made some mistakes, bounced back and is a living example that you can make it despite the odds.

Colin Powell, George Bush, Laura Bush, Mother Teresa, Jimmy Carter, and Lee Unkrich, co-director of *Finding Nemo,* were also mentioned. Notice how many mothers and fathers are in the list. Notice the qualities women admire; giving back to society, selflessness, caring, determination, honesty, talent, and patience. From celebrities, to business folks, to politicians, women wrote about people who touched their lives in a positive way. These people were recognized for the value each one brought to society as a whole.

To the delightful young woman who wrote this reply about the 20th century woman she admires most: "My mother. She is determined and ambitious. When she sets her mind to something she does everything possible to achieve her goal. Hopefully I have inherited some of her determination," this Mom thanks you.

WHAT WE LEARNED IN THIS CHAPTER
- o We learned that *Dickless Marketing* is the new millennium way to court the largest group of shoppers on the Web today.
- o We learned that the largest group of shoppers online today is women.
- o We learned that you should have an 800 number, a privacy statement, an easy, functional shopping cart, and free shipping.
- o We learned that today's women like computers and shopping online.
- o And we learned that if women like you and your Web site, we have the power to make you the next Wal-Mart, the next Gucci, or the next Amazon.com.
- o What's not to like about that?

Acknowledgements

The writing of any book requires more physical labor than most people understand. The hundreds of hours spent typing away on a computer keyboard, eyes focused on a computer monitor trying to craft meaningful paragraphs—using the right words to get the right message to the right people—can cause back pain, eye strain, and the loss of feeling in one's lower limbs.

The people who assisted me in making this book come alive know and understand those issues well. They all spend much of their days at the computer, writing, reading, and conducting business. I owe them all a mountain of thanks.

Listed in alphabetical order, thanks go to:

Dr. Mark Anderson for his continued support and witty additions to the content, none of which survived for reader viewing. More's the pity. Dr. Anderson is the Honors Director at SUNY Brockport and is intimately familiar with reading, writing, and conversing over a computer cable.

Jamie Bigelow who stepped in at the last minute to do a fabulous job on the book cover. When other graphic designers were unable to do what I wanted, I turned to a member of my own family, my nephew, Jamie, who took on the challenge without hesitation. See, I actually practice what I preach.

Thomas Collins for his unfailing encouragement and support. Tom is studying Informatics at Buffalo State in order to help lawyers get a grasp on this new technology. He was vital in contributing thoughts, edits, and information to the final draft of *Dickless Marketing*.

Victoria Dravneek who was Victoria Jerman when the book began. Victoria came into my life at just the right time, straight from New York City, a former content writer for iVillage. She understands women and the Internet better than most. Without her reviews of each chapter, and her gentle but firm advice on one paragraph or another, this book might have reached well over 900 pages.

Ronald George for his valuable insight into what *Dickless Marketing* really means—and it doesn't mean beating up on Dick. Ron is responsible for the logo, the book cover design, and the Web site. Without his clear focus and his understanding of what I was trying to accomplish, coupled with his keen eye for detail, this book and its attendant Web site would be less perfect than they are.

Shirley Malone for her excellent proofreading skills. Had I not met Shirley when I did, Microsoft might be getting credit for spell-checking this book, and we all know how well MS spell-check works!

Diana Robinson a good friend and professional coach who also turned out to be an excellent editor! Diana was instrumental in catching inconsistencies and confusing content. She wrote dozens of pointed comments in her reviews of each chapter; comments that helped me focus on seeing the book from the reader's eyes. Many of Diana's notes were personal, about her life growing up in England, and I enjoyed them all. I encourage her to write a book of her own.

My family, each and every one of them; from my four sisters who cheered me on, to my children who eagerly awaited the finished product, to my Mom and Dad who merely said, "We never doubted you could do it." And to my brother, who inspires me to success each and every day. Without my family and their unwavering emotional support, this book would be languishing in a box in a closet somewhere.

All of these people endeared themselves to me not only because they participated in making this book happen, but also because they believed in me. They cared. I thank them from the bottom of my heart.

Yvonne DiVita